Abnormal Psychology

ABNORMAL PSYCHOLOGY

Aarti Dua

MD PUBLICATIONS PVT LTD
NEW DELHI

For information:

MD Publications Pvt Ltd
'MD House', 11, Darya Ganj
New Delhi - 110 002
Phone : +91-11-41563325 (Customer Service)
+91-11-41562846 (Editorial)
E-mail (orders): contact@mdppl.com
Website: www.mdppl.com

ISBN: 978-81-7533-139-6

Published and Printed by Mrs. Rajni Gupta on behalf of **MD Publications Pvt Ltd** at Times Press, 910, Jatwara Street, Darya Ganj, New Delhi.

Contents

PREFACE

The history of abnormal psychology began with the research of the famous ancient Greek philosopher Plato in the fourth century B.C. During his time, most believed that the strange behaviors and actions that psychologists study today were caused by evil spirits. Plato believed this to be false and spoke his ideas of these behaviors being caused by a "natural madness, usually caused by a disease". Unfortunately his words had no affect on the common people of his age. During the Dark Ages, the idea of the behaviors being caused by evil spirits escalated to the idea that people were being possessed by demons. Many people were exercised by the churches or burned at the stake for possessing these "demons". Over approximately one hundred thousand innocent people were killed for the same reasons by the Inquisition. It wasn't until early 19th century that the idea of evil spirits and demons was tossed aside, and the idea of these behaviors being caused by illnesses in the mind was finally embraced.

A more religious approach to the animistic beliefs of abnormality is the practice known as exorcism. Performed by religious authorities, exorcism was thought of as another way to release evil spirits whom were causing the pathological behavior within the person. Most patients or individuals with mental disorders, were exhiled or banned from society. Witchcraft currently viewed at as a psychosis or state of delirium was punished by death. Most witches ended up on the pile. The church made a manual that told the people what to do with witchcraft and abnormal behavior. That manual is known as the witchhammer, official Latin name: Malleus Maleficarum. Witch was one of the first books actually published in Germany that held a taxonomy of the abnormal or deviant behavior, of course that work was revised by now and banned by the church in late 15th century. Throughout time, societies have proposed several explanations in hopes of understanding abnormal behavior within human beings. Throughout "pre-modern" societies, people firmly believed that abnormal behavior was a direct result of animism, the belief in the existence and power of a spiritual world. The idea that people demonstrating abnormal behavior was possessed by malevolent spirits led to a practice known as trephination. The process of trephination involved cutting a hole into the individual's skull in order to release the malevolent spirits.

The amount of different theoretical perspectives in the field of psychological abnormality has made it difficult to properly explain psychopathology. The attempt to explain all mental disorders with the same theory leads to reductionism. Most mental disorders are composed of several factors, which is why one must take into account several theoretical perspectives when attempting to diagnose or explain a particular behavioral abnormality or mental disorder.

I am very much grateful to Mr. Pranav Gupta, Director of MD Publications Pvt Ltd, for his kind cooperation and support for this book.

Aarti Dua

1

Abnormal Psychology: An Introduction

Definition and Meaning

The philosopher Plato, in the 4th century BC, distinguished natural madness, resulting from physical disease, from that given by divine gift. He insisted that mental disturbance should be treated within the family, which led to special temples being set aside as retreats for the mentally ill. Hippocrates, a Greek physician writing at the same time (often considered to be the father of modern medicine), described five forms of madness (hysteria, epilepsy, acute mental disturbance with and without fever, and chronic mental disturbance), all of which he considered to be medical in origin and treatable by procedures such as emetics, bleeding, purges and dietary change. These procedures were aiming to reduce the excess of bodily fluids, or humours, which Hippocrates thought were responsible for mental disorder. An excess of black bile was thought to lead to depression (melancholy); an excess of yellow bile to irritability and anxiety (choleric); an excess of phlegm to indifference (phlegmatic); and an excess of blood to mood shifts (sanguinity). Thus some of the modern categories of disorder had clearly been identified even then.

The Greek physician Galen, in the 1st/2nd century AD, studied anatomy in his search for explanations, but is often considered to be the first person to suggest that abnormal behaviour could also have psychological origins.

The Middle Ages and Demonology

The demonological view had taken over in Europe, and madness again became linked with possession by evil spirits. This represented a reversion to earlier ideas about evil spirits, but the ideas had been embedded in the context of Christianity. Such individuals were more likely to be subjected to exorcism or burnt at the stake than treated medically. The Inquisition was an institution set up by the Roman Catholic Church to discover and suppress heretics (those people who held opinions opposed to those of the church). In 1484, the Inquisition began in earnest with the publication of the *Malleus Malleficorum*, the witchhunter's guide to diagnosing witches. This was one of the first books to be printed and widely circulated. According to Spanos as many as 100,000 persons were dealt with in this way between 1450-1600. Not all were mentally disordered of course (many were eliminated as the result of political or economic rivalry), but it is likely that many would have been.

However, at about the same time there was also the first attempt to provide secure places for mentally disordered persons. Until this time lunatics (as they were generally known) had either been accommodated by their own families or simply cast out to fend for themselves. Bethlem hospital, opened to lunatics in London in 1403, was the first in Europe, and it was followed by another in Spain in 1408, in North America in 1639 and France in 1657.

These two views of madness, as disease or as demonic possession, continued to conflict for many centuries; only recently has the latter approach been replaced by a broader, 'moral' view of such behaviour that is less reliant on religion.

The 'Age of Reason' and Moral Treatment

During this period in history, science and rationality were believed to hold the key to making progress with solving human problems. Hence it has become known as the Age of Reason. Physical treatments, based on 'scientific' principles and administered by physicians, gradually gave way to moral treatment based on rational argument.

In the early 18th century lunacy was regarded as an illness, and following the Poor Laws of the late 17th century, lunatics were to be protected in asylums. As these asylums became more and more overcrowded, however, the use of chains and restraints increased. By the late 18th century, as the 'Age of Reason' prevailed, religious fervour had cooled off, and the inadequacy of physical treatments had also been recognised. There were several reasons for the latter. First, physical treatments such as the whirling chair had proved ineffective. (This was a device into which patients were strapped and rotated at speed, allegedly until blood ran from their ears.) Second, in the Bethlem scandal of 1814 it was discovered that a patient called James Norris had been kept in irons for 10 years for attacking his 'keeper'. (As usual, of course, it has been noted that there were two versions of this scandal that Norris was an extremely violent patient, and that when chained he was kept supplied with reading materials and even had a pet cat. Nevertheless, the case roused public opinion against the use of chains in asylums, especially when such neglect was found to be common).

Third, the madness of King George III (noted in letters dated 1788) had failed to respond to the available medical treatments of bleeding, blistering and purging. His problem turned out to be porphyria, a hereditary disease that produces abdominal pain and mental confusion. At the time, it was unrecognised. The rejection of the religious and medical approaches to dealing with mental disorder led to a third response to abnormal behaviour; the moral approach. This is considered to have originated with Francis Willis, a clergyman who was called in to treat George III. He placed great emphasis on physical remedies such as diet, exercise, physical restraint (using chairs or straitjackets) when required, and lectures on morality designed to make the patient see the error of his ways. The importance of this is that madness no longer appears to be considered to be purely physical or demonological in its origins. It is also possible, of course, that the use of different treatments does not necessarily indicate a shift in ideas about the origins of mental disorder.

The moral approach was also reflected by Chiarugi in Florence, Italy in 1788. He removed all restraints from patients and provided them with activities to occupy them. This could be considered to be the start of occupational therapy. In the Bicetre hospital in Paris, the superintendent of the incurables ward, a layman called Pussin, had similarly unchained patients and forbidden staff to beat them in 1784. He extended these reforms with the aid of Pinel, who was appointed physician in 1793 (and generally gets the credit for the improvements).

In England, the Quaker William Tuke (1732-1822) opened the York Retreat in 1796, which proved to be highly successful. It was based on moral therapy, an attempt at resocialisation that emphasised kindliness, orderliness and occupation. No physicians were employed there, and restraint was used only if absolutely necessary. The term 'moral insanity' was coined by the Englishman Pritchard in 1835 to refer to people who do not live in acceptable ways. It has been suggested that this was subsequently used as a convenient excuse to incarcerate unwanted relatives, particularly women who had an inheritance coming to them.

This conflict between the moral and the medical approaches replaced the earlier conflict between the religious and the medical approaches. This diversity can still be seen today in the different therapeutic approaches to mental disorder.

In response to these developments, Parliament passed legislation in 1808 regarding care for the insane, but it was not until the Lunatics Act of 1845 that it became mandatory to provide asylums. These were considered to be centres for cure rather than restraint. Prior to that, many mentally disordered individuals were incarcerated in prisons or the workhouse if they couldn't afford private care. In America, the physician Benjamin Rush (1745-1813) devoted his career to the study of mental problems, and the reformer Dorothea Dix (1802-1887) campaigned for special humane facilities to be provided for the mentally ill, raising sufficient funds to found 32 mental hospitals.

The Modern Era and Mental Illness

Considerable expansion in provision occurred between 1860-1900, and the medical view prevailed once again. The first textbook of psychiatry was published by Kraepelin in 1885, and established abnormal behaviour as a manifestation of mental illness, a physical disease or dysfunction in the individual that should therefore be treated by physical means. To some extent this optimism was lost subsequently, as the asylums became more and more overcrowded and madness became regarded as incurable.

Another pioneer from this period was Freud, who studied hysteria with the neurologist Charcot in Paris. Hypnosis had had some popularity as a treatment for mental problems since it was first introduced by Mesmer some years before in the guise of mesmerism. Freud used it briefly, but then rejected it and developed his own system. Known as psychoanalysis, it was the forerunner of modern psychotherapies, and also reinforced the view that mental illness was curable and need not necessarily be medical in origin.

After World War II (1939-1945), the hospital population reduced again with the advent of drug treatments. The neuroleptics (major tranquillisers) in particular produced a major revolution in treatment and a liberalisation of care. Medicated patients were much better equipped to deal with everyday activities, and many could remain in the community. From the 1950s onwards, with the social psychiatry movement gaining ground, hospitalisation came to be seen as an inappropriate way to deal with the problem of mental disorder. The World Health Organisation adopted the label 'mental disorder' to replace the term 'mental illness', emphasising the fact that a physical basis had not been found for many of the conditions involved. As a result of this, and the requirement in the Mental Health Act of 1959 and the Community Care Act of 1990 for local authorities to provide more community services, many mental hospitals have now closed.

Underpinning these responses to abnormal behaviour, Halgin and Whitbourne have identified three different explanations for that type of behaviour: mystical; scientific; humanitarian. These are equivalent to the religious, medical and moral views identified earlier. The mystical view is that it results from demonic possession; the scientific view is that it results from biological factors such as faulty genes or brain disease, or psychological factors such as learning or stress; the humanitarian view is that it results from social conditions. Treatments have broadly speaking been either 'medical' or moral/religious, illustrating physical and mental (psychological) approaches, respectively. What is interesting here is the similarity in the way that mental disorder has been dealt with over time. Although the approaches have been reframed according to prevailing societal values (e.g. religious/moral) they have remained much the same for centuries. These are apparent in the attempts to define and classify and in the different models used to understand abnormal behaviour, which we will be discussing in the rest of this chapter. Finally, most of what has been written about the history of mental disorder has focused on the way in which society has varied in its treatment of those whom it has labelled as abnormal. A more difficult issue to address is whether there has been any real change in the nature of the behaviours that evoke such labels.

Criteria for Defining Abnormality

Any discussions in this area depend on the existence of an agreed definition of what constitutes abnormal behaviour. Such a definition should ideally be able to cover all behaviours that are generally agreed to be abnormal; should exclude all normal behaviours; should provide a basis for objective measurement of behaviour; and should be applicable to everyone irrespective of culture.

Progress Exercise

Ask a sample of people (about six should do) from different backgrounds what types of behaviour they would regard as abnormal. Then ask them which of those behaviours are criminal (bad) and which are 'mad'. What types of behaviour have they identified? How much agreement is there? Is there an overlap between 'mad' and 'bad'? How can they be distinguished?

Legal Criteria

It might be thought that the legal system, which is responsible for making compulsory treatment orders for those who display abnormal behaviour, would have agreed a suitable definition. The law differs in different countries; in Britain the 1983 Mental Health Act offers the following definition of mental disorder: 'Mental illness, arrested or incomplete development of mind, psychopathic disorder and any other disorder or disability of mind.'

Mental illness is not defined further, but is left up to the judgement of the professionals involved in treating such disorders. The underlined statement is similarly vague. 'Arrested or incomplete development of mind' is further defined as a state 'which includes severe/significant impairment of intelligence and social functioning and is associated with abnormally aggressive or seriously irresponsible conduct on the part of the person concerned.' Psychopathic disorder is 'a persistent disorder of, or disability of mind (whether or not including significant impairment of intelligence) which results in abnormally aggressive or seriously irresponsible conduct on the part of the person concerned.'

Some of these definitions give indications of the kinds of behaviours that are regarded as troublesome impaired intelligence (though not always); impaired social functioning; abnormally aggressive and seriously irresponsible behaviours. However, the qualifiers (impaired, abnormally, seriously) leave a great deal of scope for subjective judgement. What is judged to be impaired social functioning by one person may be considered acceptable by another. Consider regular bouts of excessive drinking, for example.

Progress Exercise

In the light of the legal criteria, consider what level of intelligence you think constitutes 'severe/significant impairment'. Is it an IQ of 50, or 75 for example?

What is ' abnormal' aggression, and what is normal aggression? Does it have to involve physical violence, and if so to what degree? When *is* aggression justified?

What is 'seriously irresponsible conduct'? Should it include such behaviours as being seriously in debt? Not paying maintenance for children? Using 'dirty tricks' to eliminate business rivals?

Statistical Criteria

In an attempt to address some of the issues raised earlier, statistical criteria have been introduced for some behaviours, based on the normal distribution curve. If the mean score of the population on any given measure of behaviour is known, together with the average variation from that mean (known as the standard deviation) it is possible to identify mathematically which scores would be achieved by only a small proportion of the populace. These could then be regarded as abnormal. For example, given that the population mean score for IQ is 100, and the standard deviation (a measure of the average deviation from the mean) is 15, it could be argued that an IQ score of below 70 is abnormal, since it will only be obtained by about 2% of the population.

This system has the advantage of objectivity, in the sense that categorising the individual is done solely on the basis of the test score, without recourse to the clinician's judgement. There are also difficulties, however. First, the clinician must still decide which behaviours to measure in the first place, and exactly where to place the cut-off point, i.e. how much deviation is acceptable. Another problem is that population means may not exist for many behaviours that are thought to be relevant, such as irresponsible behaviour. It has also been shown that many mental disorders are statistically quite common.

Approximately of Americans will suffer from some form of mental disorder at some stage of their lives. In Britain, the lifetime prevalence for mood disorders is 15% and for women in inner London this rises to 70% for depression alone. The final weakness of the statistical criterion is that it is value-free (in theory, if not in practice). There are many people who differ from the average in ways that are considered desirable; members of Mensa, for example, would probably take exception to being labelled as abnormal, and generally they are labelled in this way. This means that as well as being statistically rare, the behaviour concerned must be regarded as undesirable; a value judgement is made.

Deviation-from-the-norm Criteria

This approach takes the population norm, rather than the average, as the starting point for determining abnormality. What is important is whether the individual differs from *expected* ways of behaving. Thus depression, which is statistically quite common, would be regarded as abnormal because it is not expected of us (except in particular situations such as bereavement, and then only for a certain period of time). In some societies, such as the Zulu for example, hallucinations or screaming in the street are regarded as normal behaviour.

Landrine has identified a syndrome known as 'drapetomania', which used to be an acknowledged disorder in America. It was the tendency of slaves to run away from their masters. Homosexuality is a good example of a behaviour that is no longer generally regarded as abnormal in our society, and has always been perfectly acceptable in other cultures such as the Mohave Indian. According to some writers such an insistence on adherence to the norm could be used to justify persecution of minority groups. Soviet Russia, for example, has been accused of treating political dissidents as if they were mentally disordered. Drapetomania can clearly be seen as a syndrome that serves the aims of one social group who wish to oppress another. Progress exerciseConsider the positive and negative outcomes of insisting on adherence to social norms.

Mental Health Criteria

Jahoda proposed a set of criteria for mental health. Rather than focusing on undesirable behaviours, like the other approaches discussed here, this is a list of desirable characteristics and behaviours. Abnormality could be indicated by their absence. These criteria are as follows:

1. The absence of mental illness.
2. Being able to introspect about yourself, being aware of what you are doing and why.
3. Growth, development and self-actualisation (achievement of potential).
4. Integration of different aspects of the person (e.g. a balance between id, ego and superego in Freudian theory).
5. The ability to cope with stress.
6. Autonomy - being able to function independently.
7. Seeing the world as it really is.
8. Environmental mastery - adaptability to change, and the ability to love, work, play and have satisfactory relationships.

This is a useful way of identifying those people who would benfit from psychological help. However, it is in many ways just as prescriptive an approach as those outlined earlier, and has the additional problem that most of us would probably fail to meet all of these criteria. Many may be present to some extent, so the issues of cut-off points and difficulties with measurement also arise. Cultural variation may also be a problem. For example, collectivist sccieties do not value autonomy in the same way that Western, individualist societies do. They place more emphasis on family and community values and social co-operation.

Psychological and Social Criteria

Rosenhan and Seligman have produced a list of undesirable behaviours, and argue that if several of these exist at any one time the individual may be considered to be in need of help. The list includes such things as suffering, personal and social maladaptiveness, unpredictability and loss of control, unconventionality and irrationality, observer discomfort, and violation of moral and ideal standards. These criteria benefit from the inclusion of personal suffering, so that judgement about the individual is not solely based on the responses of other people. However, many of the criteria mentioned are difficult to measure and therefore leave a great deal to the subjective judgement of the clinician. Suffering and unconventionality are good examples.

Individual objections can be raised against the behaviours listed as well. Suffering, for example, is not always apparent. Some mentally disordered individuals (such as those who have some types of personality disorder) do not suffer themselves, although they may upset others. Unconventional behaviour may be displayed by nonconformists as well as those who are mentally disordered. Refusal to wear clothes in public places is a good recent example of this. Irrational behaviour is also not uncommon in some circumstances - if people are worried or physically ill, their behaviour may appear irrational to others. Finally, observer discomfort will vary with the observer and with the culture concerned.

The Four D's

Comer has suggested that what many of the above systems have in common can be covered by just four points:

- deviance (different, extreme behaviours such as severe depression, sexual deviance, etc.);
- distress (behaviours that upset the individual concerned, e.g. paranoia);
- dysfunctional (behaviours that interfere with everyday functioning, e.g. substance abuse, agoraphobia);

- dangerous (potentially damaging behaviours, e.g. aggression, eating disorders).

Although these seem to cover a wide range of problems, they are still not universally applicable. Some behaviours fulfil these criteria but are nevertheless acceptable; for example, the alcohol consumption of many students may be regarded as extreme, causes them distress and dysfunction, and could be dangerous. However, it is regarded as acceptable for this group of individuals, at this stage in their lives. Thus the context, as well as the content, of the behaviour must be considered.

Mental Illness Criteria

In this approach, abnormal behaviour is defined by the presence of particular clusters of symptoms. These symptom clusters are thought to indicate the presence of an underlying mental illness that may respond to treatment. The symptom clusters are laid down in the diagnostic and classification system current at the time. For example, the *Diagnostic and Statistical Manual of Mental Disorders* defines mental disorder as:

> *a clinically significant behaviour or psychological syndrome or pattern that occurs in a person and that is associated with present distress (a painful symptom), disability (impairment in one or more important areas of functioning), a significantly increased risk of suffereing death, pain, disability or an important loss of freedom. In addition, this syndrome or pattern must not be merely an expectable response to a particular event such as, for example, the death of a loved one.*

The other main classification system is the International Classification of Diseases, which defines mental disorder as 'the existence of a clinically recognisable set of symptoms or behaviours associated in most cases with distress and with interference with personal functions'. Like DSM, this focuses on the distress experienced by the individual concerned, rather than other people, and mentions symptom clusters.

In clinical practice, use of the mental illness criteria is the favoured approach. It is clear from what has been said that the identification of symptom clusters is the critical issue here. Can they be reliably identified? Do different clinicians agree on their judgements? If they can, it still remains to be seen whether or not those clusters appear to be valid, in the sense of distinguishing syndromes that have different causes and respond to different treatments.

Validity and reliability aside, there are other criticisms of this approach. Most of these are based on the argument that in many cases of mental disorder there appears to be no organic basis for the problem. Discussion of this argument in depth is beyond the brief of this text, and the reader is referred to *Psychopathology* by Stirling and Hellewell in the series. However, more and more evidence is accumulating about the physiological problems (based on genetics, brain dysfunction and biochemistry) associated with mental disorders. The difficulty for researchers is establishing whether these problems are the cause of the disorder or a consequence of it.

Another perspective on this is provided by Thomas Szasz. In an article entitled 'The myth of mental illness' he made the point that the mind itself is non-physical and therefore cannot suffer from illness. His view is that mental disorder is the result of 'problems in living', which may be simply exacerbated by the use of psychiatric labels such as 'schizophrenic'. These labels are stigmatising, and may also be self-handicapping in so far as they remove the responsibility for behaviour from the individual concerned; the 'illness' can be blamed instead, and responsibility delegated to medical professionals.

Perspectives on Abnormality

Before moving on to develop these issues further, we are going to look at some theoretical aspects of the topic. Perspectives are addressed in detail in the book Theoretical Approaches in Psychology in the series. In the AQA specification, the perspectives section is divided into issues, debates and approaches. The following sections use the same structure.

Issues

The AQA specification mentions four issues that should be considered when studying any area of psychology. Here, we will briefly consider their relevance to the study of abnormality.

The first issue is gender bias. Within our society, males and females have traditionally been considered to have different roles, with the female being the dependent, nurturing homemaker and the male the independent, assertive, worker. These roles dictate how the two sexes relate to one another as well as to the world in general. When it comes to abnormal behaviour, it is perhaps not surprising that behaviours that are considered abnormal for one gender are considered to be acceptable for the other. Dependency in women, for example, is much less likely to be seen as problematic than when it is displayed in men. What may be less obvious, however, is the perpetuation of such biases in the behaviour of clinicians. Bias has been detected in the classification systems for mental disorder, and in the diagnoses and treatments given by clinicians.

Another form of gender bias can be seen in the different rates of certain mental disorders in the two sexes. Depression, as already noted, is very much more common in women than in men. There are likely to be several reasons for this, including the possibility that the different gender roles are responsible. Powerlessness and helplessness, as we shall see, are thought to be key factors in the development of some disorders, depression in particular.

The second issue is cultural bias. We have already seen that different societies have different expectations for the behaviour of their members. Looking at behaviour purely from the perspective of one society or culture will therefore provide a biased view. What is defined as abnormal in one culture will not be regarded as exceptional in another, so any criteria for defining abnormality that fail to take this into account can be described as culture-bound. A related difficulty is raised by the debate about culture-bound syndromes. These are disorders that are seen in some cultures but are not recognised in others. Anorexia nervosa, for example, may well come into this category. Whether these result from different social conditions (such as the Western emphasis on thinness in women) or whether they represent diagnostic bias is an important issue. A weaker form of the culture-bound syndrome may be evident in the different ways that disorders show themselves in different cultures. For example, depression is more likely to be associated with somatic symptoms such as digestive complaints in some cultures.

When members of other cultural groups live in a Western society, these biases become all the more evident. If certain cultural groups seem to receive particular diagnoses and treatments more frequently than other groups, we have to consider whether this is due to bias in the classification system, bias in the clinician, or differences in social conditions and pressures. The third issue is ethics. This is the debate about what is considered right and wrong in the way that we treat one another. Clearly, when we are diagnosing mental disorder this can have profound consequences for the individual concerned. This can be considered not only in terms of treatment but also such aspects of everyday functioning as family life, housing and employment. The diagnostic label can affect the individual's self-concept (how the person sees himself or herself), usually in a negative way. This negative evaluation may well be reinforced by feedback from others, since the public stereotype of those with mental disorder is not a good one. Legal issues may also enter into this, since a diagnosis of mental disorder can provide grounds for not standing trial for crimes, or for not being held responsible for actions.

Psychiatric diagnoses may also be used deliberately to dispose of unwanted persons, for either personal or political gain. This also constitutes a contravention of ethical standards. The fourth issue is the use of non-human animals in research. Concerns here are divided into practical (whether it is admissible to extrapolate from animals to human behaviour, for example) and ethical (whether it is acceptable to use non-human animals for research purposes). Where mental disorder is concerned, this issue relates most obviously to research into the causes of mental disorders, which is not the main concern of this text. However, some of the approaches/models to be discussed in the final part of this section obviously have their roots in theories that are based on animal research. The behaviourist and biological/medical approaches are obvious examples.

Debates

Again, we will look here at the four debates mentioned in the AQA specification. These are: free will and determinism; reductionism; psychology as a science; the nature-nurture debate.

Free will and determinism is a discussion about the origins of our behaviour. As the term implies, the free will view is that we choose to act the way that we do. We are free agents and can make our own choices in life. This is a view espoused by the humanistic psychologists. Determinism is the view that our behaviour is preset by forces outside our control, including genetics and other biological factors, past learning and experiences, and social pressures. This view is advocated by the behaviourist, psychodynamic and biological approaches, for example. A compromise position is that of soft determinism, such as an imbalance in neurotransmitters (the chemicals involved in communication in the nervous system). For this reason, an eclectic approach, taking note of all aspects of the problem, is generally advocated.

Science underpins the work of psychologists in all spheres, and mental disorder is no exception to this. One key feature of the scientific approach is classification. Another is building theoretical explanations for mental disorder, and testing hypotheses derived from those theories through experimentation or other acceptable scientific methods. In both cases the concern is with achieving objectivity and eliminating sources of subjective bias. Throughout the following chapters we will be looking at the classification system, the process of assessment and diagnosis, and at specific categories such as Multiple Personality Disorder. The aim will be to evaluate them in terms of their scientific standing, particularly regarding the important criteria of validity and reliability.

Another element of the scientific approach that you may wish to consider is predictability. Science assumes that we are predictable, and that in turn implies that our behaviour is determined. However, some allowance is made for free will, in the sense that science deals in probabilities rather than certainties. Some psychologists, notably those who espouse the humanistic approach, argue that the scientific approach is not justified in psychology. This is partly because they consider that we do have free will, and partly because they feel that subjectivity (understanding what others are experiencing) is more important than objectivity.

The nature-nurture debate is taken up in the realm of mental disorder by arguments about the origins of mental problems are they present at birth (nature) or are they acquired through experience (nurture)? The interactionist position is a compromise between these two, suggesting that both are involved. This is dealt with in *Psychopathology* by Stirling and Hellewell of the series in detail, but there are some aspects that can be considered here. Perhaps the most important is the extent to which research into this topic is dependent on a reliable and valid classification system. In order to carry out research into the causes of problems such as schizophrenia, we must be able to identify schizophrenics accurately in the first place. Another important point that can be illustrated well using material from this text is the great variety of influences, both nature and nurture, which can be involved in bringing about mental disorder. This links well with the levels of analysis mentioned earlier when discussing reductionism. Cultural, social, cognitive, genetic and biochemical levels (among others) can all be seen at work in the field of mental disorder.

Approaches/models

Within psychology there are several different approaches, or models, which can be applied to abnormal behaviour. These determine which behaviours are regarded as abnormal, as well as how those behaviours are explained and treated, hence they have considerable practical importance. In this book we will be focusing primarily on the first of these areas, the others being dealt with by other books in this series. The models we will be outlining include the biological/ medical, psychodynamic, behavioural and cognitive (as mentioned in the first part of the AQA specification), the social constructionist, humanistic and evolutionary (from the second part of the specification), and the family systems and socio-cultural (from the third part of the specification). The approaches underlying these models should already be familiar to AQA students. As this topic is dealt with in *Psychopathology* by Stirling and Hellewell, only a brief outline of each will be given, and an example of an explanation for mental disorder.

The Medical (or Biomedical) Model

This approach assumes, as outlined earlier in the chapter, that abnormal behaviour exists when there is an identifiable cluster of symptoms. This cluster is indicative of an underlying physical illness, possibly involving neurological or biochemical malfunction due to genetic abnormalities, accident or disease. A biomedical explanation for depression, for example, would suggest that it may be the result of a faulty gene, a hormone imbalance, or a disorder in the system of neurotransmitters that brings about communication in the nervous system. Treatment should therefore be based on the removal of this underlying physical illness, under the direction of a physician. If it cannot be cured (e.g. by surgery), then it can be controlled by physical means using drugs or electroconvulsive shock therapy (ECT). Depression is likely to be treated using antidepressant drugs and ECT, for example.

In support of this model, it is possible to carry out scientific research to test hypotheses about medical bases for disorders. (This contrasts it with the psychodynamic model, to be discussed shortly.) Research has found support for organic involvement in some disorders. General Paresis of the Insane (GPI), for example, is known to be caused by infection with syphilis. Manic depression seems to be influenced by genes, and schizophrenics have shown abnormalities when subjected to brain scans. Physical treatments, such as drugs, have been successful in dealing with the symptoms of some disorders.

However, not all disorders have shown links with biological causes; nor is it certain that the organic changes observed in patients are causes rather than effects of the disorder. Physical treatments are by no means always successful, which again raises questions about the alleged physical basis for the disorders. We will return to this when discussing the validity of the classification systems.

The Psychodynamic Model

The view here is that we are all abnormal to some degree as a result of the inevitable clash between our innate instincts (represented by a part of the personality called the 'id') and the demands of society (represented by the 'superego'). In particular, sexual desires and the way that they are dealt with in the course of development can lead to conflicts in the unconscious mind. Although we may be unaware of these conflicts, they can have a powerful influence on our behaviour. Mediating between the id and the superego is a third part of the personality, the ego. The ego may experience anxiety as a result of pressures from these other elements of the personality. It has a variety of defence mechanisms (such as repressing distressing thoughts into the unconscious mind) that it can deploy to protect itself from this anxiety. It is the strength of the ego and its defence mechanisms that determines whether or not we will experience mental problems.

In this view, depression has been considered to be the result of the early loss of a parent. This loss may be objective (as in bereavement) or subjective (if the individual feels let down or abandoned, for example). In both cases, the anger felt at the parent for leaving has been suppressed and turned on the self.

Developing the ego's capacity to deal with conflict lies at the heart of the psychodynamic approach to treatment. This entails finding out about the client's early childhood experiences, and unearthing the resultant conflicts that reside in the unconscious (such as early loss in the case of depression). In the course of psychoanalysis the analyst provides insight to the client based on the client's free associations, analysis of dreams, and on the nature of the relationship that develops between analyst and client. In the case of depression, it may involve providing a parent-child relationship in therapy, so that the individual can experience caring and understanding from another.

This approach has been very influential, but the lack of scientific basis in the way that Freud operated has led to a great deal of criticism. The theories have been based on the case study method, which focuses on individuals. This means that generalising to the population as a whole is difficult to do. Some writers have criticised Freud for being biased in the way that he dealt with patients and wrote up the cases. Furthermore, because the unconscious remains generally inaccessible, it is difficult to put Freudian concepts to the test in scientifically acceptable ways. The psychoanalytic treatment that has been developed from these ideas appears in general to be limited in the range of disorders to which it can be successfully applied. It is much more useful with less severe disorders such as generalised anxiety than with schizophrenia, for example.

The Behavioural Model

The behaviourists as a group identified the study of observable behaviour to be the main aim of psychology in general. Not surprisingly, they see abnormality as being the demonstration of maladaptive behaviours. These behaviours they consider to have been learnt through conditioning processes, either operant (learning through reinforcement and punishment) or classical (learning through association). Anybody could learn these behaviours, given the appropriate environmental conditions.

In this view, depression may be a manifestation of learned helplessness. This is a state of apathy that results when an animal cannot escape from an unpleasant situation. It has been demonstrated in animals who are faced with aversive stimulation (such as electric shocks) from which they cannot escape. When confronted with further shocks from which they can escape, they do not do so, and the behaviours they display appear similar in some ways to those of depressive patients.

Changing the environmental conditions can also, therefore, lead to the elimination of undesirable behaviours. Behavioural therapies aim to do this through an analysis of the reinforcements (positive consequences) that are maintaining the behaviours at present. These will then be altered in the course of a therapy (there are a variety of these, such as behaviour modification, aversion, implosion or systematic desensitisation), and more appropriate behaviours will be encouraged. Targets will be set with the client, so the control is not totally in the hands of the therapist. For depression, the task of treatment is to increase the frequency of social behaviour and ensure that it is associated with pleasant outcomes.

Based on sound research, albeit mainly using animals, the behaviourist approach offers several useful therapies that have been shown to deal quickly and effectively with some mental disorders, such as phobias. However, it has been criticised for offering a 'quick fix' rather than getting to the root of the problem. It is also difficult to explain why, given the same environmental experiences, some people develop maladaptive behaviours whereas others do not, and others will develop different maladaptive behaviours.

The Cognitive Model

Cognitive psychologists such as Beck link abnormal behaviour with distorted thought patterns, which lead in turn to disordered behaviour. These distortions can include dichotomous thinking (seeing everything as either black or white) and overgeneralisation (e.g. assuming that because something has happened once, it will always happen). Depression, for example, may be associated with having a negative view of the self, the world and the future (known as the 'cognitive triad ' of depression). Such individuals maintain these biases by simply failing to notice any events that do not support their negative views. Other disorders may result from social learning processes, in which behaviour is observed in others and imitated.

Rather like the behaviourists, cognitive therapists are not concerned with the origins of these ways of thinking, so much as with changing them for more realistic and adaptive ones. Cognitive therapists aim to identify disordered thoughts and instigate programmes that will eliminate them, replacing them with more rational thought processes and behaviours. Therapies based on the cognitive model involve identifying and restructuring the problematic thought patterns. A depressive patient, for example, may be encouraged to keep a diary to identify the negative automatic thoughts that occur. These can then be challenged by logical argument and by practical tasks. Role play may also be used when it is felt that behaviours may be changed through observation and imitation.

Again the approach is a scientific one, based on theories that have been developed through research. Effective therapies have been devised to treat depression and panic disorder, for example, and more recently there is evidence that they can be used to control the hallucinations suffered by schizophrenics. However, just as the behaviourists consider that 'it could happen to anyone', there is the assumption that anyone could develop maladaptive thought processes, but the theorists fail to explain why only certain individuals seem to do so. In some cases, such as depression, the thought processes displayed are actually more realistic (they show greater accuracy when assessing risks, for example) than those of 'normal' individuals, so it is difficult to describe them as being 'maladaptive'.

The Social Constructionist Model

This approach takes the view that there is no such thing as objectivity, and that our knowledge of ourselves and the world around us is simply based on social concensus; in other words, it is socially constructed. Because we cannot separate ourselves from our culture or our period in history, we cannot have an unbiased view of the world. This can be extended to mental disorder, making the point that what is perceived as abnormal (as already discussed) may vary, and that mental disorder itself may be socially created according to societal and clinical bias.

The Humanistic/Existentialist Model

The basic premise of this approach is that people are motivated towards personal growth and self-actualisation (realising their potential). They are free to make choices about their lives and accept responsibility for what they do. Mental disorder is thought to result when this is prevented; this may be associated with refusal to accept responsibility for actions, and with a negative view of the self. Depression in this instance could be the result of a blocking of this desire to self-actualise that we all share, or too great a mismatch between the individual's perceived self and the ideal self.

Therapies place an emphasis on understanding the conscious experiences of the individual, and objective scientific analysis is not considered appropriate. The best known of these, person-centred therapy, aims to provide conditions that will encourage personal growth by being non-directive and non-judgemental. Therapy aims to be holistic, and integrate various elements of behaviour so that the person becomes a unique being with the capacity to live 'authentically' (i.e. be spontaneous, caring, open and realistic). These ideas have formed the basis of the very influential counselling movement, and have proved to be useful in dealing with the less severe disorders. Because they play down the role of the 'therapist-as-expert', they have been associated with the growth of community-based self-help groups in many spheres. Where clients are more severely disordered, and may not be very articulate, they have proved to be less useful. On the whole, these theorists have not carried out much scientific research in order to test their ideas.

The Evolutionary Approach

The emphasis here is on the adaptiveness of behaviour. The theory of evolution states that species have evolved through the process of natural selection. Because there is competition between individuals for limited resources, not all are able to survive. Those individuals who are well adapted to the environment will survive to pass on their genes (survival of the fittest) and those who are not well adapted will die out. The relevance here is that for mental disorder to persist in the population, it must be adaptive in some way. Depression, for example, may be adaptive when individuals are faced with situations in which it is impossible to win. Anxiety may have been adaptive when we were faced with 'fight or flight' confrontations, with dangerous animals for example. The fact that it is not adaptive nowadays illustrates genome lag, whereby genes that are no longer useful persist because insufficient time has passed for them to be eliminated. This approach has encouraged us to look at the functions of behaviour. However, it clearly has no application to behaviours that are not genetically determined, and the applications to treatment (genetic engineering and counselling) are ethically dubious. It is also impossible to put these ideas to the test.

The Family Systems Model

Instead of viewing the mentally disordered person as an individual, in this perspective the entire family is looked at as a social system. The idea is that mental disorder may not be located in the individual, but may be indicative of dysfunctional interaction patterns in the family as a whole. Symptoms may develop as a way of distracting attention from areas of conflict. Anorexia nervosa, for example, has been attributed to families where members are over-involved with one another and overt conflict is avoided.

Family therapies based on such explanations focus on communication patterns in families, and use feedback to show family members what is happening. This can also be related to the shared beliefs and understandings of family members. These therapies have proved useful with disturbed children, as well as with marital conflict and violence. The difficulty for theorists is that such patterns of interaction are very difficult to substantiate in scientific research, and much is therefore reliant on clinical judgement.

The Socio-cultural Model

This is the family systems approach on a larger scale, looking at cultural practices and social factors such as poverty for explanations of mental disorder. The variation in incidence of some disorders in different societies, or different groups within society (such as gender and social class), is used as the basis for arguments that social conditions can lead to psychopathology. Depression, for example, is more common in women, particularly those who live in adverse conditions with several young children. Hence it has been linked with isolation, lack of social support, lack of opportunity and feelings of powerlessness. Intervention would take the form of helping individuals to cope through, for example, building up their social support networks. Another possibility is to intervene at the level of the community or at the political level to bring about changes in social conditions.

The Feminist Model

This seeks to locate mental disorder (mainly in women) in the gender role allocated by society. The main focus has been on eating disorders. Anorexia, for example, has been linked with the powerlessness of women, and the need to strive to please, or to gain power, by focusing on their appearance. Fasting gives the satisfaction of being able to exert control over at least one aspect of life. A related view is that self-denial is an integral part of the female role. Once this is accepted, and the woman ceases to recognise her own needs, anorexia may well follow. Change, in this model, can again focus on the individual or on society. Therapy with the individual can aim to free the woman from the constraints of the role provided by society. At the societal level, the aim is to bring about change in the gender roles themselves.

The Eclectic Approach

In practice, no single model can provide all the answers to mental disorder. Clinical psychologists are encouraged to take an eclectic approach, that is, to use all of the models, as appropriate. They may, for example, use a different model at different stages of treatment a biological model initially, to bring the problem under control with drugs, followed by interventions based on behavioural and finally socio-cultural models. A biopsychosocial model represents a good integration of many of these ideas, and accommodates research evidence that all three types of factor may be involved in many disorders. One example of this approach is the diathesis-stress model, which implicates genetic vulnerability or other forms of long-term predisposition, together with environmental stress. Working within one perspective can be seen to be very limiting, especially since, as implied earlier, mental disorders may be the result of causal chains. For example, the immediate cause may be stress, but this may only be problematic for individuals who have developed cognitive biases, which may in turn depend on abnormalities in brain chemistry. This makes it all the more important for treatment to be based on the scientist-practitioner model, which places emphasis on the uniqueness of each case. Careful consideration of each case during the assessment process should then lead to a choice of treatment that is tailored to the individual. The effectiveness of the chosen treatment can then be evaluated and alterations made as required on the basis of scientific analysis. However, clinicians may have preferences or specialisations which may dominate their view of the client and influence the course of treatment chosen, so it is important to be aware of the different viewpoints. Progress exerciseIdentify, in the form of a table, the main assumptions made by each of the aforementioned models about abnormal behaviour. The models can be divided into groups as follows:

Biomedical	Behaviourist	Psychodynamic
		Cognitive
Social constructionist	Humanistic	Evolutionary
Family systems	Socio-cultural	Feminist

Summary

We have seen how the early conflict between seeing abnormal behaviour as demonic possession or as a medical illness continued to dominate thinking in this area until the Age of Reason around the beginning of the 19th century. The religious view was then replaced by a broader moral perspective. Subsequent institutional treatment varied from medical to moral, and has more recently been superseded by a community-based approach (although this still has a strong medical influence). The issue of defining abnormal behaviour has also been controversial, with legal definitions, several sets of psychological criteria and medical criteria having been considered. None of these appears to be totally satisfactory in covering all abnormal behaviours across cultures and eras. Issues and debates in psychology have been discussed in terms of their relationship to abnormal behaviour. Different psychological models of abnormality have also been described - biomedical, psychodynamic, behavioural, cognitive, social constructionist, humanistic, evolutionary, family systems, feminist and socio-cultural - and evaluated in terms of their assumptions and effectiveness.

2

Features of Anxiety Disorders

Introduction

Reliability of anxiety disorder diagnoses has been improving with each revision to the *Diagnostic and Statistical Manual of Mental Disorders*. This is due in large part to greater reliance on empirical data as opposed to theoretical models for decision making. The current list of anxiety disorders is presented in Table 2.1.

Reliability of the most recent diagnostic criteria are yet to be reported, although they are probably at least as reliable as the previous set of diagnostic criteria, of which there are two major reliability studies. Mannuzza, Fyer, Martin, Gallops, Endicott, Gorman, Liebowitz, and Klein examined reliability using the Schedule for Affective Disorders and Schizophrenia-Lifetime Anxiety Version with 104 patients who were interviewed on two separate occasions. Kappa values (coefficients for interrater agreement beyond chance alone) were as follows (current/lifetime): panic disorder .79/.86; agoraphobia .81/.90, simple phobia .29/.29, social phobia .68/.71, obsessive compulsive disorder .91/.89, and generalized anxiety disorder .27/.60. Thus, rater agreement was generally high with the exception of simple phobia and current generalized anxiety disorder. However, these results were based on a draft version of DSM-III-R, to which changes were subsequently made.

Table 2.1. DSM-IV Anxiety Disorders

- Panic Disorder Without Agoraphobia
- Panic Disorder With Agoraphobia
- Agoraphobia Without a History of Panic Disorder
- Specific Phobia
    - Animal Type
    - Natural Environment Type
    - Blood-Injection-Injury Type
    - Situational Type
    - Other Type
- Social Phobia
    - Generalized
- Obsessive Compulsive Disorder
    - Poor Insight
- Post Traumatic Stress Disorder
    - Acute/Chronic
    - With Delayed Onset
    - Acute Stress Disorder
    - Generalized Anxiety Disorder
    - Anxiety Disorder Due to a General Medical Condition
    - Substance Induced Anxiety Disorder

Using the final version of the criteria with 267 individuals who were interviewed twice with the Anxiety Disorders Interview Schedule-Revised, Di Nardo, Moras, Barlow, Rapee, and Brown obtained the following kappas for current diagnoses: panic disorder with agoraphobia .71 (panic disorder or panic disorder with mild agoraphobia .67, panic disorder with moderate or severe agoraphobia .75), simple phobia .63, social phobia .66, obsessive compulsive disorder .75, generalized anxiety disorder .53, and post traumatic stress disorder .55. These coefficients indicate fair to excellent reliability.

Several changes were made to anxiety disorders criteria with the publication of DSM-IV, including recognition that panic attacks may occur in the context of any anxiety disorder. Three different types of panic are specified: situationally bound, in which a specific situation invariably elicits a panic attack; situationally predisposed, in which a specific situation increases the likelihood of a panic attack; and uncued, or panic attacks that seem to occur without an obvious precipitant. Furthermore, changes were made to certain anxiety disorder categories (e.g., obsessive compulsive disorder, generalized anxiety disorder, specific phobia). These are reviewed in later chapters pertaining to each anxiety disorder. Also, childhood anxiety was integrated more fully with adult anxiety in order to emphasize continuity over the life span. In particular, overanxious disorder of childhood and adolescence is now subsumed under generalized anxiety disorder and avoidant disorder is subsumed under social phobia. Separation anxiety remains as the only childhood anxiety disorder.

Very few studies have examined the reliability with which anxiety disorders are diagnosed in children. Silverman and Nelles reported on the diagnostic reliability of DSM-III and DSM-III-R criteria, evaluated with the Anxiety Disorders Interview Schedule for Children -parent and child versions. Interestingly, parents viewed their children as experiencing fewer problems with anxiety than the children reported themselves. When the various anxiety disorders were collapsed, the overall kappa coefficient was high. Given a small sample size (n=51), kappas for individual disorders were restricted to simple phobia, school phobia, and overanxious disorder. The former two had moderate to high kappas, whereas the latter disorder was not reliably diagnosed. Obviously, there is need for more investigation of reliability of anxiety diagnoses in youths.

Prevalence, Course and Help Seeking

The National Comorbidity Survey is the most recent large-scale epidemiological study, with 8,098 15- to 54-year-olds from the community interviewed using the Composite International Diagnostic Interview (CIDI). This instrument is an improvement over the Diagnostic Interview Schedule that was used for the same purposes in the earlier Epidemiological Catchment Area Study (ECA), published in 1984. The NCS data are based on DSM-III-R diagnoses. Approximately 25% of the sample reported a lifetime history of at least one anxiety disorder. This figure was comparable to the rate for substance use disorder and higher than the rate for lifetime history of mood disorders (20%). Interestingly, proportionately more indicated an anxiety disorder than either a substance use disorder or a mood disorder in the last 12 months, suggesting that anxiety disorders are more chronic than either of these other two conditions. The lifetime and current (i.e., last 12 months) prevalence rates for specific anxiety disorders are presented in Table 2.2.

Estimates for obsessive compulsive disorder and post traumatic stress disorder were not included in this report. The lifetime prevalence of post traumatic stress disorder was 7.8% in a separate report from the National Comorbidity Survey. Obviously, this rate increases dramatically in veteran samples.

Weissman examined prevalence of obsessive compulsive disorder across seven different countries, to find a lifetime range of 1.9 to 2.5%, and a 12-month range of 1.1 to 1.8%. Thus, anxiety disorders overall are highly prevalent conditions, with approximately 17% of the population suffering from panic disorder, agoraphobia without panic, social phobia, generalized anxiety disorder, or simple phobia in the last 12 months, and more when obsessive compulsive and post traumatic stress disorders are included.

The typical age of onset varies across the anxiety disorders. In brief, the peak age ranges are childhood for specific phobias (with the exception of claustrophobia), adolescence for social phobia, 20s to 30s for panic disorder and agoraphobia, and 30s to 40s for obsessive compulsive disorder. Some patients with generalized anxiety report that they have been "that way all of their lives," whereas a substantial minority (approximately 35%) report a later onset. Finally, as expected, there is no modal age of onset for post traumatic stress disorder.

Anxiety disorders are not only prevalent — they are chronic. Remission from anxiety disorders (n=77) was estimated at only 17 to 30% from the Munich Follow-up Study, which followed a sample of 1,366 subjects in the community from 1974 to 1981. Also, the majority of individuals with anxiety disorders subsequently develop one or more additional diagnoses. Wittchen found a 66% risk for major depression, dysthymia, substance abuse or dependence, or other disorders in individuals with untreated anxiety disorders. A more recent prospective study known as HARP (Harvard/Brown Anxiety Disorders Research Project) examined the natural course of

Table 2.2. Lifetime and 12-month Prevalence Rates for DSM-III-R Disorders from the National Comorbidity Survey

	Male				Female				Total			
	Lifetime		12 mo.		Lifetime		12 mo.		Lifetime		12 mo.	
Disorders	%	SE	%	SE	%	SE	%	SE	%	SE	%	SE
Affective disorders												
Major depressive episode	12.7	0.9	7.7	0.8	21.3	0.9	12.9	0.8	17.1	0.7	10.3	0.6
Manic episode	1.6	0.3	1.4	0.3	1.7	0.3	1.3	0.3	1.6	0.3	1.3	0.2
Dysthymia	4.8	0.4	2.1	0.3	8.0	0.6	3.0	0.4	6.4	0.4	2.5	0.2
Any affective disorder	14.7	0.8	8.5	0.8	23.9	0.9	14.1	0.9	19.3	0.7	11.3	0.7
Anxiety disorders												
Panic disorder	2.0	0.3	1.3	0.3	5.0	1.4	3.2	0.4	3.5	0.3	2.3	0.3
Agoraphobia without panic disorder	3.5	0.4	1.7	0.3	7.0	0.6	3.8	0.4	5.3	0.4	2.8	0.3
Social phobia	11.1	0.8	6.6	0.4	15.5	1.0	9.1	0.7	13.3	0.7	7.9	0.4
Simple phobia	6.7	0.5	4.4	0.5	15.7	1.1	13.2	0.9	11.3	0.6	8.8	0.5
Generalized anxiety disorder	3.6	0.5	2.0	0.3	6.6	0.5	4.3	0.4	5.1	0.3	3.1	0.3
Any anxiety disorder	19.2	0.9	11.8	0.6	30.5	1.2	22.6	0.1	24.9	0.8	17.2	0.7

Table Contd....

	Male				Female				Total			
	Lifetime		12 mo.		Lifetime		12 mo.		Lifetime		12 mo.	
Disorders	%	SE	%	SE	%	SE	%	SE	%	SE	%	SE
Substance use disorders												
Alcohol abuse without dependence	12.5	0.8	3.4	0.4	6.4	0.6	1.6	0.2	9.4	0.5	2.5	0.2
Alcohol dependence	20.1	1.0	10.7	0.9	8.2	0.7	3.7	0.4	14.1	0.7	7.2	0.5
Drug abuse without dependence	5.4	0.5	1.3	0.2	3.5	0.4	0.3	0.1	4.4	0.3	0.8	0.1
Drug dependence	9.2	0.7	3.8	0.4	5.9	0.5	1.9	0.3	7.5	0.4	2.8	0.3
Any substance abuse/dependence	35.4	1.2	16.1	0.7	17.9	1.1	6.6	0.4	26.6	1.0	11.3	0.5
Other disorders												
Antisocial personality	5.8	0.6	-	-	1.2	0.3	-	-	3.5	0.3	-	-
Nonaffective psychosist	0.6	0.1	0.5	0.1	0.8	0.2	0.6	0.2	0.7	0.1	0.5	0.1
Any NCS disorder	48.7	0.2	27.7	0.9	47.3	1.5	31.2	1.3	48.0	1.1	29.5	1.0

Notes: Prevalence rates for obsessive compulsive disorder and post traumatic stress disorder are not included.

anxiety disorders. The probability of panic disorder patients achieving an eight-week remission from panic attacks over the course of one year was .42. Probabilities of remission were lower for patients with panic attacks and agoraphobia (.15). From the same data set, Keller reported that of those who remitted, patients with panic disorder and panic disorder with agoraphobia had relatively high probabilities of relapse (.31 and .35, respectively). In other words, remission rates are generally low, and a substantial proportion of those who remit subsequently relapse.

Costs of untreated anxiety disorders have been stated to some degree already comorbidity with depression and substance abuse. Suicidality is another cost. A recent study of inpatients found a high rate of suicide among "pure" anxiety neuroses. Nearly one third of all deaths before the age of 70 were from suicide, suggesting that the risk of suicide for *inpatients* with anxiety disorders may be as high as for patients with depression. Obviously, the rates are considerably lower among less distressed groups. For example, Goisman noted that 9% of patients with panic disorder or agoraphobia in the HARP study reported ever having made a suicidal attempt or gesture.

Other costs include financial burdens. Anxiety disorders account for 31% of total mental health costs, exceeding those due to mood disorders (22%) and schizophrenia (20%). Panic disorder in particular is associated with increased health care utilization. For example, Swinson, Cox and Woszcyna found that in the last year, nearly one third of 128 panic disorder and social phobia patients had seen three or more different health care professionals, and one fifth with panic disorder had gone to an emergency room. In addition, panic disorder is associated with increased use of welfare, impaired marital and social functioning and impaired work productivity and employment status. From a sample of 65 patients with panic disorder, Siegel, Jones, and Wilson estimated that seven times as many physician visits occurred, twice as many work days were lost, and overall life satisfaction and number of good days were lower than in the general population. Finally, there is evidence for increased cardiac, respiratory, gastrointestinal, and neurological illnesses and mortality with anxiety disorders, although again these data refer mostly to panic disorder.

Despite the serious consequences of untreated anxiety, most individuals do not seek treatment. Only 20% of 65 young adults with anxiety disorders in Zurich had received treatment within the last 12 months. From the ECA study, only 27% of those with agoraphobia and 16% of those with some other kind of phobia had sought assistance for mental health within the last six months. Similarly, Pollard, Henderson, Frank, and Margolis found that of a sample of 142 individuals, only 40% of those with agoraphobia, 28% with obsessive compulsive disorder, and 8% with social phobia reported having sought professional assistance. Furthermore, treatment that is obtained is not necessarily effective treatment. Fewer than 15% of almost 800 volunteers for panic disorder research had previously received appropriate behavioral therapy or tricyclic antidepressants. Swinson, Cox noted from their clinic sample that only 11% with panic disorder and 4% with social phobia had received cognitive-behavioral therapy in the past. Finally, the HARP study found that of 562 patients with panic and/or agoraphobia followed for one year, only 15% received behavioral therapy and 16% received cognitive therapy (both of which have demonstrated efficacy), whereas 33% received psychodynamic therapy (a therapy that has not been demonstrated to be effective for panic disorder). These data illustrate the need to disseminate information regarding effective treatment to patients and clinicians alike.

Comorbidity

Sanderson, Di Nardo, Rapee, and Barlow examined comorbidity in a sample of 130 patients presenting to an anxiety disorders treatment facility. Seventy percent received at least one additional Axis I diagnosis, most commonly simple phobia and social phobia. Taking a more conservative approach by excluding subclinical diagnoses, de Ruiter, Rijken, Garssen, van Schaik, and Kraaimaat found a very similar result. These data suggest a strong tendency for anxiety disorders to cluster together.

Mood Disorders

There is considerable evidence for clustering of anxiety and depression. In the previous two studies, dysthymia and major depressive episodes were the next most common comorbid diagnoses. Angst, Vollrath, Merikangas, and Ernst examined the prevalence rate for simultaneous manifestation of anxiety and mood disorders as part of the Zurich Study. They found that the joint presentation of anxiety and depression occurred at a rate that was three times higher than chance expectations and that the combination was nearly as common as the occurrence of anxiety alone. A particularly strong association was noted between panic disorder and depression, occurring at a rate that was five times greater than chance. Furthermore, anxiety usually preceded depression: 62% were first diagnosed with anxiety and later developed depression, whereas 18% showed the reverse pattern. A strong relationship is found between anxiety and depression among children as well.

The fact that depression most commonly follows rather than precedes anxiety suggests that depression may be a response to anxiety; that is, individuals become depressed as a result of impairment and distress imposed by anxiety disorders. Alternatively, Watson and Kendall and Alloy, Kelly, Mineka and Clements attribute the association between anxiety and depression to shared features, including negative affect, irritability, decreased energy, disorganization, performance deficits, restless sleep, helplessness, worry, and negative self-evaluation. Others note that anxiety and depression may share basic biological and psychological predispositions. For example, Alloy proposed the Helplessness-Hopelessness model of comorbidity between anxiety and depression, which views anxiety and depression as sharing an expectation of uncontrollability but differing in negative outcome expectancies. Pure anxiety is hypothesized to result from a helplessness expectancy regarding ability to control important future outcomes, although the expectancy is uncertain (i.e., neither stable nor global). Uncertain expectancy generates a state of preparation, or increased arousal, vigilance, and anxiety. As the attributions become more negative, a mixed anxiety-depression emerges, in which one is convinced of helplessness but still uncertain about the likelihood of important negative events in the future. Finally, with certain helplessness and certain hopelessness (i.e., the conviction that negative outcomes will occur), the presentation shifts into pure depression, characterized by despair, loss of interest, and suicidality.

Occurrence of depression with an anxiety disorder increases severity of presentation in several ways. For example, patients with panic disorder or generalized anxiety disorder combined with major depression show greater psychopathology; are less likely to respond to conventional antidepressants, placebo therapy and psychological therapy; and are less likely to recover over a period of 2 years. Furthermore, Wittchen reported greater psychosocial impairment when major depression was also present. This was particularly interesting given that the symptom course for depression was more episodic than for anxiety. Wittchen suggests that a history of depression, even if currently remitted, confers greater impairment because of long-lasting psychological aftereffects of depression.

Personality Disorders

Others have noted elevated rates of personality disorders among individuals with anxiety disorders. As expected, the most commonly diagnosed personality disorders are from Cluster C (i.e., avoidant, dependent, and obsessive compulsive), which raises the possibility that "personality disorders" are a function of anxiety disorders. In support of this hypothesis, scores on personality measures tend to change with improvement in agoraphobia. Unfortunately, this area of research is beset with measurement problems (such as instrument variability and reliability), so that the extent to which personality features are precursors to or the result of anxiety disorders remains questionable. Furthermore, unreliable measurement of personality probably accounts for the wide range in comorbidity across studies. For example, estimates range from 26% to 58% among panic disorder patients.

With the reliability caveat in mind, we can consider several studies that compare personality disorders across the various anxiety disorders. Sciuto, Diaferia, Battaglia, Perna, Gabriele, and Bellodi found slightly higher rates of personality disorder in obsessive compulsive patients (68.8%) than panic disorder patients (60%). From a sample of 347 patients with a principal anxiety disorder diagnosis, Sanderson, Wetzler, Beck, and Betz found that 35% met criteria for at least one personality disorder. This was particularly so for patients with social phobia and generalized anxiety and least so for patients with simple phobia. Similarly, data from the HARP study show that generalized anxiety and social phobia were most frequently associated with personality disorders. Reasons for the different rates across anxiety disorders are not clear.

As with comorbidity with depression, comorbidity with personality disorders is associated with more severe psychopathology. For example, comorbid presence of personality disorders may reduce treatment efficacy. In addition, the presence of personality disorders is associated with more severe depression. In fact, there is some evidence to suggest that depression is a mediating variable that increases the risk for personality disorders in anxious individuals. For example, Alnaes and Torgersen and Reich found that patients with anxiety and depression had more frequent and more severe personality disorders than anxious patients who were not depressed. Also, Klass, Di Nardo and Barlow noted that anxiety patients with personality disorders were more depressed than those without personality disorders. However, the causal pathways are yet to be fully determined, and a reciprocal relationship remains equally plausible, whereby an initial anxious or depressed mood engenders maladaptive personality styles that in turn generate more anxiety and depression.

Substance Abuse

Comorbidity occurs between anxiety and substance use disorders, although the rates may differ across the anxiety disorders. For example, Himle and Hill reported that although 12% of 2,371 individuals with lifetime diagnoses of mixed anxiety disorders (ECA study) also met criteria for lifetime history of alcohol abuse or dependence, the rates were particularly high and above general population rates for panic disorder with agoraphobia (30%). Similarly, Bibb and Chambless and Reich and Chaudry reported high rates of alcoholism among patients with agoraphobia and panic disorder. In contrast, rates with simple phobias may not differ from the general population.

Also, anxiety disorders are common in substance-abusing populations, as is use of substances to cope with anxiety. For example, alcoholics in the ECA study were twice as likely to have panic disorder compared to the general population. In comorbid samples, substance abuse most commonly follows rather than precedes anxiety or mood disorders. This pattern suggests that substance abuse is most often a reaction to anxiety disorders. On the other hand, Weissman noted that despite gender differences, anxiety and alcoholism show similar symptoms and tend to co-occur in families. In support, family studies of patients with agoraphobia show a larger than expected number of relatives with alcohol difficulties, and there is an elevated risk of panic disorder in co-twins of alcoholic probands.

Models of Comorbidity

Comorbidity among anxiety, depression, substance abuse, and personality disorders might reflect shared predispositions or distinct pathologies that co-occur but develop in chronological sequence. With respect to the latter, anxiety in childhood may contribute to maladaptive interpersonal styles (or the foundations of personality disorders) that in turn contribute to the development of anxiety and depression in adulthood. Depression may also be engendered directly by chronic anxiety. Anxiety and depression in turn may lead to reliance on substances as a method of coping, which in turn contributes to continued anxiety and depression. Although accounting for the usual course, this model does not explain the above-chance risk for alcoholism in biological relatives of patients with anxiety disorders, and vice versa, which suggest shared biological and/or environmental predispositional factors.

Fear and Anxiety in Children

Transitory fears are very common and part of normal child development. The number of intense fears averages 11 to 13 for 6- to 18-year-olds. Most studies show a decline in the number of fears with increasing age.

Also, fears tend to change over time, shifting from immediate, tangible fears to anticipatory, less tangible fears. In children of very young ages, fears of loud noises, being dropped or startled, loss of support, and separation from mother predominate. These are followed by fears of strangers as the child learns to recognize the difference between others and the primary caregiver. Fears of imaginary creatures and small animals develop during toddler years, followed by fears of darkness in the fourth year, and social fears during the fifth to sixth years. For children from around age six through adolescence, fears remain relatively constant and consist primarily of fears related to injury, natural events, and social anxiety.

The 10 most common fears for youths in 1985 were being hit by a car or truck, not being able to breathe, fire getting burned, death or dead people, bombing attacks being invaded, getting poor grades, having my parents argue, being sent to the principal, a burglar breaking into our house, and falling from a high place.

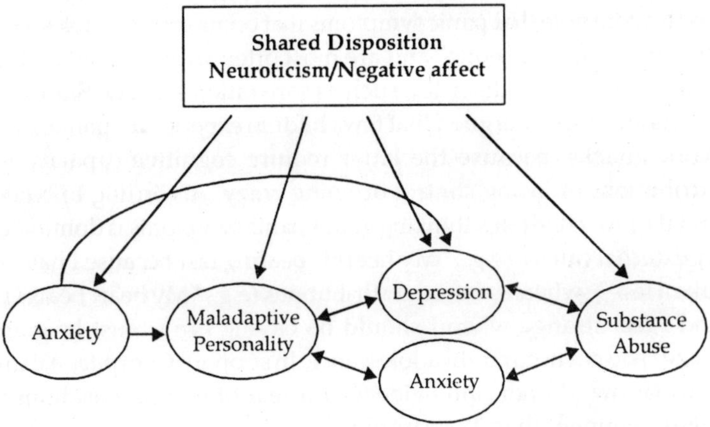

Fig. 2.1. Shared disposition and developmental model of comorbidity.

Ollendick posit that fears change throughout childhood as a result of cognitive development and abilities to recognize and understand dangers in different situations: The child is increasingly able to perceive potential dangers but has neither advanced to the point of understanding the situation fully nor become fully able to exercise control over the situation. Thus, fears are adaptive, or possess survival value. However, as reviewed in the next chapter, normal development may be arrested by reinforcement patterns from significant others, so that fears that would normally subside as the child develops become reinforced and continue long after their adaptive value has lessened. Obviously, fears and anxieties that persist and impair functioning develop into anxiety disorders.

A recent interest is the phenomenon of panic in children and adolescents. King, Gullone, Tonge, and Ollendick examined the incidence of panic attacks in a group of 534 adolescents aged 13 to 18. Almost 43% reported having a panic attack (i.e., sudden and unexpected fear) at some time in their lives. However, as with adult samples in the general population, the vast majority were not perturbed by these experiences, and only 6.8% indicated that the panics created "quite a bit or very much" interference in their lives. Using more conservative definitions of panic, Hayward found that 5.3% of 754 adolescent girls reported a history of at least one panic attack involving four or more symptoms. Interestingly, the incidence increased with sexual maturity, regardless of age. Last, Perrin, Hersen and Kazdin note that panic symptoms that occur prior to adolescence are rarely "spontaneous" and are most often an associated feature of another anxiety disorder, such as separation anxiety. Similarly, Nelles and Barlow argued that few children experience spontaneous panic attacks, because the latter require cognitive capacity for attributions of losing control or going crazy. According to Nelles and Barlow, children's thinking about panic symptoms is dominated by external causes (e.g., "My heart is beating fast because I have to take a test"), whereas internal attributions (e.g., "My heart beats fast and I feel strange when I should be having fun I must be going crazy") do not occur until adolescence. In support, Chorpita, Albano and Barlow did not find evidence for fear of bodily sensations in youths younger than 12 years old.

Anxiety disorders are among the most common psychiatric diagnoses among children and adolescents. Among preadolescent children, estimates range from .7 to 12.9% for separation anxiety, 2.7 to 12.4% for overanxious disorder, 2.4 to 9.2% for simple phobia, 1.0 to 1.1% for social phobia, and .3% for obsessive compulsive disorder. Among adolescents, the ranges are as follows: 2.0 to 3.6% for separation anxiety disorder; 2.4 to 7% for overanxious disorder, 1.9 to 4.0% for obsessive compulsive disorder, .6 to 4.7% for panic disorder, 3.6% for simple phobia, and 1.1% for social phobia. Prevalence estimates generally increase with age, particularly for social phobia, which reaches 11.1% by 18 years. However, as can be seen, estimates vary considerably across studies, possibly due to unreliable diagnoses.

As with adults, there is strong comorbidity among anxiety disorders in children. For example, up to 50% of clinic-referred children and adolescents with either separation anxiety or overanxious disorder have another anxiety disorder. Similarly, in the general population, comorbidity among anxiety disorders is found for up to 39% of children and 14% of adolescents. Also, children with anxiety disorders frequently experience depression, as well as attention deficit disorder and conduct/oppositional disorders. Consistent with the adult literature, specific phobias among youths tend to be associated with the least pathology overall, whereas overanxious disorder has the highest rate of comorbidity.

Although the diagnosis may change over time, children with anxiety disorders tend to retain an anxiety syndrome or mood disorder, often developing new anxiety disorders. Three to four years following initial diagnosis for clinic-referred children and adolescents, 82% no longer met criteria for their initial anxiety disorder. Separation anxiety disorder had the highest recovery rate (96%), and specific phobias the lowest (69%). However, during the follow-up period, 30% developed new psychiatric disorders and half of these developed new anxiety disorders.

Instability in specific diagnoses is apparent over shorter time frames as well. Beidel, Fink and Turner examined stability of diagnostic, selfreport, and psychophysiological data over a six-month interval in 75 boys and 75 girls, aged 7 to 12 years. Of the 12 children diagnosed initially with social phobia, 4 (33%) still met diagnostic criteria, 5 (41%) continued to endorse social fears but did not meet criteria (i.e., subthreshold), 2 (16%) were diagnosed with overanxious disorder, and 1 (8%) had no diagnosis six months later. Of the 12 children diagnosed initially with overanxious disorder, 6 (50%) still met criteria, 3 (25%) were diagnosed with social phobia, and 3 (25%) had no diagnosis. Of the 72 children without an Axis I disorder at initial assessment, 61% continued to report little or no distress, whereas 39% reported subthreshold features of either social phobia or overanxious disorder.

Data concerning the development of anxiety from childhood to adulthood are scant. Extrapolating from research presented above, one might surmise that anxiety and fear are likely to continue into adulthood, but the specific anxiety disorder and clinical versus subclinical status may shift over time, and the role of depressed mood may become more prominent. Some recent data suggest that 21-year-olds with anxiety disorders have a history of anxiety disorders more often than not (Newman, Moffitt, Caspi, Magdol, Silva, & Stanton, 1996), as shown in Figure 2.2

Nevertheless, childhood anxiety neither guarantees nor is necessary for the development of adult anxiety. For example, only

54% of 194 adults with panic disorder retrospectively reported a history of childhood anxiety disorders. There are probably a plethora of social and psychological factors that moderate the relationship between childhood and adulthood anxiety. Also, if anxiety does persist into adulthood, the degree to which the symptoms of adult anxiety are similar to the anxiety disorders of childhood and adolescence is not clear.

Anxiety in the Elderly

Examination of childhood anxiety is a relatively recent endeavor, and even more recent is the study of anxiety in the elderly. Anxiety disorders are less common in the elderly than in younger age groups, but nevertheless, as a group, they remain more common than mood disorders. "Across the eight community surveys conducted to date on individuals ages 60 and older, prevalence rates ranged as follows: phobic disorders, 0% to 10%; GAD, 0.7% to 7.1%; Obsessive Compulsive Disorder, 0% to 1.5%; and Panic Disorder, 0.1% to 1.0%". Anxiety in the elderly is particularly important given negative effects on health status, increased use of pain-relieving medications, increased disability and pain, and increased health care costs associated with anxiety, some of which have been directly assessed in elderly samples.

Most elderly who seek treatment for anxiety disorders receive pharmacological treatment, and evidence suggests that benzodiazepine use is more common among the elderly, despite the potential negative effects of psychotropics in combination with metabolic changes with aging and medical comorbidity. Psychological treatments have only just begun to be investigated. Obviously, this area is in need of a great deal more research attention, including modifications to current effective treatments to suit the needs and medical comorbidities of the elderly.

Gender Differences

Much of the following section is reviewed by Craske and Glover (in press). Epidemiological research clearly establishes that females are more at risk than males for fears. This gender bias is apparent as early as 9 to 12 years of age, when the average number of fears endorsed (mild or greater) is 50 for girls and 40 for boys. Also, girls score higher on measures of general anxiety symptoms and report more distress after natural disasters than boys. In adult samples, women score higher than men on scales such as the Fear Survey Schedule, although adult males report as many fears of public speaking or social-evaluative situations.

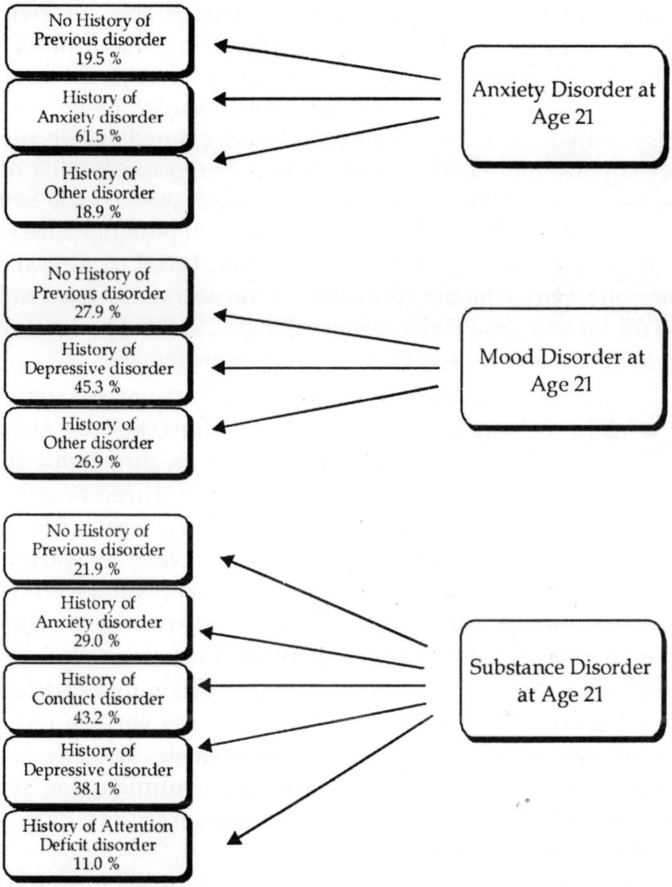

Fig. 2.2. History of anxiety disorders and other disorders in a 21-year-old cohort with anxiety disorders as well as histories for those with mood disorder and substance disorder at age 21. From Newman, D. L., Moffitt, T. E., Caspi, A., Magdol, L., Silva, P. A., & Stanton, W. R. Psychiatric disorder in a birth cohort of young adults: Prevalence, comorbidity, clinical significance, and new case incidence from ages 11 to 21.

In addition, women are more at risk than men for most anxiety disorders. The gender ratio for anxiety disorders was at least 2:1 (F:M) in the Zurich study. The NCS study reported lifetime prevalence rates for any anxiety disorder (excluding obsessive compulsive and post traumatic stress disorders) of 30.5% for females and 19.2% for males. As found in the earlier ECA study, female-to-male discrepancies were least apparent for social phobia, but twice or more as many women than men met criteria for panic disorder with and without agoraphobia, agoraphobia without panic disorder, specific phobias, and generalized anxiety disorder. Other research suggests that, like social phobia, obsessive compulsive disorder is only slightly more common in women. For example, 60% of the obsessive compulsive sample in the ECA study were female. Several studies indicate that women are more at risk for post traumatic stress disorder than men. For example, Breslau, Davis, Andreski, and Peterson reported lifetime prevalence estimates of 11.3% for women and 6% for men, and Helzer reported that 72% of the post traumatic stress disorder sample in the ECA study were female.

Gender patterns among adult patient samples are similar to patterns in the general population. In contrast, anxious children seeking treatment are more likely to be equally distributed across genders, despite clear female versus male differences in the community. This suggests a bias among caregivers. That is, caregivers may be less likely to perceive anxious behaviors as warranting therapeutic intervention in girls than boys. Shyness and withdrawal may be considered more normative for girls than boys, resulting in anxious behaviors being dismissed or minimized in girls.

Gender differences are apparent *within* certain anxiety disorders also. For example, gender ratios differ across varying levels of agoraphobic avoidance. The proportion of females increases as level of agoraphobia intensifies. However, after controlling for level of agoraphobia, few gender differences emerge in self-reported panic disorder symptomatology.

In addition, gender ratios differ across the various subtypes of specific phobias. Himle, McPhee, Cameron, and Curtis found a preponderance of females in patients fearful of animals and choking-vomiting, whereas approximately equal numbers of female and male patients were fearful of blood, injections, and injury and of situations such as driving, flying, heights, enclosed places, and crowds. As with panic disorder, severity of distress associated with specific phobias does not differ between men and women in clinic samples. The same is true in socially phobic and generalized anxiety disorder patients.

Significant gender differences emerge in associated psychopathology such as substance abuse. Males with panic disorder and agoraphobia report significantly greater use of alcohol and more reliance on alcohol than females. The fact that male relatives of individuals with panic disorder and agoraphobia are more likely to suffer from alcoholism than female relatives suggests that gender differences in substance use may involve more than preferred coping style.

Whereas males are more likely to report substance abuse, females are more likely to suffer depression in combination with anxiety disorders. For example, Ochoa, Beck, and Steer examined comorbidity in a large series of 1,051 patients to find that rates for pure anxiety disorders were 9.1% among female patients and 7% among male patients, whereas rates for anxiety disorders comorbid with secondary mood disorders were 14.9% among female patients and 9.3% among male patients. Greater comorbidity between anxiety and depression for females has been reported by others as well.

Gender Roles and Expectations

Cameron and Hill point out that observed differences in gender ratios could be artifacts of reporting bias or diagnostic methodology. That is, males may underreport and/or females may overreport anxiety psychopathology, creating an apparent gender difference when no such differences exist. Pertinent to this issue is a study by Speltz and Bernstein. They examined gender differences in avoidance behavior, by comparing male and female college students who were fearful of snakes. Participants were assigned to high or low demand conditions of approach to a live snake. Overall, highly fearful males achieved closer proximity to the snake than highly fearful females. However, according to behavioral observations of overt motor fear, such as extraneous hand and arm movements, hand tremors, emotional verbalizations, and accelerated breathing, males and females experienced the same degree of psychological distress. Furthermore, highly demanding conditions increased the proximity with which females approached the snake. These data suggest that overt behavior under fearful conditions is in part a function of gender role expectations and that stronger expectations for approach may account for the greater willingness on the part of fearful males to approach phobic objects, but that females will also approach given sufficiently strong expectations. Like overt avoidance behavior, public declaration of fear might be affected by gender roles and expectations, thus producing apparent gender differences in prevalence.

These processes may help explain the progressive predominance of females as level of agoraphobia increases. In support, Chambless and Mason found that differences between 68 men and 334 women in agoraphobic avoidance behavior were due mostly to masculinity traits. They acknowledge, however, that lower "masculinity" may be either a cause or a result of agoraphobic behavior. Furthermore, one would expect fear scales to correlate with measures of social conformity if indeed gender roles influence fear reporting. The evidence is equivocal. Finally, as Cameron and Hill note, a gender response bias would be expected to operate across all anxiety disorders; that is, a reporting bias does not explain why gender differences are more apparent for some anxiety disorders than others.

Alternatively, females have fewer opportunities for exposure to situations such as travel away from home and being alone. Consequently, they may have less opportunity to habituate to or extinguish their fears. The fact that they probably have as much opportunity as men for exposure to social situations may explain why gender differences are less apparent for that category of stimuli. Another commonly cited reason for gender differences is that males are less likely to seek help than females. However, the data do not support this hypothesis. In contrast to expectations, Pollard found the same ratio (2:1) of females to males among anxiety disordered individuals in samples of persons who did not seek help and samples of those who did seek help. Similarly, epidemiologists note that "once a phobia has become established, men appear to be no different than women in seeking professional help".

Oei found gender differences in clinician-rated scales of symptomatology of agoraphobia, despite the absence of gender differences in self-reported symptomatology. They attributed this to a clinician bias toward rating male agoraphobics as less severe than female agoraphobics, given that clinicians generally rate females as more symptomatic than males. (Note the contrast with the notion that caregivers are less inclined to seek treatment for anxiety symptoms in girls than boys.) Such biases for adults may operate at the level of diagnostic assignment as well, with clinicians more likely to diagnose the same behavior as a sign of an anxiety disorder in women.

Traumas and Stressors

Gender differences may arise from a higher incidence of acute and/or chronic traumas or stressors in women as a result of their lower status politically, economically, and socially in most cultures. A traumatic event to which men and women are differentially vulnerable is physical or sexual abuse. Incidence rates suggest that females experience greater threat of this sort of abuse than men. Results from law enforcement agencies, national random surveys, and representative samples of college students suggest 12.9 to 15.4% of all women in the United States have been raped at least once during their lifetime, and actual incidence rates may be considerably higher. Also, 16 to 34% of women report at least one occasion of physical abuse from male partners. Physical and sexual abuse is obviously associated with increased risk for post traumatic stress disorder. The degree to which such abuse increases the risk for other anxiety disorders is not known, but an increase is expected.

Even if women are not victims of rape or assault, the potential risk for such events may influence their perceptions of threat. In a survey of 1,200 urban Israelis asked to select the most anxiety-provoking scenario in everyday life, women selected situations involving physical threat whereas men selected property-threat scenarios. Also, Koss and Mukai reviewed evidence showing that fear of rape is highly prevalent among women and it is a fear not shared by men.

Other traumatic events include natural disaster, robbery, seeing others seriously hurt or killed, and sudden injury or accident. More women (27%) than men (13%) in the "high exposure" category developed major depression, generalized anxiety, or post traumatic stress disorder following the Mount Saint Helens volcano. Also, from a sample of over 1,000 21- to 30-year-olds, males were 1.46 times more likely to encounter traumatic events, but among those exposed to traumatic events, women were 1.77 times more likely than men to develop post traumatic stress disorder.

The role of less traumatic negative life events, such as divorce or job loss, is less clear. Contrary to expectations, Kessler and McLeod found from their meta-analysis of community surveys that men and women reported comparable numbers of undesirable life events. Perhaps women are more vulnerable to specific types of daily negative events. For example, Kessler and McLeod noted that "network life crises" events, such as the death of a friend or other close relative (other than child or spouse), were associated with more psychological distress in women than men. Russo and Green reviewed the impact of important events such as menstruation, pregnancy, childbirth, abortion, and menopause on women's mental health in general. However, the relationship between these types of events and anxiety disorders is unknown due to the scarcity of well-controlled experimental research.

Biological Features

Perhaps females are more physiologically predisposed to experience fear and anxiety. However, the evidence does not support this hypothesis. Basic experimental research shows that male rodents are more sensitive and physiologically reactive to stress than females. A particularly interesting set of findings was reported by Blanchard, Shepherd, de Padua Carobrez and Blanchard, who studied natural defensive patterns in rats exposed to a cat (a natural predator of rats). Defensive patterns were assessed under two conditions: during the predator's presence ("actual threat") and following predator removal ("potential threat"). The potential threat condition involved exposure to cat odors and other aftereffects of the cat's presence. When the cat was present, males and females behaved similarly, engaging in almost no movement or observable behavior, indicating high fear. However, under "potential threat" conditions, females behaved more defensively than males, suggesting greater female reactivity to risk of threat. These results raise the interesting possibility that females may be more distressed by potential threat, which may retard their recovery from acute stressors and contribute to their greater risk for fears and anxiety disorders. On the other hand, several studies with nonprimates and humans show that the genders do not differ in their rate of fear acquisition to discrete conditional stimuli (e.g., tones paired with the delivery of shock).

Very few studies have examined gender as a factor in human psychophysiological response to fear-provoking stimuli, and the available data are contradictory. Haskins found that female college students showed greater electrodermal activity than their male counterparts when presented with innocuous tones, an arithmetic problem, and blood drawing from the antecubital vein. The gender difference was particularly pronounced in the latter two anxiety-producing conditions. In contrast, Katkin and Hoffman found no differences in skin conductance when spiders were presented to equally fearful males and females. Furthermore, several studies report stronger skin conductance reactivity in males, as measured via rates of habituation, responding during classical conditioning, and responding during the vicarious threat of observing others receive shock. Finally, Stoney, Davis and Matthews concluded from their meta-analysis that females have a higher heart rate at rest and during challenge than males. However, males show higher systolic blood pressure at rest and in response to challenge.

Other researchers have studied adrenaline and noradrenaline (catecholamines, also referred to as epinephrine and norepinephrine) as indicators of emotional arousal. Frankenhaeuser's review found no evidence for gender differences under resting conditions. However, when stressed (e.g., taking a test under a time pressure or performing an attention-demanding task), both adult men and boys increased their output of epinephrine, whereas epinephrine levels for women and girls remained relatively stable. Similarly, Elwood, Ferguson, and Thakar found that boys were more likely to respond to stressors with increases in catecholamine (adrenaline; noradrenaline; and 3-methoxy-4-hydroxyphenylglycol, or MHPG) than girls. Thus, with the possible exception of heart rate, males may have greater physiological response during acute behavioral stress than females.

Cognitive Processing and Appraisals

There is now strong evidence that anxiety enhances attention to threat-relevant stimuli and decreases attention to neutral or positive stimuli. Once anxious, individuals tend to focus on danger-laden aspects of their internal or external environment and to interpret ambiguous events as threatening. Very little research has directly examined gender differences with respect to attentional and cognitive processes of these kinds. One study shows no gender differences in reactions to ambiguous arousal, suggesting women are no more likely to interpret ambiguous arousal caused by exercise as negative than men.

However, these information-processing biases are central to the construct of worry, and worry is gender related. That is, most self-reported worriers are women and females score significantly higher than males on worry scales. Perhaps women's tendencies to worry lower their autonomic reactivity to acute stressors. Stavosky and Borkovec hypothesize that worry is fundamentally a fear of failure and rejection. They suggest women worry more because they experience more situations in which potential failure is a real possibility. Women's status (e.g., less power, lower socioeconomic levels, and less economic freedom) leads to feelings of lack of control and frustration. This frustration occurs when there is a discrepancy between expected or hoped-for goals and perceived reality. Gender-stereotypical roles of feminine passivity and dependence may encourage worry and discourage overt problem-solving action. Consequently, stressful events may be more anxiety inducing in women than men, consistent with previously cited evidence regarding reactivity to "potential threat" and the development of post traumatic stress symptoms after traumas.

Also, worry shares features in common with "rumination" a construct proposed by Nolen-Hoeksema and colleagues in which gender differences are clearly apparent. They define rumination as behaviors or thoughts that focus attention on depressive symptoms or their consequences, in contrast to diversion of attention onto pleasant or neutral topics (e.g., Nolen-Hoeksema. Morrow and Nolen-Hoeksema proposed that rumination prolongs a negative mood by generating more negative interpretations and outcome expectancies and/or interfering with effective problem solving and decision making. Females are more likely to ruminate than males in response to depressed mood. One might expect the same for anxious mood. Indeed, rumination prolonged anxious moods relative to distracting conditions, although gender differences were not measured in this study.

Feelings of uncontrollability are central to the clinical presentation of anxious patients. Barlow proposed that perceived lack of control over negative events underlies much of the anxious apprehension about the future that characterizes anxiety disorders. Also, Bandura emphasizes that perceived self-efficacy to exercise control over potential threats is central to anxiety. There are some reports that women are more fatalistic and have a lower sense of personal control over their lives than men. Furthermore, women may not accurately perceive their own abilities or may have unreasonably low self-efficacy. For example, in a study of test anxiety, Furst, Tenenbaum, and Weingarten found that women tended to underestimate their actual test performance whereas men overestimated their performance.

Also, Foa and Riggs assign a prominent role to the sense of uncontrollability in their etiological model of post traumatic stress disorder. Women who view themselves as incompetent or unable to control the world are at high risk for the development of post traumatic stress disorder following a traumatic incident, according to this model. Interestingly, also at high risk are women who believe they are competent and always in control because the traumatic incident disconfirms these assumptions. Women not at high risk for post traumatic stress disorder are hypothesized to be those who hold neither extreme view of the world and themselves but instead recognize that sometimes they cannot control aversive events. However, experimental studies of gender differences in this paradigm have yet to be conducted.

Conclusion

In summary, various factors may be implicated in the higher risk for fears and anxiety disorders among females. Gender role expectations may encourage males to display less fear and avoidance behavior than females, although willingness to seek help does not differ across genders. Also, gender role stereotypes may influence the diagnostic process, such that clinicians are more likely to assign higher levels of symptomatology and an anxiety disorder diagnosis to women than men. In terms of precipitating events, females are more prone to traumas of physical and sexual abuse and are more likely to suffer long-term anxiety reactions (i.e., post traumatic stress disorder) than males, given the same trauma. In addition, females may experience more "network crises" (such as death of a friend or close relative) and suffer the impact of such crises more than males.

Physiological data are contradictory, possibly due to methodological inconsistencies across studies. Basic experimental research with nonprimates suggests that males are more reactive to acute stress, although they are no more likely to develop conditioned fear. Female nonprimates appear more reactive to potential threat. Research with humans is mixed and sparse. However, the evidence generally points toward males being more physiologically reactive to stress, suggesting that males may be predisposed to be more acutely fearful than females.

Finally, several lines of research suggest that women are more prone to worry and to engage in forms of cognitive processing, such as rumination, that prolong negative affect. These cognitive styles appear consistent with enhanced reactivity of female nonprimates to potential threat after being traumatized and with the greater long-term impact of traumatic events on women than men. It is conceivable that although males show stronger acute fear, females are more prone to remain anxious about the recurrence of aversive events after being traumatized, thus contributing to the development of long-lasting fears and anxiety disorders. These factors are summarized in Table 2.3.

Cultural Differences

Only recently have researchers begun examining anxiety disorders across cultures and ethnicities. Good and Kleinman outline the complexities in cross-cultural research and conclude that it is "abundantly clear that anxiety and disorders of anxiety are universally present in human societies. It is equally clear that the phenomenology of such disorders, the meaningful forms through which distress is articulated and constituted a social reality, varies in quite significant ways across cultures".

Cross-Cultural Differences

Several studies compare different cultural groups in terms of standard measures of trait anxiety. From these studies, it appears that American students are less anxious than students from Japan, Britain, Italy, France, India, and Poland. However, Good and Kleinman question the validity of these findings for several reasons. These include reliance on measures developed in one culture and language that are simply translated into another language without consideration of the different ways in which anxiety may be expressed in different cultures and without separate norms.

Table 2.3. (Factors that Contribute to Gender Differences in Anxiety)

Factor	Gender difference
Gender role expectations	Females display and report more fear and avoidance Diagnosticians more likely to assign diagnosis of anxiety disorder to women (Males and females equally likely to seek help for anxiety)
Life events	Females subject to more physical and sexual abuse or threat thereof Females more likely to develop distress and post traumatic stress symptoms following trauma Females more distressed by network life crises
Physiology	Males more physically reactive to acute stress Female nonprimates more reactive to potential threat
Cognition	Females more likely to worry and ruminate

Others have compared the prevalence of anxiety disorders across different cultures. Diagnostic surveys show that anxiety disorders are generally diagnosed at a rate of 12 to 27 per 1,000 persons in most cultures, although, according to most recent statistics, these rates are lower than estimates for North American culture. A major exception, according to Good and Kleinman, is Australian Aborigines: Only one of a sample of 2,360 Australian Aborigines was considered to show persistent apprehension and restlessness, despite the common experience of short-lived fear. Also, there is some evidence for comparatively lower rates of anxiety in China, the Philippines, and Korea. Lower rates in China were attributed to stable family and social support systems. However, the complexity of issues is not matched by research sophistication, rendering these results of questionable validity.

The form and content of anxiety tends to be expressed in culture-specific idioms. For example, dreams are more often expressed in some cultures and bodily complaints in other cultures. Also, cultures influence the focus of anxiety. For example, a study in Qatar found that panic disorder typically involved fear of after-death rather than dying per se, due most likely to the emphasis in Islamic religion on torture after death for wrongdoings. In addition, sociocultural factors influence the labeling of "disorder" and help-seeking behavior. Kirmayer, Young, and Hayton note that whereas agoraphobia is common among samples of phobic individuals in the United States, only 8% of women with phobias in Qatar report agoraphobia, perhaps because it is unusual for women in Qatar to leave the home unaccompanied by at least one male adult.

Similarly, in societies where ritual plays an important role in religious life, repetitious behavior and anxious preoccupation with avoiding "pollution" and with doing things correctly may be misdiagnosed as OCD [obsessive compulsive disorder]; on the other hand, such societies may predispose individuals to obsessive-compulsive symptoms and mask the disorder when present. Fears of contamination, which often are interpreted as symptoms of OCD, are common among peoples where much religious emphasis is placed on purity and many rituals and practices exist to avoid pollution and cleanse the self. Here, again, it may be very difficult to judge where zealous religious practice shades into obsessive preoccupation.

A variety of culture-related forms of anxiety seem to overlap with anxiety disorders as conceptualized by Western societies. Examples include *koro* in South and East Asia and semen-loss anxiety (*dhat* and *jiryan* in India, *sukra praneha* in Sri Lanka, *shen-k'uei* in China). The syndrome of koro involves intense, acute fear that the penis is shrinking into the body and that when this process is complete, the individual will die. It most commonly occurs in epidemics, and for women is represented by a fear of nipples retracting and breasts shrinking. Symptoms of panic are attributed to these fears. Another example is latah, which occurs in Malay cultures, and is characterized by an exaggerated startle, often with exclamations of obscenities; it is more typical in persons of lower socioeconomic status, who are publicly ridiculed and provoked to startle. Good and Kleinman note that propensity to acute startle reflexes is probably normally distributed in the population, but in some societies, "It acquires great symbolic significance, is responded to in a culturally specified manner and is socially and culturally constructed into a major illness form" whereas in other societies the same physiological propensity is relatively ignored.

Taijin kyofusho (TKS) is a Japanese form of social phobia. A core symptom of TKS is fear of offending or making others uncomfortable through inappropriate social behavior, emitting an offensive odor, or having a physical blemish or misshapen features. This presentation is consistent with Japanese concerns about public presentation of self in society. "Japanese cultural values put an emphasis on harmonious relationships within a complex status hierarchy that demands skill and vigilance on the part of social actors to successfully negotiate". TKS differs from core features of social phobia in Western societies, in which the major fear is being the object of scrutiny, humiliation, or embarrassment, as opposed to causing offense to others.

Another culture-related anxiety syndrome is *ataques de nervios,* found among Puerto Ricans and other Hispanic Caribbean peoples. The symptoms resemble panic disorder but prominently feature uncontrollable shouting and attacks of crying, along with trembling, heat in the chest rising into the head, and verbal or physical aggression. These ataques usually follow immediately on a stressful event, to which they are attributed.

Cultural Subgroups within North American Culture

Overall, the ECA study found few significant differences with respect to race in prevalence of anxiety disorders. The main exception was phobias. Brown, Eaton, and Sussman found a higher rate of phobic disorders among African Americans than Caucasians. For example, rates for simple phobia and agoraphobia in Baltimore were 27.6 and 13.4 for African Americans, and 17.4 and 7.2 for Caucasians. Racial differences remained even when controlling for specific demographic, socioeconomic, and sociocultural factors. They conclude that heightened vulnerability for phobias may reside in the stress of minority status. Similarly, Neal and Brown suggest that to be poor and a member of a minority in the United States places one at a higher risk for chronic stress and negative life events, which may render African Americans more vulnerable to the development of specific fears and phobias. On the other hand, these differences were not replicated in the National Comorbidity Survey.

Paradis, Hatch and Friedman note that other anxiety disorders are underdiagnosed in African Americans or are misdiagnosed as more serious forms of mental illness. In other words, they suggest that a strong diagnostic bias exists. Most perturbing was a report by Friedman and Paradis. In a small sample of 15 African American adults with panic disorder, they found chart evidence for some unnecessary psychiatric hospitalizations due to misdiagnosis of severe panic attacks as forms of psychosis. On the other hand, Horwath, Johnson and Hornig found similar prevalences for panic disorder, despite socioeconomic differences, across African American and white community samples from the ECA data. Perhaps the diagnostic bias discussed by Paradis is more evident in clinical settings or with more severe presentations of anxiety.

Cultural differences may reside not only in prevalence but in associated features of anxiety disorders. Neal, Lilly, and Zakis compared fears reported by African American and white children, primarily from workingclass and low-income families. Eight of the 11 most common fears were the same for both groups, suggesting that fears reported by children transcend race and culture. However, factor analyses of the Fear Survey Scale for children revealed only a three-factor solution for African American children, in comparison to the usual five-factor solution. This result occurred mainly due to the absence of school fears for African American children. Interestingly, using a clinic rather than a community sample, Last and Perrin found a very similar result. They compared 30 African American children to 139 white children who were referred to an anxiety clinic. Although the two groups were more similar than different diagnostically, sociodemographically, and in clinical features, a difference occurred with respect to school refusal. White children from lower socioeconomic backgrounds were more likely to report school refusal than their African American counterparts. The researchers attribute this to lower levels of performance anxiety around school-related tasks in African American children. Also, there was a trend for the latter group to show more post traumatic stress disorder, which was attributed to lower socioeconomic backgrounds. Finally, in accord with community data, African

American children endorsed more fears, even after correcting for age and socioeconomic status.

Studies of other racial groups are almost nonexistent. Ginsburg and Silverman compared symptoms among children from Hispanic (n=99) versus Caucasian (n=143) backgrounds who were seeking treatment for anxiety. Overall, these two groups were judged more similar than different. The primary difference was that a higher proportion of the Hispanic group presented with separation anxiety disorder.

Finally, cultural differences emerge with respect to treatment seeking and treatment response. African Americans with anxiety disorders are less likely to seek help from mental health professionals. Furthermore, Friedman and Paradis note that African Americans who were treated with behaviorally oriented psychotherapy did less well than their white counterparts. Similarly, Williams and Chambless reported a nonsignificant trend for African Americans to show less treatment benefit in terms of mobility, anxiety, and panic attacks than white Americans. They suggest that abundance of stress in daily life for African Americans creates a state of arousal that impedes habituation during in vivo exposure and makes it more difficult to achieve the self-discipline needed to carry out practice sessions and adhere to a behavioral treatment. On the other hand, Friedman, Paradis and Hatch replicated their original study with larger sample sizes to find equivalent treatment outcomes across the two groups. Thus, effects of race on treatment outcome remains uncertain.

Conclusion

In summary, anxiety is universal, although some cultures may experience less anxiety than others. However, the quality of research in this area is generally questionable. It is clear that anxiety is expressed differently across different cultures, in connection with culture-specific beliefs. Notably, this contrasts with evidence for universality of physiological and behavioral indices of fear. Within the American culture, cross-cultural comparisons are limited mostly to Caucasian versus African American samples. African Americans may be more vulnerable to specific phobias than their Caucasian counterparts and may differ on other associated features of anxiety disorders such as school refusal among youths. However, there are more similarities than differences. Clinicians may overpathologize anxiety in African Americans with more severe anxiety disorders, and African Americans may respond less well to current treatments for anxiety. But these findings are based on a limited number of mostly uncontrolled studies and await further investigation, as does the entire issue of cultural variables in the expression and treatment of anxiety disorders.

The presentation of anxiety disorders in youths, adults, and the elderly and across genders and cultures were reviewed in this chapter. Associated features of depression, personality disorders, and substance abuse were also considered. Each anxiety disorder is characterized by states of fear/panic, anticipatory anxiety, and worry, depending on imminence of threat. Differences among anxiety disorders reside largely in the *source* of threat. Nevertheless, as reviewed in the next chapter, individuals probably differ in their proneness to worry, anticipate, and become afraid. Moreover, some anxiety disorders may be more strongly associated with certain points along the threat imminence continuum than others, due largely to the predictability and controllability of the sources of threat.

3

Methods and Treatments of Abnormal Psychology

Introduction

The treatments for anxiety disorders target states of worry, anticipatory anxiety, and fear and their associated profiles of physiological, behavioral, and cognitive responding. The latter include passive avoidance and active escape behavior, reliance on safety signals, other maladaptive coping behaviors, muscular tension, autonomic arousal, and cognitive distortions that overestimate danger or underestimate ability to cope with danger. Empirically validated psychological treatments are broadly classified as behavioral or cognitive. They include exposure therapy, applied relaxation training, systematic desensitization, response prevention, behavioral rehearsal, and cognitive therapy.

Empirically Validated Treatments

Clinical researchers have emphasized empirical derivation for years, but the dissemination of this approach into clinical practice has been slow. In an attempt to enhance the dissemination of empirically derived approaches, David Barlow, as president of Division 12, American Psychological Association, established a task force to "consider methods for educating clinical psychologists, third party payers, and the public about effective psychotherapies" (Task Force on the Promotion and Dissemination of Psychological.

This task force was composed of experts from various theoretical perspectives, including psychodynamic, interpersonal, and cognitive-behavioral. Although they recognized that no treatment is ever fully validated, they provided a set of criteria by which to judge which treatments were "well established" empirically, as well as "probably efficacious."

As can be seen, manualization is one criterion. The task force notes that since the Beck, Rush, Shaw, and Emery volume that marked the beginning of availability of treatment manuals for specific patient problems (aside from earlier behavioral treatments presented in detail in journal articles and chapters), treatment manuals have become required for psychosocial research. Treatment manuals successfully standardize treatments and reduce methodological problems caused by variable therapist outcomes. Furthermore, manualized treatments may even result in more successful outcomes. For example, Schulte, Kunzel, Pepping and Schulte-Bahrenberg obtained more effective results from standardized versus "tailor-made" behavioral therapy for phobias. Future attempts to replicate these findings would be well worthwhile.

Notably, the list of "well-established," empirically validated psychological treatments covers many treatments for anxiety disorders: cognitive-behavioral therapy for panic disorder, with and without agoraphobia; cognitive-behavioral therapy for generalized anxiety disorder; group cognitive-behavioral therapy for social phobia; exposure treatment for agoraphobia; exposure treatment for social phobia; exposure and response prevention for obsessive compulsive disorder; and systematic desensitization for specific phobias. Also notable is the fact that these treatments are limited to behavioral and cognitive-behavioral procedures, thus highlighting the general absence of empirical support for insight-oriented approaches for anxiety disorders. In contrast, interpersonal therapy, for example, is effective for depression and bulimia.

The same is true for "probably efficacious" treatments for anxiety disorders, which included applied relaxation for panic disorder, applied relaxation for generalized anxiety disorder, exposure treatment for post traumatic stress disorder, exposure treatment for simple phobia, stress inoculation training for post traumatic stress disorder, group exposure and response prevention for obsessive compulsive disorder, and relapse prevention programs for obsessive compulsive disorder. These lists represent advances in the treatment for anxiety disorders since the 1970s. The following discussions of treatment methods and mechanisms are limited to empirically validated cognitive-behavioral approaches.

Behavioral Treatment Methods

Behavioral treatments for anxiety disorders emphasize extinction of conditional responses and mastery development through self-confidence building and skill deficit correction.

Exposure Therapy

Conditioning theory led to a set of procedures called exposure therapy, which entail systematic and repeated confrontation with phobic stimuli. Traditionally, exposure was limited to situations such as social encounters for social phobia; distance from home for agoraphobia; and snakes, spiders, and other circumscribed objects or situations for specific phobias. However, exposure can be applied to any anxiety disorder once the primary focus of concern is identified. Thus, exposure may occur to feared bodily sensations, such as increased heart rate in the case of panic disorder; feared images of contamination in the case of obsessive compulsive disorder; images of catastrophe for generalized anxiety disorder; or images of trauma for post traumatic stress disorder.

There are several variations in the way exposure is conducted. Efficacies of these varied approaches are discussed in later chapters relevant to each disorder. They include the modality through which stimuli are presented: imaginal (e.g., in the case of systematic desensitization), virtual reality, and in vivo (in real life). Also, the intensity of exposure varies, ranging from graded exposure (progressing from the least to the most feared exposure task) to intense flooding therapy, or exposure to the most intensely feared stimuli for protracted lengths of time. Exposure tasks are typically ranked according to difficulty level or level of anxiety anticipated in each situation, thus generating a hierarchy of progressively more anxiety-provoking situations. Third, the rate at which exposure is conducted varies from a massed schedule (e.g., once every day for several weeks) to a spaced schedule (e.g., once every week for several months). Spacing can even be applied to the rate at which each trial of exposure is conducted on a given day. For example, exposure to driving might entail three drives immediately one after another or three drives spread out over the course of the day. Fourth, variations occur in parameters used to determine the length of each exposure. For example, exposures may be continued the length of time required for fear to diminish fully or partially. Alternatively, trials may be ended at the point of heightened anxiety, followed by reexposure after anxiety has subsided. Termed *controlled escape,* this is discussed in more detail below. Another alternative is continuation of exposure for a predetermined length of time regardless of level of anxiety. Fifth, exposure can be conducted with the aid of a therapist or other person, who serves as a safety signal to promote exposure, or by oneself alone in a self-directed manner. Finally, exposure can be conducted with the aid of relaxation, in the form of applied relaxation or cognitive techniques.

Relaxation

Relaxation has been a mainstay of behavioral treatments and encompasses an array of strategies, including autogenic training, progressive muscle relaxation training and various forms of meditation and yoga. Most treatments for anxiety rely on progressive muscle relaxation, although in a condensed form of 8 to IS sessions instead of the lengthy training (50 sessions) initially developed by Jacobson. Progressive muscle relaxation training involves tensing and relaxing of major muscle groups in progression, followed by deepening of relaxation through slow breathing and/or imagery. The data clearly show that muscle relaxation is anxiety-reducing overall, although the degree to which relaxation is necessary in the context of exposure is questionable.

Applied relaxation involves cue-controlled relaxation for the management of anxiety in anxiety-provoking situations. For this procedure, complete progressive muscle relaxation is gradually reduced to very brief relaxation; the initial set of 16 muscle groups is reduced to 8 muscle groups, then to 4 muscle groups, and finally to cue-controlled relaxation. The latter entails repetition of a word (e.g., "calm" or "relax") that has been previously associated with the relaxation phase of the tenserelax cycles and consequently has developed conditional properties for inducing relaxation. After mastering cue-controlled relaxation, patients practice confronting anxiety-provoking situations while applying relaxation to manage their anxiety.

Wolpe's systematic desensitization similarly combines relaxation and exposure to feared stimuli. Individuals progress through increasingly more anxiety-provoking imagined encounters with phobic stimuli while utilizing relaxation as a reciprocal inhibitor of rising anxiety (although, as described later in this chapter, this mechanism has been questioned). A basic premise of systematic desensitization is that imaginary experience generalizes to real life. In other words, imagining fearful stimuli is assumed to be equivalent to actually confronting fearful stimuli. As relaxation is intended to compete with and inhibit the anxiety response, it is essential that anxiety remains weak; hence, the value of a graded exposure format. Hierarchy generation is based on careful assessment of dimensions relevant to the expression of fear. For example, formality of the setting, preparation time, size of the audience, familiarity of the audience, and the topic being presented may be relevant for public speaking fears. Once the dimensions are identified, a representative sample of 10 to 20 very concretely described situations is derived from the total list of possible anxiety-provoking situations. Although Wolpe emphasized multiple hierarchies for different areas of anxiety (e.g., public speaking, job interviews, dating), themes can be merged into single hierarchies as well. After hierarchy generation, systematic desensitization continues by testing imaginal skills, such as by imagining naturally anxiety-provoking images (e.g., an impending crash in a flight). Inclusion of responses (e.g., racing heart) and meaning (e.g., "I will die") elements into imagined scenarios typically enhances imaginal anxiety. Systematic desensitization proceeds by repeated pairing of the least anxiety-evoking image with subsequent relaxation. This pairing is repeated the number of times necessary until the hierarchy item can be imagined with minimal or no anxiety, at which point the next item on the hierarchy is imagined. In its original form, imagining of fearful scenes was limited to no more than 15 seconds or until anxiety was felt, whichever came sooner, at which point there was a return to the relaxation state. Goldfried developed a self-control version of desensitization. Instead of removing the image and returning to a relaxed state, the patient is encouraged to maintain the image and practice relaxation to remove tensions and anxiety. That is, desensitization is viewed as an opportunity to rehearse coping skills.

One version of desensitization that has received much attention since 1989, when it was first described in published form, is eye movement desensitization, in which imagining the fear-provoking stimulus is combined with rapid movements of the eye. Several studies report successful treatment of post traumatic stress disorder and specific phobias. However, eye movement desensitization is not yet considered an empirically validated treatment according to the task force described earlier.

Mastery Exposure Therapy

Although proponents of self-efficacy theory rely heavily on in vivo exposure to overcome phobias, their approach emphasizes skills and mastery acquisition versus extinction of conditional fear. Hence, the term *guided mastery therapy* is used in place of exposure therapy. Performance accomplishment provides the most potent evidence of one's capabilities, in contrast to vicarious experience, imaginal practice, or self-talk. Therefore, the therapist's role is to promote performance success, whereas duration and level of anxiety during exposure are relatively unemphasized. Williams lists the following mastery induction methods during exposure: Therapists perform tasks jointly with patients, model approach to tasks, set subtasks to be accomplished sequentially, graduate tasks and treatment settings, and provide physical and mechanical support. Proficiency and flexibility of performance are enhanced by helping patients to abandon defensive rituals (e.g., holding the rail of a balcony for patients fearful of falling from heights) and varying performance (e.g., walking over a bridge in a variety of different ways, such as fast and slow). Finally, independence of performance is fostered by using the least assistance needed, withdrawing assistance as soon as possible, and training patients to be their own therapist. Williams and his colleagues have shown this type of mastery exposure to be more effective than usual exposure methods.

Response Prevention

Response prevention is a specific technique for the treatment of compulsive behavior. Basically, patients are prevented from carrying out their usual compulsive rituals. That is, they are dissuaded from performing compulsive rituals during sessions and encouraged to relinquish all avoidance behavior and rituals outside of therapy sessions. Originally, Meyer, Levy and Schnurer implemented response prevention in an inpatient setting with continual supervision by nursing staff who prevented patients from carrying out rituals. However, simply instructing patients to relinquish rituals is almost as effective, perhaps especially for less severe compulsions. Response prevention was based on the notion that obsessions evoke anxiety, compulsions reduce anxiety, and compulsions preserve obsessional anxiety because they disrupt habituation to the obsession. In addition, because compulsions tend to alleviate anxiety, they are reinforced and maintained over time. Although these theories have been questioned, the combination of response prevention with exposure therapy is more effective than exposure therapy alone for obsessive compulsive disorder.

Behavioral Rehearsal

Other behavioral treatments include social skills and assertiveness training, utilized mostly for social anxiety, generalized anxiety disorder, and agoraphobia. Skills such as giving and receiving compliments, requesting information, and refusing requests are taught through instruction, modeling, and role play and feedback, as therapist and patient play out different roles. As with exposure procedures, a hierarchy of situations is usually devised for the purposes of role playing and behavioral rehearsal. However, items are rank-ordered by behavioral complexity rather than by anxiety. Behavioral rehearsal itself relies on principles of operant conditioning and shaping. For example, the complexity of behaviors involved in social interaction are divided into components, each of which is the focus of separate behavioral rehearsals. That is, each situation on the hierarchy is practiced, with emphasis on a particular behavioral component and feedback after each role play. Therapist modeling is incorporated when patient performance is extremely deficient or not responsive to corrective feedback.

Sometimes covert rehearsal is used instead of overt rehearsal, such as when overt rehearsal is not appropriate (e.g., sexual intimacy). Following mastery in-session, the new behaviors are practiced in in vivo situations. Although Wolpe construes social skills and behaviors taught through behavioral rehearsal as reciprocal inhibitors of fear, others propose a response deficit correction model. That is, social skills are taught to overcome deficits in behavioral repertoires. Alternatively, behavioral rehearsal may constitute another form of exposure therapy.

Another behavioral skills technique is problem solving, which has been observed to have some benefits for generalized anxiety disorder. Patients are taught a general set of skills for approaching problems of everyday living, intended to replace ruminative, nonproductive worry. Steps involved in problem solving include problem definition and formulation, generation of alternatives, decision making, and verification.

Cognitive Treatment Methods

Cognitive therapy assumes that emotions are based on cognitive processes that can be corrected or manipulated via conscious reasoning. McNally asserted that cognitive therapies are unlikely to be effective due to the unconscious and involuntary nature of anxious cognitive processes. In response, Beck and Clark argue that verbal mediation is necessary but not sufficient to correct "primal" or automatic modes of information processing. In their view, "one of the most effective ways of deactivating the primal threat mode is to counter it with more elaborative, strategic processing of information resulting from the activation of the constructive, reflective modes of thinking". Indeed, there is evidence that elaborative cognitive processes, such as those rehearsed in cognitive therapy, can override involuntary, automatic processes. For example, Davey and Siddle and Bond cite evidence showing that instructions alone alter conditioned responses. Furthermore, as reviewed in later chapters, cognitive therapy is effective for many anxiety disorders.

In its early stages, cognitive therapy consisted of relatively simplistic selfstatement training. Cognitive procedures have become more sophisticated over time, particularly with the manualization of cognitive treatments by Beck and colleagues. Several variants of cognitive therapy exist. In paradoxical intention, patients are instructed to exaggerate and magnify their fears, so that, paradoxically, their fears lose strength and meaning. The exaggeration is intended to bring humor to the situation. Ellis's rational-emotive therapy assumes that actively and directly disputing negative self-statements (or core irrational beliefs) is effective, especially when patients are taught ways of disputing their own statements. In self-instruction training, Meichenbaum modifies internal dialogues to include coping, task-oriented (i.e., preparing, confronting, coping, and reinforcing) self-statements. Beck targets dysfunctional beliefs and faulty information processing in what is generally referred to as cognitive therapy. Beck's treatment follows a course of collaborative empiricism, in which patient and therapist work together to identify and label errors in thinking; evaluate the evidence; and generate alternative, more realistic hypotheses. Because Beck's approach has received the most empirical support, it is described in more detail.

Typically, cognitive therapy begins with discussion of the role of thoughts in generating emotions, to provide a treatment rationale. Next, thoughts are recognized as hypotheses rather than fact and therefore open to questioning and challenge. Detailed self-monitoring of emotions and associated cognitions is instituted to identify specific beliefs, appraisals, and assumptions. Once relevant cognitions are identified, they are categorized into types of typical errors that occur during heightened emotion, such as overestimations of risk of negative events or catastrophizing of meaning of events. The process of categorization, or labeling of thoughts, is consistent with a personal scientist model and facilitates an objective perspective by which the validity of the thoughts can be evaluated. Thus, in labeling the type of cognitive distortion, the patient is encouraged to use an empirical approach to examine the validity of his or her thoughts by considering all of the available evidence. New evidence is collected using behavioral experiments referred to as hypothesis testing. Therapists use Socratic questioning to help patients make guided discoveries and question their anxious thoughts. Next, alternative hypotheses are generated that are more evidence based. In addition to surface-level appraisals (such as, "That person is frowning at me because I look foolish"), core-level beliefs or schemata (such as, "I am not strong enough to withstand further distress" or "I am unlikable") are questioned in the same way.

Recognition of behavioral experience as possibly the most powerful means of modifying cognitions leads to an inevitable overlap between cognitive and behavioral treatment methods. In other words, most cognitive therapies employ behavioral techniques, including exposure to feared situations and behavioral rehearsal, as vehicles for testing and modifying beliefs.

Pharmacological Treatments

Pharmacological treatments are reviewed in more detail in relation to specific anxiety disorders in later chapters. In general, six classes of drugs are effective for anxiety disorders. These include heterocyclic antidepressants, intended to block locus coeruleus activity, such as imipramine (Tofranil) or nortriptyline (Pamelor). Selective serotonin reuptake inhibitors include fluoxetine (Prozac), sertraline (Zoloft), paroxetine (Paxil), and fluvoxamine (Luvox). Benzodiazepines are widely used, including alprazolam (Xanax), lorazepam (Ativan), clonazepam (Klonopin), and diazepam (Valium). Monoamine oxidase inhibitors include phenelzine (Nardil), and azapirones include buspirone (Buspar). Finally, beta blockers, such as propranolol (Inderal), are sometimes used for performance-based anxieties.

In general, medications are assumed to alter underlying pathogenic neurochernical dysregulation. These are hypothesized to include dysregulation of brain stem respiratory control centers, which seem to have the most relevance for panic disorder. In addition, noradrenergic dysfunction has been implicated, possibly involving an alpha 2 adrenergic receptor hypersensitivity and the locus coeruleus. Again, this dysregulation is of particular relevance to panic disorder. Serotonergic dysfunction has been implicated in panic disorder and obsessive compulsive disorder. Hyperactive sympathetic nervous system functioning and abnormality in the hypothalamic-pituitary axis have been associated most with post traumatic stress disorder.

Interesting psychological effects of medications exist. These are evidenced by the efficacy of placebo medications for 20 to 70% of individuals with anxiety disorders. Further illustration of psychological effects of medications derives from McLeod, Hoehn-Saric, Zimmerli, de Souza, and Oliver, who compared physiological and subjective changes over the course of six weeks of either alprazolam or imipramine for patients with generalized anxiety disorder. Although both drugs produced significant *decreases* in symptom reports, alprazolam produced corresponding reductions in physiology whereas imipramine was associated with *increases* in heart rate, blood pressure, muscle tension, and norepinephrine. Similarly, others note increases in heart rate, norepinephrine, and other measures from tricyclic antidepressants. McLeod attribute positive subjective effects to expectations of improvement. That is, expectations for improvement may generate searches for confirmatory evidence, resulting in less symptom reporting despite elevated physiological arousal. Interactions between medications and psychological treatments, including potential advantages and disadvantages of adding medications to behavioral treatments.

Mechanisms of Behavioral Treatments

Although behavioral treatments developed mostly from theories of conditioning and mastery acquisition, a variety of theories of fear reduction exist. Most of these theories pertain to exposure therapy.

Habituation

Habituation was first applied to fear reduction through exposure therapy by Lader and Wing. The term *habituation* refers simply to reduction in response strength with repeated stimulus presentations. In their dual-process theory, Groves and Thompson suggested that observed behavior reflects the summation of habituation and sensitization (the latter refers to increased responding to repeated stimulation). Sensitization is considered largely reflective of and influenced by the state of the organism, or "general levels of excitation, arousal, activation, tendency to respond, etc.". In contrast, the process of habituation is believed to be specific to certain stimuli. Groves and Thompson further stated that although sensitization and habituation are independent systems, they interact to produce behavioral outcomes. The strength of habituating and sensitizing processes for any given stimulus depends on parameters of intensity and frequency. Sensitization is more pronounced at high stimulus intensities, especially with more frequent presentations. Habituation is inversely related to stimulus intensity and directly related to stimulus frequency.

Habituation models were used as a descriptive framework for predicting responses during systematic desensitization, especially because patterns of self-report and physiological responding over repeated exposure trials tend to be consistent with habituation. That is, most data show a general linear decline in self-reported fear and physiological arousal across exposures, although self-reports of distress tend to habituate at a slower rate than physiological arousal. Foa and Chambless distinguished between habituation curves for imaginal and in vivo exposure. The former were more curvilinear, due to initial delay in fully experiencing the image, whereas the latter were more linear, because the stimulus is immediately present and potent.

Several theories of habituation have been proposed, many of which are reviewed by Mackintosh. Wagner proposed a particularly interesting model, in which habituation was explained by memory representations of stimuli and comparator models. However, Mackintosh concluded from his review that there is no compelling evidence to support comparator models. Instead, Mackintosh suggests that the more parsimonious stimulus-response (S-R) pathway models are more consistent with the data: Habituation occurs because with every presentation of a stimulus there is a decline in the efficiency of transmission along a S-R pathway.

Traditionally, habituation was viewed as a transient process; dishabituation (or sensitization) was expected to inevitably follow habituation. Consequently, habituation could not account for long-lasting fear reduction from exposure therapy. However, several theoreticians discriminate shortterm from long-term habituation. Groves and Lynch proposed different brain areas: Long-term habituation was associated with the frontal cortex and hippocampus, whereas shortterm habituation was associated with the brain stem. Similarly, Foa argued that long-term habituation is dependent on higher, or more elaborate, cognitive processes. She suggested that within-session (i.e., from the beginning to the end of an exposure session) habituation represents mostly autonomic dampening, whereas between-session (i.e., from the end of one session to the beginning of the next session) habituation represents changes in expectancy or the realization that the stimulus can be experienced without much fear. Most recently, Mackintosh evoked conditioning to explain long-term habituation, at least with respect to stimuli of biological significance. Long-term habituation is attributed to conditioning of a compensatory reaction or "opponent process" in which affectively significant stimuli initially elicit responses of one affective sign that then give way to compensatory responses of the opposite sign. Long-term habituation is the result of this compensatory reaction occurring progressively earlier as it is reliably elicited by contexts that predict biologically significant events.

Support for the role of habituation in exposure therapy includes the finding that specific phobics who show more physiological habituation during exposure achieve a better outcome overall than nonhabituators. On the other hand, recent findings from my laboratory, described later in this chapter, contradict this finding. Other supportive evidence is that a number of independent variables effect habituation and fear reduction during exposure in the same way: depressant drugs, level of arousal, rate of stimulation, attenuation of stimuli, regularity of presentation, and complexity of stimuli. Finally, dishabituation provides a good account for return of fear (i.e., partial increase of fear following successful fear reduction), as reviewed in the next chapter. However, there are a number of limitations. For example, habituation models do not adequately account for persistence of some fears despite repeated stimulus presentation and the efficacy of flooding therapy despite the induction of intense distress that should impede habituation. Additionally, Barlow and Rachman note that habituation does not account well for desynchrony, or weak correlations, between verbal reports and physiological responding in fear reduction and return of fear. Finally, Rachman notes some tautology in that both habituation and success of exposure treatment are defined by a reduction in fearful responding. Currently, habituation processes are typically incorporated into models of fear reduction but are rarely considered to be the sole or primary agent of change.

Toughening Up

A physiological explanation for exposure effects is based on differential noradrenergic activity during periods of acute versus chronic stress. Learned helplessness effects arise from acute exposures to uncontrollable stress. The phenomenon of "toughening up," as explained by Weiss, Glazer, and Pohorecky and Weiss and later adopted by Gray, refers to elimination of the learned helplessness effect by chronic exposure to stress. In other words, individuals experiencing chronic stress toughen up and are more resistant to anxiety, in comparison to individuals having experienced only acute stress. Briefly, the biochemical mechanism for this phenomenon is posited to involve overall increases in whole brain levels of noradrenaline upon brief exposures to stress, versus overall decreases in noradrenaline upon repeated, chronic exposures. Weiss proposed that chronic stress results in a rise in tyrosine hydroxylase activity, which in turn increases noradrenaline levels in the locus coeruleus. This produces a rise in autoreceptor-mediated inhibition in the locus coeruleus and a reduction in noradrenergic brain transmission in the forebrain.

In terms of exposure therapy, the toughening up hypothesis assumes that repeated exposures to feared objects increase resistance to anxiety. In addition, the toughening up hypothesis has been used to explain the wide variability in response to exposure, given that individual differences may exist in rates of receptor desensitization and other biochemical changes necessary for toughening up to occur. However, the toughening up hypothesis cannot account for the success of exposure procedures of short duration or without full evocation of the fear response (e.g., controlled escape exposure) and has not been directly empirically evaluated in humans.

Extinction

Extinction refers to decrements in responding through repetition of unreinforced responding. That is, repeated encounters with feared stimuli without aversive consequences result in repeated presentations of the CS without the US. Thus, the person who is fearful of heights (CS) learns by repeated exposures that he or she does not fall (US). Extinction accounts are supported by the finding that a single lengthy exposure session is generally more effective than a series of short exposures for the same total duration, as lengthy exposure provides sufficient time to learn that aversive outcomes do not occur. Therefore, like habituation theory, extinction models suggest the importance of continuation of exposure until fear declines. There are additional reasons to continue exposure until fear declines. Kahneman, Fredrickson, Schreiber, and Redelmeier exposed individuals to a cold water hand immersion test for 60 seconds or for 90 seconds that ended with gradually increasing water temperature in the last 30 seconds. When given the choice for a third trial, participants reliably chose the latter over the former. The authors claim that we use an averaging model for global evaluations of aversiveness based on peak intensity at the end of the experience. Thus, how exposure ends may significantly impact future anxiety and willingness to confront feared situations again.

Wolpe attributed extinction to counterconditioning or reciprocal inhibition. Specifically, when a response antagonistic to anxiety can be made to occur in the presence of anxiety-provoking stimuli and results in a complete or partial suppression of the anxiety response, then the bond between the stimulus and the anxiety response is weakened. His model has been criticized because exposure can proceed effectively without including specific antagonists to anxiety. Wolpe's response to this criticism is that there are many unintended reciprocal inhibitors, including the presence of the therapist, that work to compete with anxiety during exposure therapy. However, this awaits empirical examination.

Recent conditioning models maintain that extinction involves learning of new, inhibitory CS-no US associations as opposed to unlearning of the original CS-US associations. Thus, Bouton and colleagues propose that the original excitatory *meaning* of the CS is not erased during extinction but rather an additional inhibitory *meaning* is learned. The resulting dual meaning of the CS creates an ambiguity that is resolved only by the current context of the CS. Bouton uses the analogy of an ambiguous word. That is, reaction to the word "fire" depends largely on the context in which it occurs; "fire" may elicit a panic reaction in a crowded theater and elicit very little reaction in a carnival shooting gallery. Thus, the context determines which meaning is expressed at any given time. In terms of anxiety treatments, bodily sensations may mean "sudden death" when alone at home in contrast to "unpleasantness but harmlessness" in the medical setting. Specifically, Bouton proposes an "AND" gate: A stimulus and context occurring together activate an AND gate, which is the mechanism to activate inhibitory associations (i.e., nonfearful meanings) with the US. Without the joint presence of the stimulus and the context, the inhibitory path is not activated and the excitatory path controls the response to the US. This model is explained in more detail in the next chapter.

This conceptual development, which is supported by extensive animal experimentation and some limited support from human samples, has direct treatment implications. Basically, exposure is best conducted in as many contexts as possible to minimize context specificity of fear reduction and enhance the likelihood of inhibitory or nonfearful meanings in whatever context the stimulus is encountered once treatment is over. Contexts relevant to treatment of fear include extinction contexts, such as presence of therapist, location of exposure, and internal sensations and mood states and drug states throughout exposure, as well as contexts associated with the original fear acquisition. Return of fear, for example, may be minimized by lengthy exposures to the full variety of contexts in which USs occurred in the past, as well as exposures to settings in which USs are most likely to occur in the future. Return of fear is more likely if exposures are restricted to certain contexts, such as presence of a therapist or a particular drug state.

It is noteworthy that the context ambiguity model emphasizes a continuous struggle between fear generalization, as emphasized by adaptive conservatism, and context specificity of extinction. In other words, acquired fears will generalize, whereas extinguished fears will not. It also implies that return of fear is a strong possibility. In support, partial return of fear commonly occurs. On the other hand, long-term results from exposure therapies remain generally impressive, and unexpected in light of the notions of adaptive conservatism. The long-term success of fear reduction techniques suggests that mechanisms in addition to context-specific extinction may be taking place. The finding of enduring generalized benefit to distinct untreated agoraphobic fears similarly suggests mechanisms in addition to extinction.

Compliance

According to habituation, toughening up, and extinction models, compliance with instructions to practice exposure should predict a more positive outcome. Interestingly, research examining the relationship between treatment adherence and outcome is relatively sparse, and extant data are somewhat equivocal. Several studies examine compliance with respect to social phobia treatment. In a relatively detailed analysis, Edelman and Chambless found that adherence to instructions for between-session practice did not relate to overall treatment outcome at the end of treatment, but those who adhered fared better at follow-up in terms of anxiety during a speaking task and overall reductions in anxiety and phobic avoidance. Similarly, engagement during treatment sessions did not relate to outcome at posttreatment but was positively related to self and observer ratings of skill during a speech and conversation role play at follow-up. Most recently, Leung and Heimberg found that compliance with homework during the first and latter periods of cognitive-behavioral treatment for social phobia was associated with lower levels of anxiety after treatment. Interestingly, however, the reverse was found for compliance during the middle portion of treatment.

In the treatment of agoraphobia, some studies show a positive relationship between adherence and outcome, some show no relationship and others find mixed support. Finally, O'Sullivan, Noshirvani, Marks, Monteiro, and Lelliott reported that obsessive compulsive patients who were more compliant with homework assignments, according to therapist ratings, reported lower levels of ritualizing six years after behavioral treatment. However, as Edelman and Chambless note, O'Sullivan did not objectify their measurement of compliance.

In summary, although most studies report the expected relationship between exposure practice and outcome, the data are somewhat equivocal. Unfortunately, this area of research is beset with methodological problems, including measurement of compliance and the degree to which compliance with exposure is distinguished from compliance with other aspects of cognitive-behavioral treatment. These limitations cast doubt on the findings to date and speak to the need for more research in this area, especially given the direct derivation from several prominent theories of fear reduction.

Endogenous Opioids

Another learning theory account of fear reduction emphasizes endogenous opioids, or endorphins. These are natural substances, released in response to fear or pain, that serve an analgesic function

Release of endogenous opioids in response to fear may reinforce approach behavior and thereby promote extinction, reduce the aversiveness of exposure, or directly increase approach behavior because endorphins increase exploratory behavior. In support, Egan, Carr, Hunt, and Adamson found that pharmacological blockade of endogenous opioids, via naloxone, impeded imaginal exposure relative to saline, in a group of six specific phobics. However, a second and larger study by Merluzzi only partially replicated these findings. Although naltrexone, another opioid antagonist, resulted in higher maximum heart rate and more time to complete one exposure task in spider phobics, in comparison to placebo, there were no differences in average heart rate or blood pressure. Another group of researchers showed that naltrexone during exposure resulted in more relapse one week after treatment for spider phobia, although the effect was limited to avoidance measures and was not observed in terms of anxiety. Furthermore, high versus low doses of naltrexone did not influence fear acquisition or extinction of fear of a tone. Despite the mixed results, Carr claims support for the role of beta endorphins (notably, he does not review the studies by Arntz and colleagues). In particular, Carr hypothesizes that stress, in the form of exposure, induces adrenocorticotrophic hormone (ACTH) release as well as beta endorphins. Initially, the endorphins are blocked by ACTH, but ACTH subsides quickly, resulting in a delayed anxiolytic effect from the endorphins. However, as noted, the paucity of evidence in this area precludes definitive conclusions regarding these hypothesized mechanisms.

Emotional Processing

In 1980, Rachman proposed the concept emotional processing to account for therapeutic change: "A process whereby emotional disturbances are absorbed, and decline to the extent that other experiences and behaviors can proceed without disruption". He suggested that incomplete processing, evidenced by persistence or return of fear, is overcome by evoking the emotion in therapy so that it may be processed.

Foa and Kozak extended this notion by stating that treatment depends on modification of pathological fear structures in memory via habituation and cognitive change. They hypothesized two necessary conditions for fear reduction: full activation of the fear structure and incorporation of new material that is incompatible with the old structure so that a new structure is formed. The former condition is supported in part by evidence that heightened initial arousal (assumed to reflect full fear activation) is predictive of superior outcome. The most effective method for activating fear structures is direct exposure to feared stimuli. The model states that with repeated exposure incompatible information is derived from short-term physiological habituation that dissociates stimulus and response (i.e., recognition that the stimulus can occur in the absence of arousal). Between-session habituation is attributed to changes in the meaning of the stimulus and response (i.e., risk of harm is lowered and affective valence becomes less negative). That is, outcome expectancies are altered. Thus, there are three indicators of emotional processing: evidence of initial physiological arousal and self-report distress (i.e., fear activation), reactions gradually reducing during exposure (i.e., within-session habituation), and initial reactions to the stimulus reducing across exposures (i.e., between-session habituation). Fear structures before and after emotional processing are depicted by Foa and Kozak in Figure 3.1.

Emotional processing is impeded by elements that interfere with access to fear structures or with integration of new information. Foa and Kozak suggest that such interference would arise from distraction, excessively high or very low levels of anxious arousal, or overly brief exposure durations, each of which have received some support. However, the data are equivocal.

With respect to distraction, Borkovec and Grayson stated, "Objective presentation of stimuli does not guarantee functional exposure to those stimuli". Seven studies since then examined the effects of distraction during exposure, although two were not centrally focused on the role of distraction in relation to fear.

The results of the other five studies are contradictory. Grayson employed a crossover design in which patients with obsessive compulsive disorder held their most feared contaminant stimulus throughout 90 minutes while either conversing with the therapists regarding aspects of the stimulus and their own discomfort or being distracted by playing video games. The group who underwent distraction during the first exposure session showed more fear at the start of the second session than the group that began with focused exposure. These authors replicated this study using a between-groups design. The distracted exposure group showed more within-session fear reduction, but both groups evidenced return of fear at the start of the second session.

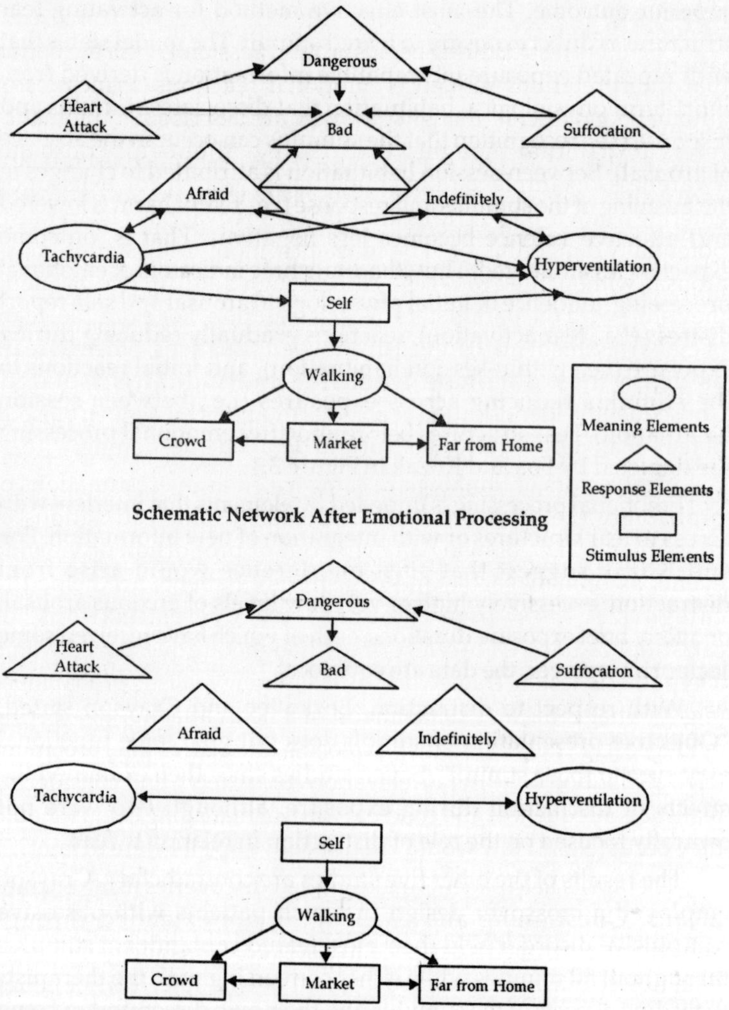

Fig. 3.1. Relationship among stimulus, response, and meaning elements a fear network before and after successful emotional processing (i.e., fear reduction). That is, successful treatment "disintegrates the fear structure."

Heart rate data were mixed as well. Colleagues and I examined distraction versus attentional focus versus control conditions over three six-minute exposures for individuals fearful of snakes and spiders. Focused exposure resulted in higher fear than either of the other two conditions, which did not differ from each other. Return of fear was not examined. In a treatment outcome study, 11 group sessions of distracted or focused exposure were compared for patients with panic disorder and agoraphobia. In the focused exposure condition, patients were trained to monitor bodily sensations and to use thought stopping and self-focusing statements to interrupt distraction. In contrast, patients in distracted exposure were trained to engage in cognitive distraction tasks such as word rhymes during exposure and to use thought stopping and task-oriented self-statements to interrupt internal focusing of attention. Both conditions improved, with the distracted group tending to show greater improvement by posttreatment. However, the focused group continued to improve over the six months after treatment, whereas the distracted group tended to deteriorate. Finally, distraction in the form of affective and neutral slides interfered with fear reduction during high-intensity exposure to snakes and spiders Behavioral Approach Task (BAT) Fear Ratings.

This result persisted during behavioral approach tests after completion of exposure. In contrast, as seen in Figure 3.2, distraction had no impact under low-intensity conditions.

Reasons for the contradictory nature of these findings include lack of an operational definition of distraction. For example, what aspects of attentional focus should be demanded by the distracter? Should the feared stimulus remain within the visual field while cognitive effort is being distracted or should the feared stimulus be out of the visual field and cognitively avoided? Is distraction from the threatening stimulus different from distraction from the feared response? The affective quality of the distracter may be important as well. For example, the competitive nature of the video games used by Grayson may have proved stressful. Other methodological issues in this area include the measurement of fear: Should fear be measured while the stimulus remains absent or the person is distracted or should the stimulus be presented intermittently for recording purposes? Grayson intermittently prompted participants in distracted conditions to visually examine the phobic stimulus and provide fear ratings. However, this assessment procedure may have inadvertently produced a series of brief exposure trials that led to sensitization. Finally, as my colleagues and I found with our 1995 study, stimulus intensity is another variable that complicates the effects of distraction. Thus, in contrast to tenets of emotional processing theory, the role of distraction is not fully clear.

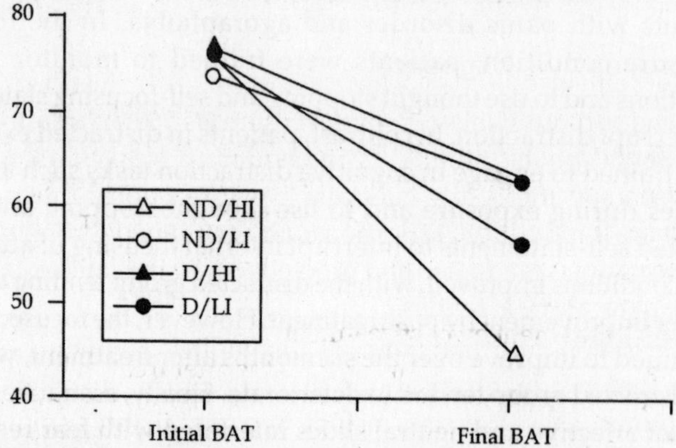

Fig. 3.2. The effect of distraction (0-100) during brief exposures to spiders and snakes was apparent in the change from pre- to postbehavioral approach test only in the group that received high-intensity exposure. (D=distraction; ND=no distraction; HI=high intensity exposure; LI=low intensity exposure).

Other tenets of emotional processing theory also have received only mixed support. Evidence for within-session habituation derives from Beckham, Vrana, May, Gustafson, and Smith; Grayson and Hecker. In addition, Foa, Grayson, and Steketee reported that between-session habituation correlated .43 with outcome. On the other hand, Kozak et al. conducted perhaps the most detailed evaluation to find that within-session habituation for obsessive compulsive features did not correlate with treatment outcome, and between-session habituation occurred for self-report indices but not for physiological indices of fear. Moreover, Riley found that indices of within-session habituation, toward the beginning, middle, or end of an eight-week treatment program for panic disorder with agoraphobia, did not relate to outcome. However, their treatment was confounded by the addition of mild to moderate doses of alprazolam. My colleagues and I conducted two studies in which indices of emotional processing throughout exposure treatment (i.e., initial physiological activation and between-session habituation) predicted *poorer* long-term outcome.

Emotional processing theory faces several conceptual difficulties, such as return of fear; it is unclear why fear structures, once modified, would return to their original state. The notion that fear structures *modify* contrasts with evidence for permanence of long-term memory and particularly fear memory. As suggested by Bouton, generation of an additional nonfear structure is, perhaps, more likely than modification of an original fear structure. Finally, emotional processing theory does not account for controlled escape exposure, in which physiological habituation and information about the harmlessness of high anxiety are minimized.

Self-efficacy and Control

According to self-efficacy theory, therapeutic gains are dependent on the degree to which self-efficacy, or confidence to perform a certain task, is generated. Self-efficacy is defined as "the conviction that one can successfully execute the behavior required to produce an outcome". Self-efficacy is theoretically distinct from outcome expectancies, which refer to the perceived likelihood and valence of negative events. In accordance with social learning theory, in which cognitive processes are attributed a prominent role in the acquisition and retention of behavior, efficacy expectations are claimed to influence the choice of activities and settings and determine the degree of effort expended and persistence in the face of obstacles or aversive experiences. In other words, self-efficacy is believed to influence coping in threatening situations. Self-efficacy judgments are posited to derive from four main sources of information: performance accomplishment, verbal persuasion, vicarious experience, and physiological arousal. The strongest source is the first, as it is through performance accomplishment that one obtains the most evidence for personal achievement and skills. Bandura claimed that all therapeutic modes operate by raising and strengthening percepts of self-efficacy. Thus, in contrast to previously reviewed mechanisms, self-efficacy explains treatments other than exposure therapy.

Overall, self-efficacy predicts treatment outcome. Moreover, Williams and colleagues find that self-efficacy is predictive of behavioral indices of treatment outcome regardless of treatment method, even after controlling outcome expectations of danger or anxiety, across targeted and nontargeted phobic stimuli. Similarly, Hoffart found that changes in selfefficacy accounted for changes in agoraphobic fear over and above the effects due to catastrophic beliefs or feelings of perceived control.

A strength of self-efficacy theory is its explanatory power for controlled escape exposure, in which participants may terminate an exposure trial when anxiety reaches unduly high levels. However, the theory has been criticized along several lines, such as for being tautological and epiphenomenal. Williams counters this argument by noting that self-efficacy is predictive of therapeutic gain from imaginal or symbolic/vicarious treatments in which there is no direct behavioral experience with the phobic object; that phobic behavior after treatment is more accurately predicted by selfefficacy judgments than by level of behavioral accomplishment during treatment; and, finally, that generalization of treatment gains to untreated phobic targets is predicted by self-efficacy. Nevertheless, none of these conclusively demonstrate that self-efficacy is the primary causal agent of therapeutic change. For example, imaginal and vicarious exposure to fear-provoking stimuli may alter physiology that in turn increases self-efficacy. Also, Teasdale argues that "by including the words 'successfully' and 'require to produce outcomes' in his definition of efficacy expectations, Bandura combines belief about the ability to make a response with expectations concerning the outcome of the response". In addition, self-efficacy has not been well separated from other influences such as skills and incentives. Furthermore, Rachman describes an example of fearfulness accompanied by confidence and courage in war situations, or simultaneous self-efficacy and fear, thus contradicting the tenets of self-efficacy theory. Although strong relationships exist between self-efficacy and fear behavior, the relationship with self-report and physiological arousal is less clear. Kendrick, Craig, Lawson and Davidson found that self-efficacy correlated only with behavioral outcome measures from a cognitive-behavioral treatment for anxious musicians. Furthermore, selfefficacy did not correlate with physiological measures in another study of anxious musicians.

Finally, self-efficacy theory has difficulty accounting for response desynchrony.

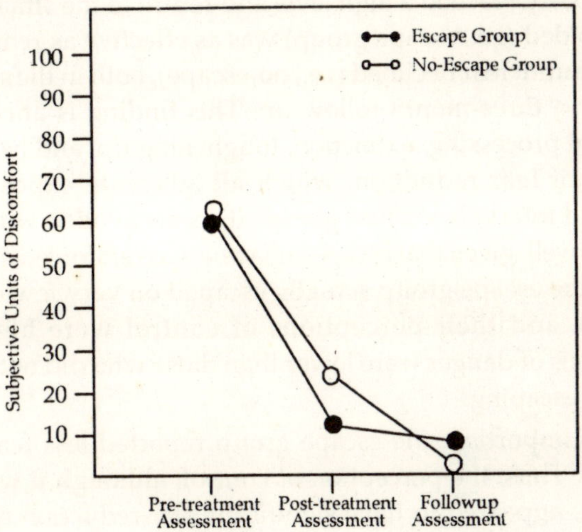

Fig. 3.3. Self-ratings of discomfort (0-100) during behavioral testing at pre, post, and follow-up assessments in groups with agoraphobia that received No-Escape (n=7) or Escape (n=7) instructions during exposure treatment. Note that the groups improved equally well.

Barlow emphasized the development of a sense of control for fear reduction. He posited that reversal of the fear action tendency, or reduction of escape urges or behaviors, leads to a sense that events or emotions are no longer proceeding uncontrollably, which in turn lessens fear and anxiety. This process can be set in motion by preventing the fear action tendency or by introducing specific competing tendencies, such as those characteristic of positively valent emotional states (e.g., humor). The fearreducing properties of veridical and perceived control have been demonstrated experimentally. For example, Starr and Mineka showed that fear of a CS declines over the course of avoidance learning when the organism has control over US termination. This effect was not due simply to absence of CS-US pairings, given that yoked animals, who had the same amount of exposure to USs but did not have control over their termination, did not show the same fear reduction.

The set of procedures previously referred to as "controlled escape" seem to illustrate the therapeutic effects of perceived control.

Rachman replicated an earlier set of results by de Silva and Rachman in showing that allowing patients to terminate an exposure practice when anxiety reached a high level and return to the situation after fear subsided (i.e., escape group) was as effective as remaining in exposure until fear declined (i.e., no-escape), both in the short term and over a three-month follow-up. This finding is at odds with emotional processing, extinction, toughening up, and habituation theories of fear reduction, which all advocate exposure over prolonged intervals. At first glance, it seems at odds with control theory as well, given that escape behavior was reinforced. However, those in the escape group actually escaped on very few occasions (13/128), and their perceptions of control were higher and perceptions of danger were lower than those who did not have the option of escaping.

Most important, the escape group reported less fear during exposure. Thus, the perception of control, although it was rarely exercised, appeared to have significant fear-reduction effects. In contrast, Marshall found that exposure that was terminated during a state of high anxiety was inferior to exposure that was continued until anxiety reduced. However, there were some key differences between the studies. For example, Marshall used flooding as opposed to the graduated exposure used by my colleagues and me. Also, in our study, patients took more control in determining when to escape, and we employed lengthier exposure durations. Nevertheless, the primacy of anxiety reduction versus achievement of control continues to be debated.

Predictive Accuracy

Rachman introduced the notion of match versus mismatch between expected fear and experienced fear that phobias are maintained by overestimations of the amount of fear to be experienced. From this model comes the possibility that therapeutic effects of exposure are due to disconfirmation of overprediction of fear, especially given the evidence that predictions become more accurate with repeated exposures to the same stimulus. Not too dissimilar is Kirsch's proposal that exposure functions by providing experiential feedback that confirms expectancies of fear reduction.

However, fear predictions are less likely to become accurate during repeated exposure to differing stimuli. Furthermore, actual fear decreases regardless of matches or mismatches between predicted and actual fear levels, although Arntz argues that further experimental evaluation is needed on this issue. Moreover, specific feedback about inaccuracies was not beneficial for analog fear reduction, according to Arntz. Finally, there are risks involved in reducing overpredictions; by reducing overpredictions, one is more vulnerable to underpredictions, which in turn have damaging effects of subsequent anticipatory anxiety and avoidance. Therefore, although it is clear that fearful individuals overpredict and that overpredictions may increase anticipatory anxiety and avoidance, it is not clear that increased accuracy of predictions explains the effects of exposure therapy.

Mechanisms of Cognitive Treatments

Cognitive theorists hypothesize that treatment is effective to the degree that information-processing distortions and underlying tacit beliefs and assumptions are altered, and that this is the basis of therapeutic change whatever the modality of change. Obviously, these notions overlap with concepts of emotional processing, self-efficacy, and predictive accuracy accounts of behavioral treatments. Evidence for cognitive mechanisms are reviewed in two ways. First, is treatment outcome mediated by cognitive shift, and, second, do cognitive therapies achieve this shift more than behavioral therapies?

Cognitive Mediation of Treatment Effects

Evidence to suggest that cognitive modification predicts outcome from treatment is accruing. Mostly the evidence is indirect, showing either no difference from nonanxious controls at posttreatment or reductions in cognitive biases among anxious patients from before to after treatment. For example, measures of catastrophic thinking about panic predict outcome for patients with panic disorder regardless of treatment modality. Also, Clark found that cognitive functioning after treatment for panic disorder was more predictive of follow-up status than other posttreatment measures. Similarly, Bruce, Spiegel, Gregg and Nuzzarello found that change in fears of bodily sensations from baseline to post-alprazolam taper correctly classified drug status (a return to medications or not) in 85% of the cases, suggesting that treatments that fail to reduce fears of bodily sensations have higher rates of relapse. On the other hand, as noted earlier, Williams and colleagues find that self-efficacy predicts changes in agoraphobic behavior over and above the effects of shifts in catastrophic cognitions.

With respect to social phobia, Mattia, Heimberg and Hope showed that responders to cognitive-behavioral treatment, medications, and placebo had significant reductions in modified Stroop response latencies for social threat words. Also, changes in Fear of Negative Evaluation scores and Irrational Beliefs Test scores predict outcome for social phobics treated with cognitive therapy, behavioral therapy, or a combination of the two. Indeed, changes in Fear of Negative Evaluation scores account for most outcome variance. On the other hand, this test is considered by some to be a measure of anxiety rather than cognition and Mattick note that approximately 65% of outcome variance was unexplained, suggesting that factors other than cognitive modification are important as well.

Most of the research on cognitive mediation of treatment effects pertains to generalized anxiety disorder. Recovered generalized anxiety disorder patients interpret ambiguous statements in much the same way as controls, with relatively benign meanings, in comparison to currently anxious patients. Also, recovered patients are more likely to complete stems of words with neutral than with threatening words in comparison to currently anxious patients. Furthermore, one study found that recovered patients do not show attentional vigilance in dot probe detection tasks, although Mathews, May, Mogg, and Eysenck showed that even recovered generalized anxiety disorder patients were affected by a "threat" distracter in these tasks. All of the above studies used between-group rather than repeated measures designs. Mathews tested the same group before and after treatment on an array of cognitive measures. As patients improved with treatment, the extent of interference from threatening distracters decreased. Finally, Mogg examined the effects of cognitivebehavioral treatment on nonconscious processes, using the modified Stroop task at subthreshold as well as suprathreshold conditions of stimulus presentation. Again, treated generalized anxiety disorder patients did not differ from controls. However, changes in cognitive bias correlated only with changes in anxious thoughts and did not correlate with changes in anxious and depressive symptornatology.

Superior detection of anxious words in a dichotic listening task disappeared after behavioral treatment for obsessive compulsive disorder. Also, change in irrational beliefs correlates (.44) with improvement in anxiety and discomfort for obsessive compulsive disorder. Evidence for cognitive mediation exists for specific phobias as well. Watts, McKenna, Sharrock and Trezise found that Stroop interference effects due to phobic words were removed after systematic desensitization for a sample of individuals phobic of spiders. Also, reductions in negative cognitions after cognitive therapy, in vivo exposure, or interoceptive exposure correlated with claustrophobic fear reduction.

Rachman and Whittal noted 10 instances (out of 60) cf very abrupt changes in fearfulness during treatment. They proposed that these are more characteristic of insight learning than the usual gradual progression of trial-and-error learning. Insight learning may occur as a result of a cognitive shift. That is, cognitive modification does not have to occur gradually, as would be predicted from extinction theory or emotional processing theory.

Nevertheless, all of the evidence for cognitive mediation of treatment effects is subject to alternative interpretations. Rachman notes the difficulty of establishing a causal role for cognitions. That is, do cognitions precede or follow fear reduction? This question is especially difficult to answer because change is often slow and may occur between treatment sessions, rendering observation of the sequence of events problematic. Furthermore, measures of cognitive change are mostly limited to self-reports, which are subject to responder bias and may confound cognitions with anxiety in general (such as the Fear of Negative Evaluation scale). Also, Costello criticizes cognitive accounts for concepts that are indistinguishable or incontrovertible. For example, he questions the degree to which concepts of "cognitions" differ from "bodily sensations" in panic disorder research. He cites factor analytic research showing that semantically related descriptions of cognitions and bodily sensations load on the same factors. Furthermore, he refers to work by Smith and Allred and Zurawski and Smith, who found that measures of irrational beliefs had higher correlations with measures of distress than with each other. According to Costello, efforts should be redirected away from incontrovertible concepts such as negative or danger-laden schema and toward more controvertible concepts that refer to pathogenic structure rather than content, such as selectivity of attention.

Others refute cognitive accounts, arguing that by discussing and imagining feared stimuli, cognitive therapy represents a degraded form of exposure that allows processes of habituation, extinction, and mastery to occur. Even degraded forms of exposure are capable of activating cohesive fear structures, according to bioinformational theory. Furthermore, cognitive therapy can be couched in conditioning terms of US revaluation. That is fear is reduced when USs are devalued by socially or verbally transmitted information (e.g., information to suggest that the US is unlikely to recur, or altered outcome expectancies) or through reevaluating reactions to the US or CS (e.g., strengthening of self-efficacy). The overlap between conditioning and cognitive models is very apparent from this perspective.

Finally, Robins and Hayes ask in effect, "If cognitions are responsible for treatment outcome, what exactly has changed?" For example, does the schemata alter (as suggested by emotional processing theory and cognitive theory)? Is a new schemata generated (as suggested indirectly by Bouton's context specificity model)? Or are compensatory skills taught to deal with the schemata (as suggested by self-efficacy theory)?

Cognitive Change Through Cognitive Versus Behavioral Treatment

In contrast to expectations, most evidence suggests that cognitions are changed to the same degree by behavioral and cognitive treatments. For example, Emmelkamp, Brilman, Kuiper and Mersch; Michelson and Williams and Rappoport found that cognitive therapy versus exposure or relaxation for agoraphobia did not differ in terms of cognitive outcome measures. These effects may have been mitigated by poorly implemented cognitive treatments, and sometimes the cognitive change was very small. On the other hand, similar results have been reported with more recent and well-implemented cognitive treatments. Moreover, Williams and Falbo reported that performance-based exposure type therapy was more effective in reducing panic-related cognitions than cognitive therapy.

The results are more mixed with respect to social phobia. Several studies found no cognitive differences at posttreatment between cognitive and behavioral treatments. Similarly, in a very detailed analysis of cognitive and behavioral change throughout short-term pure cognitive versus pure exposure treatment for public speaking anxiety, no differences were found on any measure at midtreatment, posttreatment or follow-up. On the other hand, Mattick found more within-group change and more improvement on cognitive measures at follow-up from cognitive treatment, and Emmelkamp, Mersch, Vissia, and van der Helm and Butler, Cullington, Munby, Amies, and Gelder found that exposure therapy did not produce cognitive changes. Again, however, these latter two studies may have been limited by poorly developed cognitive therapies. Conversely, Mersch obtained greater improvement of irrational beliefs with in vivo exposure only relative to a combination of rational emotive therapy, social skills training, and in vivo exposure. Similarly, Hope, Heimberg, and Bruch found that cognitive change was more broad based for exposure alone versus a combination of cognitive therapy and exposure. However, these authors temper their conclusions because of an unusually poor response to the combined treatment condition in their study. Finally, from their review of 15 social phobia studies, Feske and Chambless concluded that there was generally no difference in cognitive outcome between cognitive-behavioral therapy versus exposure alone.

With respect to generalized anxiety disorder, two studies show patterns of greater improvement on cognitive measures after cognitively oriented treatment relative to behavioral treatment. In terms of obsessive compulsive disorder, two studies report greater change on a measure of irrational beliefs after cognitive treatment relative to behavioral treatments. However, in both studies, the measure used to assess beliefs was not specific to obsessive compulsive disorder. New obsessive compulsive belief scales now exist.

Finally, studies with specific phobias are mixed. Booth and Rachman found that three sessions of in vivo exposure, interoceptive exposure, and cognitive therapy for claustrophobia were equally effective in terms of cognitive change. Emmelkamp and Felten compared one session of exposure alone to exposure plus self-instruction training for acrophobics. Although both treatments reduced heart rate and increased performance, exposure alone did not change cognitions whereas the combination treatment did. However, the brevity of treatment limits the value of both data sets.

In summary, the majority of studies show no difference in cognitive outcomes from cognitive versus behavioral treatments. However, Feske and Chambless note that cognitive therapy may require more therapist training than exposure therapy, and studies to date have not assessed treatment adherence or competency sufficiently to know if more competent cognitive therapists achieve more cognitive change than equally competent exposure therapists.

To explain the success of exposure therapy that is conducted without cognitive therapy, Rachman suggests, "With each exposure, the patient acquires fresh, disconfirmatory evidence (e.g., no heart attack, did not lose control). The accumulation of this personal, direct, disconfirmatory evidence weakens the catastrophic cognitions". The overlap with emotional processing and self-efficacy theories is obvious; that is, cognitive change occurs as a result of experience, without the need for direct cognitive intervention strategies. However, it remains to be shown whether the exposure experience changes cognitions and thereby lessens anxiety or whether lessened anxiety renders such cognitions less likely to arise.

A final difficulty for cognitive theories is desynchrony; how can changes in behavioral or physiological reactions be explained if unaccompanied by changes in cognitions, as was found by Emmelkamp and Felten? Conversely, how can the relative absence of behavioral change be explained when cognitive shifts have occurred, as was found by Emmelkamp and Mattick?

Therapeutic Relationship Mechanisms

Generally, behavioral and cognitive-behavioral therapies devote very little attention to the role of patient-therapist relationship. As alluded to previously, Wolpe attributes nonspecific or placebo effects to therapist effects, in conditioning terms. In particular, reciprocal inhibition offered by the calmness induced via a good patient-therapist relationship is assumed to reduce fear. However, this particular hypothesis awaits empirical investigation. Recently, Keijsers, Schaap, Hoogduin, and Lammers reviewed findings regarding therapist relationship factors and behavioral outcome. They conclude that empathy, warmth, positive regard, and genuineness assessed early in treatment predict positive outcome. Second, patients who view their therapists as understanding and respectful improve the most. Also, patient perceptions of therapist expertness, self-confidence, and directiveness relate positively to outcome, although not consistently. In their own study of junior therapists who provided cognitive-behavioral treatment for panic disorder with agoraphobia, Keijsers found that therapists used more empathic statements and more questioning in Session 1 than later sessions. In Session 3, therapists became more active and offered more instructions and explanations. In Session 10, therapists employed more interpretations and confrontations than previously. In fact, directive statements and explanations in Session 1 predicted poorer outcome. Empathic listening in Session 1 related to better behavioral outcome, whereas empathic listening in Session 3 related to poorer behavioral outcome. Thus, they demonstrated the advantages of different interactional styles at different points in therapy.

Conclusion

The proliferation of theories for fear reduction through exposure therapy indicates lack of satisfaction with the original habituation, extinction, and response deficit correction models. Recent theories of exposure incorporate cognitive mediation in the form of outcome expectancies regarding dangerousness of phobic stimuli (emotional processing theory), expectancies of anxiety (emotional processing and predictive accuracy), and self-efficacy and control. A most promising advance in extinction theorizing considers the "meaning" of stimuli in interaction with the contexts in which they are encountered. A particular strength of this context disambiguation model of extinction is its explanatory power for return of fear and relapse. Clearly, these "behavioral" theories overlap with cognitive theories of fear reduction. Evidence supports the role of cognitive modification in fear reduction, regardless of whether treatment is primarily behaviorally or cognitively oriented. There is even some evidence that cognitive shifts are stronger with behaviorally oriented treatments. However, it remains to be determined whether cognitive modification precedes or follows anxiety reduction. Also, much of the research to date is based on self-reported changes in cognitive content (e.g., fears of bodily sensations or negative evaluations, or self-efficacy). As noted by Costello, research efforts may be more fruitfully directed toward more controvertible cognitive concepts, such as those concerning structure rather than content of cognition. These might include concepts such as context disambiguation, attentional selectivity, and memory biases. Another debatable issue concerns the primacy of perceptions of control versus anxiety reduction. Extinction and habituation models emphasize fear reduction, whereas self-efficacy and theories of control emphasize achievement of control. Finally, the role of physiological variables such as neurochemical toughening up and endogenous opioids is interesting but awaits further investigation.

Thus, there may be a variety of ways in which fear, or threat imminence, is reduced: by achieving perceptions of control over fear-provoking stimuli or control over one's reactions to fear-provoking stimuli or by changing perceptions of danger attributed to fear-provoking stimuli. In other words, it is likely that a variety of factors are responsible for fear reduction just as fear acquisition is multimodal, so may be fear reduction, as well as return of fear, to which we turn next.

4

Theory of Abnormal Personality: Basic Structure

Introduction

The interests of researchers are mobilized by themes or areas which appear new and important at the moment; but sooner or later these prove to be sterile or exhausted and they are abandoned". "These widespread self-doubts about goals, methods, and accomplishments have been expressed recently within personality research".

There is a chaotic literature in the field. Thus there is no agreement on what should be taught in the field, that is, what knowledge is to be transmitted to students. Textbooks generally review some of the theories of personality. On the other hand, courses sometimes are organized to sample the many research studies in personality, a separate body of knowledge. What this indicates is that there is not, at present, a framework conception for the field that indicates what its subject matter is, how to go about furthering knowledge of that subject matter, and the theories and methodologies that are appropriate for the task.

The theory of personality to be presented here was developed in a quite different manner than any of the others. The goal of the work that led to the present theory was not that of constructing a personality theory. Rather the work was begun with the goal of constructing a general behaviorism that could comprehensively deal with human behavior. However, the program produced theoretical, empirical, and methodological developments that progressively led to a general theory of personality. As a result of the manner of its development, the PB theory of personality is part of a broad theory that generally applies to psychology.

Important parts of the developmental history of the PB theory of personality have already been given in presenting the first four levels of study on which the theory is based. Several additional steps in this development will be indicated to illustrate how PB concepts and principles were progressively applied to personality phenomena and to constructing the theory itself.

Developments in the PB Theory of Personality

Psychological behaviorism began with a goal of applying learning principles to the study of human behavior. As knowledge collected in this work, new developments were suggested. For example, PB applied learning principles to the analysis of language. Beginning with Watson other behaviorists had analyzed parts of language or considered phenomena like semantic generalization. None of these accounts was based on or led to an empirical program of study. PB's analysis of language, however, began with empirical study of how language is learned. On the basis of such study PB analyzed language into repertoires, which provided the conceptual basis for seeing the relationships of language to other parts of psychology.

Language Principles and Concepts

This work thus produced a conceptual framework that offered new considerations. For example, when analyzing different psychological phenomena such as communication, problem solving, originality, and scientific reasoning it could be seen that the language repertoires played a basic role. From this a new concept was derived, that of *language function*. It became important to study not only what language was and how language was learned, but also how language functioned for the individual, and between individuals, in the analysis and *explanation* of different types of human behavior. Problem solving was seen to involve labeling the problem objects, verbal associations to the labeling, and the verbal-motor repertoire that provides problem-solving actions. Communication was analyzed as the functioning of the language repertoires, as was originality (creativity). Scientific work was seen to involve the learning of repertoires, including language repertoires (theory), that resulted from new experiences (observations) for the scientist that, in turn, led to additional developments and new repertoires. Mathematics learning was analyzed in terms of specific language repertoires. These developments, and the more basic analysis of other cognitive phenomena in terms of language function, established a bridge to the consideration of cognition. The PB position became that cognitive phenomena consist largely of the functioning of learned language BBRs. This aim of this unification is characterized in its title *Learning, Language and Cognition*.

Defense Mechanisms

In turn, the human learning analyses of language function and language repertoires provided new principles and concepts that could be employed as bridging materials in advancing to the analysis of more complex human phenomena. With these bridging materials PB was able to analyze personality concepts in traditional psychology that were derived from clinical observations. An early PB analysis treated Freud's defense mechanisms. His conceptualization was that humans defend themselves from anxiety by developing ego defense mechanisms.

Radical behaviorism considers the ego, including its defense mechanisms, as traditional mentalistic concepts. The psychoanalytic personality concepts are inferred from behavior and then are considered to explain that behavior. They are thus mentalistic in nature. Mentalistic concepts are generally rejected in radical behaviorism, along with the work that has produced the concepts. The PB "behaviorizing" approach, in contrast, is to ask if the behaviors that are involved are important. If so, then the area should be subjected to a psychological behaviorism analysis. The observations underlying the concept of the defense mechanisms are indeed valuable, because Freud was an astute observer of human behavior. In PB terms the defense mechanisms can be seen to involve the functioning of complex language repertoires (largely) in a way that reduces negative emotionality the person would otherwise experience.

For example, rationalization, one of the "defense mechanisms," may be considered as an aspect of the verbal-labeling repertoire. The individual in rationalizing is labeling her actions in a way that increases positive, or decreases negative, social response. The individual, for example, rationalizes her defeat in a tennis match by saying she had hurt her back. There is a general "rationalizing repertoire" that people learn to widely differing degrees. The PB behavior analysis also added another principle with respect to the rationalization repertoire, namely that rationalization behavior determines other behaviors of the individual. "However, it must be remembered that the individual's own labeling and verbal response sequences also have an important function in mediating his own problem solving behavior and if they are too distorted, the behavior mediated may be maladjustive". If one can rationalize away one's misbehavior, for example, this subtracts from the stimuli that would lead to changing that misbehavior. In the long term this may be maladaptive. Importantly, as will be indicated, this analysis moves PB toward explaining the causal characteristic of the concept of personality.

Similar analyses were also made of the other defense mechanisms. Projection, as another example, involves ways by which we "(1) transfer the blame for our own shortcomings, mistakes, or misdeeds to others, and (2) attribute to others our own unacceptable impulses, thoughts, and desires". PB's analysis of the language repertoires involved added to the understanding of how "untrue" language sequences can produce problems in the individual's behavior. "Again, although the behavior may be considered 'adjustive' because it reduces immediately aversive stimuli (which accounts for the maintenance of the behavior), it may have detrimental consequences if it later mediates inappropriate behavior". To reason and plan well about life's problems the individual's language behavior must be sufficiently truthful or "realistic."

Repression may be considered as the case where certain of the individual's statements elicit in her a strong negative emotional response. Avoiding making those statements that is, thinking about something else removes the unpleasant thoughts (statements), and is thereby reinforced. The individual thus learns not to make those statements, even to herself, thus being unaware (unconscious) of them. Eriksen and Kuethe showed that subjects who were shocked when they made a particular word associate to a stimulus word later did not give that word associate. Since they were not aware of why they no longer had that word associate, it could be said that punishment led to repression. The problem with repression is that one cannot reason about problems if the necessary labels are not available.

The defense mechanism of fantasy was treated in PB as verbal behavior that elicits images that elicit positive emotional responses, and are thus reinforcing. "It is suggested that a life situation in which there are few reinforcers contingent upon the individual's 'realistic' [verbal] behavior would not be expected to maintain 'realistic' behavior in good strength, and the relatively small reinforcers of fantasy might serve to strengthen fantasy behavior until it becomes much more dominant". In addition, "Fantasy behaviors, however, since they are not problem-solving in nature [in the sense of pertaining to the events of the world], would not ordinarily contribute much to the adjustive behaviors the individual must emit in society. Thus, a preponderance of behavior of the fantasy type would have drawbacks for the individual's adjustment" (Staats, 1963a, p. 394). In each case the defense mechanism is seen as a repertoire acquired via conditioning principles that nevertheless can be maladjustive when it mediates maladjustive behavior.

The Self-Concept

To continue in the development of PB's behavioral concept of personality, the language repertoire (cognitive) principles and concepts were employed to make a theoretical analysis of the self-concept. The self concept was considered to consist of the individual's *learned* verbal labels to herself. Individual differences in those verbal labels were said to differentially elicit emotional responses in herself and in others, varying from negative to positive. If the individual's self-labels elicit positive emotional responses in others, the individual will have more social power, that is, serve as a positive directive stimulus that elicits positive behaviors in others. The reverse will pertain if the individual's self-labels elicit a negative emotion in others.

In addition, the statements the individual makes about himself would be expected to function as a stimulus that would control his own behavior.... It would be expected that different reasoning sequences would ensue if the individual labeled his own behavior in positive rather than negative terms. For example, the individual who makes derogatory self-statements may "conclude" in a problem-solving sequence not to attempt tasks at which he might otherwise be successful. He may thus not present himself for situations in which he might develop new skilled behaviors. On the other hand, the individual who makes "confident" self-statements may, other things being equal, attempt the task on the basis of his reasoning and be successful. As a consequence, these two individuals as they progress through life may have different opportunities to gain experience, and their behavior would be shaped accordingly. The self confident individual might well have many more experiences (again, other things being equal) where he is reinforced for emitting certain skill behaviors. The former individual might not develop those skills in the same measure. The self-confident individual may also, because of his verbal behavior, tend to gain more attention, social approval, and social rewards such as raises and honors. These experiences could reinforce the verbal behavior and produce further "self-confident" self-description.

This analysis displays PB's behavioral interaction conception that is integral to its theory of personality, as will be indicated. That is, in the PB analysis the self-concept verbal behavior is produced by the environment. But it produces emotional responses in the individual that affect other behaviors of the individual. Those behaviors (as well as the self-statements) affect the social environment, which in turn acts back on the self-concept of the individual. The interactions are complex and continuing, and must be taken into account in constructing a conception of personality and human behavior generally. The PB formulation also specified that the self concept is learned.

The child [is] trained to make appropriate verbal responses to the stimuli produced by his own behavior. He learns to label his own movements actions and his own social behavior. The individual's self statements should to some extent depend upon the physical properties of the individual and the behavior he emits. In addition, however, the child's training to make statements about himself may be to some extent independent of what he is and does. This discrepancy arises when an individual who behave[s] in a certain way has not been trained to describe verbally his behavior in commensurate terms. A child might be reinforced for labeling his skills as low level, whereas they are really very capable. On the other hand, it is equally possible to shape verbal behavior that is unrealistically flattering.

Other discriminative stimuli besides those of the individual himself and his behavior seem also to determine statements about the "self." One's statements about oneself thus may vary from situation to situation.

The heuristic value of the PB analysis of the self-concept was demonstrated in the development of other behavioral approaches.

In the social learning analysis of cognitive development, conceptions about oneself and the nature of the environment are developed and verified through different processes. People derive much of their knowledge from direct experience of the effects produced by their actions. However, results of one's own actions are not the sole source of knowledge. People develop and evaluate their conceptions in terms of judgments voiced by others. In addition to the expectancy determinants analyzed thus far, situational circumstances affect [self] efficacy expectations. As a result of such differential reactions, children eventually come to respond to their own behavior in self-approving and self-critical ways, depending on how it compares with the evaluative standards set by others. Social learning theory defines negative self-concepts in terms of proneness to devalue oneself and positive self-concepts as a tendency to judge oneself favorably.

As another example, Hayes has introduced a behavior therapy that features the self-concept. In PB theory the theory of the self-concept was constructed on the foundation of more basic analyses of language and emotion, and how both can affect the individual's behavior. However, radical behaviorism has rejected the analysis of how the individual's own behavior (such as language, or emotional responding) can be a cause of overt operant behavior. This position if it was consistently followed, which it is not would rob the concept of the self-concept of its causal (personality) functions.

Intelligence, Interests and Values

The defense mechanisms and the self-concept in traditional psychology are conceptual developments derived from naturalistic and clinical observations. There are also personality concepts that have emerged in psychometric study. For example, there are psychological tests that measure interests, values, and intelligence. Very early PB analyses began to deal with such topics.

For example, interests were considered in PB in the same framework as attitudes and values, as stimuli that elicit emotional responses the emotional response elicited then determining whether the stimulus will be positively or negatively reinforcing as well as whether the stimulus will be approached or avoided. Items on the interest test were considered to measure the emotional response the individual had to the stimuli referred to in the items. The interest test was considered to measure aspects of the individual's "reinforcer system" (an early name for the emotional-motivational repertoire). The same analysis was made of tests of values. Later MacPhillamy and Lewinsohn composed a test of people's reinforcers that provided empirical definition of the concept of the "reinforced system".

Another example of PB's early analysis of psychological tests was shown in its incipient theory of intelligence, based upon my study of children's learning of important language-cognitive repertoires. "Intelligence may be considered to refer to a wide sample of [learned] basic behavioral skills the child (or adult) has acquired which are important to the acquisition of further skilled behaviors." This account continued by saying that, "Intelligence may be considered as a dependent variable (an effect) and an independent variable (a cause) within the same analysis." Another principle was that "we are interested in this basic behavioral repertoire in the first place because we can observe that children who have the constituents of such a repertoire do well in their life tasks and problems".

In addition, consideration of these complex individual difference characteristics also provided the basis for constructing a taxonomy of abnormal behavior. To illustrate, certain types of psychological disorders (such as schizophrenia, psychopathy, and sexual deviations) were considered to involve deficit and inappropriate aspects of the reinforcer system, that is, the emotional-motivational system or repertoire. The individual's reinforcer system was being employed as an explanation of these behavior disorders.

Elements for a Theory of Personality: Beginning Framework Theory

This was the beginning. Two works *Learning, Language, and Cognition* and *Child Learning, Intelligence and Personality* stipulated additionally the concept of the basic behavioral repertoires, the conditions by which BBRs are learned, and made more clear the concept of the basic behavioral repertoire as a personality concept. The concept and principles of cumulative-hierarchical learning were introduced. Analyses were made of the empirical phenomena that define various personality concepts. As occurs in science, the various developments constituted a foundation for and a growing press for a full behavioral theory of personality.

These developments were furthered in the 1975 book *Social Behaviorism* and the conceptual framework was advanced and stipulated. For one thing, the multilevel theory construction methodology was made more formal. The position taken by PB, from the beginning, was that laboratory study of animal behavior can yield fundamental principles of learning. But it does not yield knowledge about personality and complex behavior in general. The realization was deepened that clinical observations and findings, those of psychometric research, and other human behavior study needed to be utilized. Moreover, bridging theory had to be constructed by which to do so. That became a program of PB, the elaboration of a psychological behavioral theory that utilized, among other things, observations of human behavior gained in clinical, abnormal, educational, social, and child psychology.

The concept of the basic behavioral repertoire is an example of a central bridging theory development needed for that program. The concept opened a new way of viewing the schism between traditional psychology and behaviorism. The schism occurs because personality is traditionally seen as a cause of behavior (an independent variable), but behaviorism customarily considers personality only as behavior, as a dependent variable. The basic behavioral repertoire, in being both a dependent variable and an independent variable, provides the element to resolve this fundamental schism. The *BBRs* are learned, but they also help determine the individual's behavior. Thus, language was analyzed as it was learned, as a dependent variable. But language was also analyzed as it functioned as an independent variable in problem solving, intelligence, and the self-concept. Here was a basis for very generally bringing together the *psychological* and the *behavioral*.

PB's Basic Theory of Personality

With the behaviorizing goal, the multilevel framework theory construction methodology, and with the accumulating concepts and principles, a personality theory was formed imbedded in a general behaviorism approach. Framework theory is intended to develop in successive steps, however, and much remained to be done. The theory needed to formalized, extended more broadly, with deeper and more systematic analyses. Empirical work had to be derived to extend and support the theory. New directions of research needed to be shown. Description of this extension will begin with the presentation of the PB model of personality.

PB Model

The PB conception is that the infant begins life without the basic behavioral repertoires. That is why the child displays almost no organized behavior. The child has sensory mechanisms hearing, sight, tactile sensitivity, and so on. And the child has response mechanisms. But the child's responses have no organization with respect to the stimuli that life presents. Child development, as has been indicated, consists of learning organized behavior to life's stimuli.

That learning is complex. The child learns complex sensory-motor, language-cognitive, and emotional-motivational repertoires. As this occurs the child is changed, becoming able to respond appropriately in various stimulus situations. Moreover, whereas at the beginning the child's learning is laborious, involving only the basic principles of conditioning, as the repertoires are acquired the child's *learning* comes more easily, because it now is aided by the repertoires that have already been acquired. Also the way the child *experiences* the world of stimuli depends, in large part, on the repertoires. And the way the child *behaves* depends upon the repertoires that have been learned. It is because the repertoires have those effects on the child that they are called basic behavioral repertoires. As they are acquired they give the child new characteristics.

Traditional psychology has insisted that there are some personal characteristics, some internal biological processes or structures, that are idiosyncratic to the individual, that determine the individual's behavior. Standard behaviorism has no concept that can coincide with that view of personality. The PB conception, however, is that the personal characteristics are provided by the individual's BBRs. *The basic behavioral repertoires constitute personality.* That means that personality consists of the language-cognitive, emotional-motivational, and sensory-motor repertoires the individual has learned. While one individual's BBRs may have commonalities with those learned by someone else, overall the BBRs are never duplicated in two individuals the complexity of human experience and the complexity of the human BBRs rules that out. Humans indeed have unique personalities.

The PB conception (model) of personality is presented in Figure 4.1. S_1 stands for the experience (environment) the individual has had, up to the present time, that has produced the learning of the individual's basic behavioral repertoires.

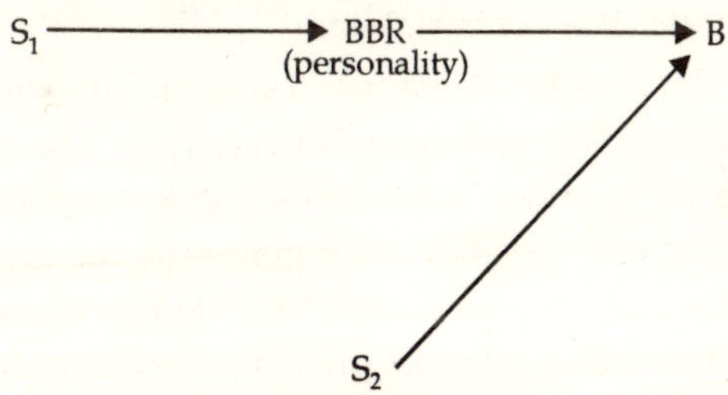

Fig. 4.1. The psychological behaviorism conception of personality. The individual's environment up to the present (S_1) results in the learning of a basic behavioral repertoire (BBR). The individual's behavior (B) is function of the life situation (S_2) and the individual's BBRs. The BBRs are a dependent variable, because they are the result of learning. But the BBRs are also an independent variable, because they act as a cause of the individual's behavior, and thus constitute the individual's personality.

As indicated, the very complex BBRs constitute the individual's personality; the BBRs are responsible for the behavioral phenomena from which the concept of personality is derived. The environmental situations (stimuli) that go into producing the BBRs contain many elements and are cumulatively very complex. At the time of behaving, which elements of the BBRs the individual will experience or act-out will be determined by the present stimulus circumstances, depicted in the figure as S_2. Thus the present stimulus situation interacts with the BBRs in producing the individual's behavior, which is depicted as B in the figure. B stands for the behavior made in an encountered situation.

This diagram is only a summary representation of the theory. It is useful for describing the basic elements of the theory. As a summary the diagram does not indicate detail or specifics. For example, we might use the model to describe a particular occasion, when S_2 stands for a particular stimulus situation. Or, we may wish to consider behavior more generally, as it exists over a longer span of time than the specific moment. For example, the individual's drinking over a period of months, after a work situation change that includes a new boss, might be considered in terms of the model. In such a case the S_2 would stand for a current life situation that extends over the relevant period, and B (the individual's drinking behavior) would refer to an ongoing, general aspect of the individual's behavior. The figure is not intended to stand for specific circumstances, but only to depict general classes of variables.

The model does not constitute a specific behavior analysis, but only a framework for making such an analysis. The conception only becomes an explanatory behavior analysis when its variables are defined in concrete specifics. As is generally the case, the model is only an abbreviation which must be filled in to constitute a real theory. The preceding chapters provide specifications of the theory, as will the rest of the present chapter and that which follows.

Biology and Personality

As in the field of child development, in personality study there has been a long-standing nature nurture schism an unfortunate opposition of the biological and environmental positions in the explanation of personality. It is important, thus, in setting forth a theory of personality, to deal with this issue.

Part of the status of biologically oriented conceptions, it should be noted, accrues because they are seen to *represent* the powerful biological sciences. Most such conceptions, however, do not actually involve biological study. What is involved is that the orientation makes assumptions that attribute personality traits (and human behavior generally) to biological processes genetics, anatomy, physiology, disease, biochemistry. The expectation is that at some time in the future the biological processes will be found. Such orientations in attributing complex traits, like intelligence, extroversion, sociability, or dyslexia, to a biological process have the effect of establishing an obstacle to a behavioral/biological unification. If a trait is laid down in the individual's biological structure, if it is prewired, then that cuts learning out of the explanatory loop.

Biological techniques of study of brain processes have advanced a great deal. This includes many studies that show that brain damage of various kinds will produce behavioral losses and change what is considered to be personality. And there are findings that drugs will do the same. Such studies are considered to support the conception that brain characteristics determine personality characteristics. But there is a theoretical jump here that is not warranted. Let me take intelligence as an example of one type of personality trait. Despite more than a hundred years of belief that some feature of the brain determines intelligence, there is little in the way of direct evidence of such causation. The fact that brain damage can subtract from the individual's intelligence does not indicate that the individual's intelligence had been produced by his brain. The fact is that huge differences in intelligence occur in people whose brains are not different. "You study the brain of a genius, and it doesn't show anything different from the brain of an idiot. Their tissue is the same, their brain waves travel in the same way. No chemical analysis, no electrical presence separates those two individuals. In a biological science laboratory, you'll never discover why one person can write so well or paint so well or do mathematics so well, and another cannot".

Because direct evidence has been lacking, many scientific resources have been devoted to gaining "circumstantial" evidence of the presumed genetic determination of intelligence. That is, many studies attempt to "prove" that biology causes a trait, not by direct evidence to that effect, but by ruling out the possibility that the trait could have been learned. For example, a favorite type of study of "genetic" effects on intelligence involves comparing the intelligence scores of identical twins (raised in different homes) to same-sex non-identical twins and to plain siblings. The correlation of IQ scores is highest for identical twins and diminishes with lessened genetic similarity. The interpretation of genetic cause in such studies rests on the assumption that being raised in different homes controls the effects of the environment. The logic of the approach will not hold water, however. The position rests on the assumption that placement into adoptive homes has been random which is not the case. Those who place children try to match the child's characteristics to those of the home, which means children are placed systematically. Moreover, identical twins will be placed in more similar homes than others. It is also the case that physical attributes of *subjects* constitute an "environmental" variable that influences the results. That is, the individual's physical characteristics affect how people respond to the individual, and that environment effects what the individual learns. Beautiful people face a different environment than do plain or odd-looking people, and big, strong, and fast males face a different environment than small and weak males. Such things affect twin studies for identical twins *share* any social environment that is produced by their shared physical attributes.

In any event, twin studies (the strongest available evidence) are indirect; they do not show just what biological processes "cause" intelligence or any other personality trait. Such studies can only have an exhortatory purpose that encourages efforts directly to find the biological mechanisms. But exhortation is not needed. Our popular as well as scientific cultures are already convinced of genetic determination of personality. Research to find biological causation of personality has been going on for some hundred and fifty years. What is needed if there really are biological variations that determine individual differences is direct evidence of what those biological mechanisms are and how they work their effects.

The same criticism may be directed at the environmentalist side, it may be added. Its traditional evidence, too, has been lacking. For example, there are studies showing that children exposed to an enriched preschool experience have higher IQ measures. As another example, Scarr and Weinberg showed that black children adopted by middle-class white parents had better than average IQs, and those adopted early had more positive IQ effects. Such studies, also, only serve an exhortatory purpose. For in such studies there is no specification regarding what the children's experience was, how it affected their intelligence, what intelligence is, or how it has its effects on behavior. The environmentalist approach, like the biological approach, has been vague. Just what personality traits are has not been specified, the learning conditions and principles that produce them, and so on.

This same weakness, it may be added, applies to behaviorists, like Watson and Skinner. They, too, have not come to grips with the study of individual differences, except by way of suggesting a general environmentalism. And that is not always clear: "A certain gene may fail in laying a proper foundation for the brain; the result will be to produce a feeble-minded individual. It is clearly proved experimentally that diverse [genetic] combinations yield diversities in behavior". The same may be said of Skinner. His statements have been taken to represent an extreme environmentalism. But he actually did not formulate such a position, or provide any substance to support one. He did not study the importance of learning in childhood, or call for this study. He did not indicate how in childhood the child learns personality traits. His work does not indicate a conviction that it is learning that produces all of complex human behavior. His position with respect to biological causation was stated in a paper entitled "Phylogeny and ontogeny of behavior". The position is that biological evolution produces adaptive behavior in the organism. The shaping of behavior, via the principles of reinforcement, is said to take over where evolution leaves off in producing adaptive behavior. This position suggests there is biological determination of behavior and that learning is like evolutionary effects in this way. But that position does not constitute a framework that unifies biological study with learning study, and thereby provide a basis for solving the nature nurture schism.

The nature nurture issue is a perennial problem in psychology. The interactionist conception that both biology and learning determine human behavior and personality only represents a "let's not fight" political compromise. No interaction approach has actually shown how learning and biological work together to produce individual differences. And, in actuality, studies and theories follow one or the other position. Some studies attempt to establish biological variables as *the* cause in a way that eliminates or trivializes the role of learning. Other studies or theories take a general environmentalist position in a way that leaves out the biological organism. No conceptual framework has been set forth indicating how to consider biology and learning as they jointly determine personality (and human behavior generally).

Evolution and Personality

The PB position is a first step toward establishing the roles of biology and learning as they operate to produce behavior. One consideration is to realize that biology is responsible for learning. Organisms operate according to the laws of classical and operant conditioning, because to do so has been adaptive in evolution. One important aspect of unification occurs is establishing the biological basis of learning and this should continue as an important problem of study. To continue, however, the increase of learning capacity has occurred over species through evolutionary principles. We recognize that certain animals have greater learning ability than others, with humans at the top. Anthropology has also shown us that the human brain has increased dramatically in volume and in other features over the species that preceded *homo sapiens*.

Evolution has also given humans general sensory systems visual, auditory, taste, smell, proprioceptive, and others. It is noteworthy that evolution in humans has produced acuity in various sensory organs, versus the greater *specialized* developments we see in the dolphin's echo-location sensory system, the smell that is so highly developed in dogs and pigs, and the sight that is so acute in eagles. In addition, evolution has given humans a hand with an opposable thumb, a bi-pedal gait, and a complex of vocal organs that compose a multifaceted, sensitive, and flexible apparatus that can produce a large variety of sounds. Evolution has endowed humans with a sensory apparatus, variously to contact the stimuli of the world, a response apparatus of wide capacity, and an enormous learning ability.

The PB position is that biological evolution also made humans more general than lower organisms in learning. There are no prewired, specific complex human behaviors (in contrast to reflexes). Here PB differs from most approaches. The PB position is that it would be non-adaptive for humans to inherit specific behaviors. Mathematics skill, playing a violin, interest in science, or love of reading would have been non-adaptive 40,000 years ago when *homo sapiens* appeared, as would courtly courtesy, answering intelligence-test items, or risking one's life to make the world safe for democracy. "Rather, such men *learned* to shape rocks, fight savagely, throw spears, club prey, make fire, plan group hunts, stitch furs, carve fishhooks, find and eat insects, discriminate subtle cues in tracking prey, communicate, and so on". In the PB view the traditional belief that humans respond to complex environmental stimuli with their complex responses because they have inherited a "hard-wired" nervous system is a poor conception from a biological orientation. Such hard-wiring would be a handicap in an evolutionary sense. The inheritance of specialized behavior patterns limits the organism to specialized environmental niches. Specialization is disadvantageous in variable conditions. A great power of humans is a universal adaptability, a variability in behavior that makes it possible to survive under a great variety of conditions. The PB theory is that the human *learns* all but the simplest (reflexes), the only S–R connections that are hard-wired. The glory of *homo sapiens* is learning ability, and the generality, as well as complexity of behavior that can be acquired. That has made it possible for humans to learn the behaviors necessary to adapt to all of the world's climates and physical features, which no other animal can do. Any position that trivializes the enormous impact of human learning in acquiring personality traits is a poor theory from a biological perspective.

Psychological behaviorism is thus very environmentalist, perhaps more than any other systematic theory of human behavior. Does that mean that PB leaves out biology? Is the role of biology finished after the evolution of learning? The answer in each case is no. Biology does play additional roles, but not as an explanation of particular behaviors or traits of behavior. *Biology provides the mechanisms for the sensing, learning, and performance of behavior*. In the PB view it is learning that explains human traits, but various biological conditions can have an effect on that learning. Figure 4.2 indicates more specifically how PB conceptualizes the relationship of learning and biology, within its model of personality.

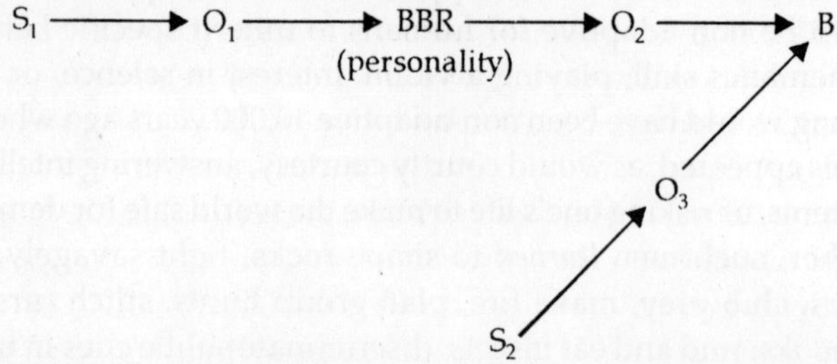

Fig. 4.2. The psychological behaviorism conception of how the biological state of the individual affects personality, perception, and behavior. The biological organism (O_1) is the mechanism by which the environment (S_1) produces the learning that results in the BBRs (personality). If there is something awry with the biological mechanism, then the learning of the BBR will be affected. In addition, if something happens to the biological organism (O_2) *after* the BBR is learned, the BBR may be affected. A change in the BBR will result in changes in the individual's behavior. Finally, the individual's behavior depends upon sensing the confronting environment (S_2). Anything awry with the individual's sensory organs (O_3) will alter the perceived environment and affect the individual's behavior.

S_1 in the figure stands for the original learning circumstances that produce the basic behavioral repertoires (BBRs). O_1 stands for the biological conditions that exist during this original learning. For example, let us take a severely brain-damaged child. Even though the environment is normal, the child will not learn BBRs in a normal manner. Similarly, genetic conditions, such as Down's syndrome, may impair brain development and hence BBR learning. Also the microcephalic child has brain development that is more severely lacking and learning is more severely limited. In a different way, the child with cerebral palsy might be neurologically capable of normal learning, but uncontrollable movement may prevent normal learning circumstances from occurring. Drugs can also alter neurological function and interfere with learning. And Ritalin has been effective in increasing the learning of hyperactive children, probably by reducing the activity, not by affecting the neurological ability to learn. The point is that the biological organism constitutes the mechanism by which learning takes place and that mechanism can be affected in various ways.

In addition to these effects, biological conditions can also play a role, at O_2, after the personality repertoires have been acquired. For learning experiences may be considered to produce neurological connections between stimulus and response events that persist. The central nervous system "carries" or "stores" the BBRs, for example, by adding neural connections. It is important to consider O_2 as that storage. At a later time, in the current environmental situation, how the individual behaves will be determined by what BBRs have been learned (stored in O_2). Thus, at this later time, the individual's biological state is an important determinant of behavior. A brain tumor, injuries, a stroke, fever, physiological conditions (such as hormone levels), drugs, or toxic conditions can affect the biological mechanism (O_2) in a way that will affect the BBRs that have *already* been acquired. As an example, an individual may have learned a rich language-cognitive repertoire. However, a head injury may literally remove that repertoire, or parts of it. Such an individual in a normal environment may not behave normally in various ways in problem solving, reasoning, planning, or learning, and on neuropsychological tests because the individual has lost the necessary BBRs through organic damage. Such losses may be temporary or permanent, depending on the organic condition involved. For example, drug effects will ordinarily wear off, but not loss of brain tissue. In this and other ways biological conditions at the O_2 time can determine behavior and individual differences in behavior.

Organic conditions, in another way, may also exert their effects on how the current environmental situation acts on the individual. By way of illustration, an individual may have fully developed language-cognitive repertoires and an intact central nervous system at O_2, such that an appropriate environmental stimulus such as a restaurant menu would ordinarily elicit the individual's reading behavior. Let us say, however, that as a consequence of aging (which happens around 40) the inflexibility of the lenses of the eyes may make it impossible to see the letters clearly enough to read without glasses in the dim light. There are various organic conditions (shown as O_3 in the figure) that can interfere with the individual's ability to respond sensorily to the current environment. The individual may have defective sight, hearing, smell, or taste through a variety of biological problems. In addition, there are other biological mechanisms that may determine how the individual responds to the current environment, without having an effect on the individual's BBRs. As an example, a man with a normal life environment and normal organic conditions has learned the normal language-cognitive, emotional-motivational, and sensory-motor repertoires necessary to make love. However, alcohol or some other drug may impair his "response mechanism," leaving him impotent in a situation in which he would otherwise perform adequately. Removal of the temporary organic condition, however, will return the individual to normal behavior because the BBRs are intact. Thus, there are organic conditions that can interfere either with the individual's ability to respond sensorily to the current environment, or with the individual's response mechanisms. In these ways organic conditions at O_3 can affect behavior. Such conditions may be permanent, as in the sensory or response losses through aging, or they may be temporary, as in illness or drug conditions.

Organic conditions, thus, are important in the PB theory of personality. *But an essential feature of the theory is that organic conditions affect behavior only through affecting learning, basic behavioral repertoire, behavior, and sensory processes.* The theory sets forth how biological study is to be introduced to the endeavor. It calls for stipulation of the organic processes in terms of how they effect how personality is acquired and how personality functions after it is acquired. General illusions to genetic, physiological, anatomical, or other biological conditions like the concepts of minimal brain dysfunction, genetically induced autism or shyness, learning disability, dyslexia, and the like do not fulfill the demands of the theory. They provide no stipulation of what is supposedly involved. In the PB view organic conditions by themselves do not produce behaviors or traits of personality of any kind.

In the PB view a biological explanation of personality or behavior is only useful if it provides specification of when and how organic conditions affect learning the BBRs, the retention of the BBRs, and the perception of the environment or ability to respond. A first step in gaining such knowledge is the realization that biological variables can have behavioral effects at the three different sites indicated in Figure 4.2. For example, although we may see that a child cannot read when presented with appropriate stimuli, it would make a great deal of difference whether an interfering organic condition had its effect (1) in early childhood, preventing the formation of the relevant basic behavioral repertoires; (2) later, in the form of brain damage, removing basic behavioral repertoires the child had already acquired; or (3) later, involving conditions (like retinal damage) that leave the basic behavioral repertoires intact, but prevent the child from sensing or responding to current situations in a way that would activate the repertoires and result in adjustive behavior.

Biology Provides the Mechanism, Learning Provides the Content

Biology thus plays its role, not as a "creator" of complex human behaviors or personality repertoires, but as the *instrument* by which those behaviors are learned. Biological problems may "delete" or disturb already learned complex repertoires—traits, abilities, talents, and so on. For example, serious biological problems may produce general behavior effects such as in Alzheimer's or Korzikoff's disease. Biological manipulations can also affect the individual's emotional responding and thereby affect behavior in general ways. But biological conditions do not create complex behaviors.

Biological development, for example, does not create language in the individual, or toilet training, social skills, altruism, ambition, suspiciousness, and reading ability. However, after the individual has learned some complex, general behavior (repertoire) a brain injury may delete that repertoire in whole or part, or disturb the display of the repertoire. Similarly, drugs cannot produce complex human behaviors or personality. However, drugs can affect brain operation and, by so doing, affect the BBRs the individual has learned, thereby affecting the individual's behavior, experience, and learning. Drugs can produce euphoria, or reduce depression, or create anxiety, and thereby affect behavior drastically. This is ordinarily a general effect that is brought on by changing the way the mechanism functions. But in this way the drugs can affect the individual's emotional response to various life stimuli. The result may be change in the individual's emotional motivational repertoire and various ways of behaving. Changes in the BBRs will be interpreted as changes in personality. Understanding what is occurring demands explication of the mechanisms. The PB conception places learning and biology into relationship in the causal process, but demands specificity.

Nurture Position

In the present view, biologically oriented approaches to personality have been "barking up the wrong tree." The field tries to establish or find the manner in which humans are hard-wired to display certain behavior traits. As has been indicated, this is a poor biological conception, as in eliminating or downplaying the importance of learning. Rather, those interested in how biology affects behavior should approach the task differently. At the basic level, there is a need to study what the biological mechanisms of learning are. There is also a need to study how biology can affect the learning of the BBRs. If mental retardation, for example, involves biological limits on learning, then it is important to ascertain just how this occurs. Do children with Down's syndrome learn basically more slowly? Or does their limitation have more to do with the quantity of learning that can occur? Can they learn early basic behavioral repertoires, but not later BBRs? Or, is it the case that they can learn BBRs but not with as many elements as is usual? What are the mechanisms by which the learning is affected? Conversely, what are the differences of these kinds in people who have very high ability? For example, if we took a large sample of newly born infants and tested their rapidity of conditioning, would it turn out that those who conditioned more rapidly would be the ones who turned out to be better learners? Are there any significant individual difference variations in the basic rapidity of primary conditioning?

In addition, the PB framework calls for research on the manner in which change of the biological mechanism can affect already learned BBRs. There has been, of course, much study of how brain damage, drugs, and other conditions can affect behavior. But such study is ordinarily used to show that brain characteristics determine individual differences in behavior (personality). It is important to establish *how* brain damage affects the operation of BBRs the individual has learned. There are localization studies that attempt to correlate area of injury with type of behavioral loss. But this study has not been used to bridge biological and learning theories. Psychological behaviorism suggests that brain localization study should be pursued as a means of finding out more about the functioning of the BBRs. For example, is the verbal-motor repertoire localized in a different place than the verbal-labeling, verbal-emotional, and verbal-image repertoires? Preliminary consideration might suggest this as a possibility, since there are emotional and sensory and response parts of the brain. The point is that if biology is involved in personality traits then there has to be a biological behavioral mechanism involved that must be ascertained.

In addition, however, other questions arise. There is a great deal of research on how alcohol and drugs affect perception and sensory-motor skill and learning. Such study could be conducted in a manner that would tie it into the PB theory of the BBRs. When depression is alleviated by drugs, what BBRs are affected? Is the effect only one of generally making the individual's emotional responding more positive? Or, are there effects on specific BBRs of the three types? When caffeine slightly increases the individual's learning ability, is this through affecting the rate of basic conditioning? Or is the effect due to some action on the functioning of the BBRs in cumulative-hierarchical learning? Or does caffeine have its affect by promoting more rapid responding, or better perception of stimuli? In what way do drugs affect the way the BBRs function, and thereby affect behavior?

In terms of O_3 there are also things to be studied in relating the theory of the BBRs to biological study. Age, drugs, and injury can affect the individual's sensory acuity – in hearing, vision, taste, smell, and so on. For example, changes in behavior as a function of aging could arise in two different ways. On the one hand, biological conditions in aging could result in losses in the BBRs. The individual's behavior losses would then be due to personality changes. Senile diseases appear to obliterate previously acquired BBRs. On the other hand, aging might have no effect on the BBRs. However, sensory losses and response losses (as in physical agility) might be the reasons for the individual's behavior losses. The old person might not be scintillating in conversation because of hearing difficulty, not because of loss of intellectual power, as one example.

The lack of research relating biology to learning, the BBRs, and behavior underlies the behaviorism/biology schism. Traditionally, attempts to use biology or learning to explain personality have been general and vague. Specificity in conception and in study can remove these qualities and replace them with definitive treatment of both types of causes and how they relate. The point is that if biology is involved in personality traits, then there has to be a learning brain mechanism involved. The PB position, thus, unlike that of radical behaviorism, has been to effect a learning biology unification.

Interestingly there are beginnings now on the neurobiology side that constitute a recognition of the importance of learning in complex human behavior.

Behavior and Personality

There are other questions that arise concerning the PB theory of personality. For one thing, the basic behavioral repertoires are composed of behaviors. Why, then, is it productive to formulate a theory that has a concept of the BBR (personality) as well as a concept of behavior? Are they not the same? Is it not sufficient to say that personality is behavior, in a Watsonian manner, which dispenses with the need for a concept of personality? The basic question, which arises within a radical behaviorism framework, is a good one. The answer, however, is that the BBR and behavior are not the same thing, in various ways that call for explication.

Differences between Behavior and the BBR

There are various reasons to differentiate the concept of the BBR from the concept of behavior in constructing a theory of human behavior, as will be briefly indicated.

Distal and Proximal Effects of the Environment

One reason is that behavior occurs in the here and now. It is the environment acting *now* that is the eliciting agent. The BBRs, however, are determined by the learning conditions that occurred in the past. In this sense the BBRs can be seen to fulfill the role of such cognitive concepts as "memory" and "personality" in traditional theory construction. In experimental psychology, the fact that the environment plays two roles one distal and one proximal is included in the traditional *learning and memory* dichotomy. There is the acquisition process and then memory keeps the learning there, waiting for later circumstances that will call it out. This has the drawback of making memory a vague mental characteristic. Standard behaviorism, with only a concept of displayed behavior, lacks a good conceptualization of the past, capable of dealing with concepts such as memory and personality.

In the PB theory the distal environment results in the *acquisition* of behaviors. The proximal environment, on the other hand, constitutes the present eliciting agent for the behavior that is displayed. Of course, the one environmental situation may have both effects, that of eliciting behaviors and of providing experience that results in further learning. This does not, however, change the need to separate the two roles of the environment.

Behavior as a Sample from the BBRs

We may record everything a person says for some extended period. This would be a large sample of the individual's verbal behavior. We would know, however, that this was just a sample. It would not constitute all of the verbal behavior that the individual could display. That can never be observed, for various reasons. Each of us, for one thing, has learned single words that we have never employed and will never employ in speech. No matter how long someone recorded our verbal behavior, the nature of our verbal labeling repertoire will never be revealed with respect to that word. There are many words like that. Moreover, that example is increased manyfold when we consider the huge number of combinations of words that we could utter, but never have and never will.

The BBR can be considered as the universe of behaviors that the individual has learned. The current situation "samples" from that universe. The behavior the individual displays in the particular situation is a function of the universe and a function of the situation, which is the sampling mechanism. But the individual could meet an infinite number of different environmental situations. Most will never occur, however. Thus the infinite number of responses that could be made to those environmental situations by virtue of her BBRs will never take place. For example, my theory represents a large BBR for me that I have, in an incipient manner, extended to various areas in outlining future papers and books. There are many more plans than I will ever have a chance to write. Even those who have the most intimate knowledge of my behavior will never know those plans.

Let me suggest that samples of the individual's life behaviors can reveal less about the nature of the individual's BBRs than would an artificial sample whose goal is the measurement of such BBRs. This is especially relevant for psychological evaluation: the PB conception says that an important part of evaluation concerns measuring the elements of the basic behavioral repertoires. Sometimes measurement of the BBRs will be better than measurements of actual behaviors. Let me suggest that people speaking to each other display smaller differences in vocabulary than will be shown on tests, because everyday speech is made up of common words to common situations. This statement thus provides us with one of the important distinctions between behavior and the BBRs. Behavior is that which occurs in specific life situations. Observations of that behavior constitute the most direct means of assessment, but not necessarily the most complete. The individual's life situations may not sample well the individual's BBRs; the contrived observations of psychological testing may yield more information concerning the BBRs, contrary to Mischel and Kanfer and Phillips.

Creativity of Personality

Behaviors displayed are actual occurrences. The BBRs are also different from behavior in constituting a *potential* for action, in several respects. One is that the BBRs are composed of elements that can be "put together" in different ways, depending upon the stimulus elements in the situations that are encountered. Novel situations can evoke new, original behavior *combinations* in the individual behaviors that have never occurred before. Behaviors in that combination will not have been learned, since the situation has never occurred before. Moreover, we might not be able to predict the behavior combination from any recording of the individual's past behaviors. Let us take a simple example. A young child may have just have been trained to say "dog" to such animals, and "running" to the stimulus of the rapidly alternating legs of a horse. Confronted with a running dog, this child may say something it has never said before, and has not been trained to say, that is "running dog," or "dog running." To predict such phenomena we need to have done something else than observe the child's behavior. This is especially the case with people who have acquired exceptional BBRs let us say an Einstein, Newton, or Freud and whose life circumstances have elicited combinations of elements that are surprisingly novel.

Since the BBRs have a great number of elements, the combinations that can occur under the action of different environmental combinations are almost infinite. For example, observing the pieces a musician has played cannot be used to predict what she can or will play for she has the potential for playing an infinite number of new compositions just by being presented with the written music. As another example, the ordinary individual is said to know from 10,000 to 80,000 words. The size of the repertoire makes the individual capable of infinite variation in combinations of words uttered in response to appropriate external and internal stimulus conditions. In these senses this language-cognitive repertoire is a capacity or potentiality, a personality (cognitive) characteristic which cannot be known from observing the individual's behavior.

Case When the BBR Is Different From the Behavior

Finally, a most important reason for introducing both the concepts of behavior and the basic behavioral repertoire is because in many cases they are different. As background for this point, an early (and continuing) behavior therapy position is that it is behavior that is the problem, in contrast to psychodynamic approaches that consider the underlying psychological problem to be the real cause. There are many cases when the behavior therapy position is correct where the problem is the displayed behavior itself. But there are many important cases where the problem is not the same thing as the behavior. Let us take as an example a child with a conduct problem in the classroom. In some cases the real problem is not the behavior itself, that is, the sensory-motor behaviors that disrupt the class. To illustrate, let us say the teacher is reading a story to the class, and the other children's attentive behavior is maintained by the reinforcement provided by the images and emotional responses elicited by the words of the story. The language-deficit child, however, will experience no images and no emotional responses, and hence no reinforcement for the behavior of sitting and listening. The result is this child's attentive behavior will not be maintained. Rather, alternative sensory-motor behavior will have been learned because they have been reinforced by disrupting such boring situations. The overt behavior of this child is unimportant, consisting of very usual sensory-motor responses. Attempts to treat the problem by reinforcing the child's attentive sensory-motor behavior and extinguishing the child's undesirable sensory-motor behavior would be ineffective and would constitute symptomatic (versus causal) treatment.

Understanding the real problem lies in understanding the relationship of the BBRs and behavior, that language BBR deficits can give rise to disruptive behavior. For many behavior problems have the BBRs as the proximal cause. The problem behaviors themselves may be very usual, ones that everyone has learned.

The concept of personality was no doubt constructed because much of overt behavior is the result of other behavioral processes of the individual, frequently within the individual where they cannot be observed. After all we experience some of these processes. Traditional psychology made the mistake of considering those internal events in different, non-behavioral, mentalistic terms. As a consequence, behaviorists rejected such considerations *in toto*. What is necessary is to recognize that personality is composed of the same *types* of events as behavior, but that personality is different from displayed behavior itself. Differentiating the two concepts behavior and the basic behavioral repertoires allows us to deal with the phenomena that have been of importance to traditional psychologists, but within an objective, unified, explanatory set of behavioral principles and concepts.

Additional Reasons Why the BBRs Constitute a Concept of Personality

There are vast individual differences in BBRs. Moreover, fitting traditional expectations, they are carried within. Behaviorism traditionally has been rejected because of suggesting that the external environment determines overt behavior. This disagrees with our common experience that personal characteristics differ and are causes of behavior. The theory of the BBRs allows us to accept that there are causal personality characteristics without sacrificing behavioristic demand for objective specification.

The BBRs fulfill that aspect of the traditional definition of personality. They are also general, not situationally specific. In the example above, attending to a teacher's story was seen to depend upon having learned verbal-motor, verbal-image, and verbal-emotional repertoires. Those same repertoires will be functional in many situations and affect the behavior displayed by the individual. The BBRs, thus, are the basic reason that individual differences in behavior can be seen across a variety of situations.

The fact that individual differences persist over time has also given support to the traditional concept of personality. Let it be said, thus, that the continuity of personality is due, in part, to the fact that BBRs generally persist over time. This occurs for several reasons. One is that the more elements compose the BBR, the less impact each new experience has on the nature of the BBR, simply because the new element is a smaller fraction of the total. The larger the BBR learned, the more learning is needed to change it.

More importantly, the BBRs provide continuity by maintaining the consistency of the individual's experience. Thus, for example, once the individual has developed a certain aspect of the emotional-motivational repertoire, this itself will determine behavior such that additional experiences will add to what has already been learned. For example, once the individual has learned a positive emotional response to classical music, the individual's behavior will be *reinforced* by such music. So music-relevant behaviors like turning on certain TV and radio programs will be maintained. In addition, music-relevant stimuli as incentives will *elicit* approach behaviors. So the individual will buy tickets to announced concerts, buy newly published books on music, enroll for classes on music appreciation, associate with friends who talk about music, and attend musical events. The experiences such behaviors yield will further ensure continuance of this BBR development and consequent behavior. Developments in the emotional-motivational repertoire affect sensory-motor behaviors.

The concept of the BBR also suggests that personality will have continuity and persist over time because one's environment ordinarily has a good deal of continuity. But, since the BBRs are learned, circumstances can occur that will produce change. For example, the music-oriented person described above may have an intense love affair with someone in the field of music that ends catastrophically. That may produce such negative emotional conditioning that the individual avoids musical occasions that may arouse those negative emotions. The avoidance behavior may lead the individual into experiences that condition her emotional-motivational repertoire in a different direction. This is to say, thus, that BBRs once learned will ordinarily tend to persist, but they are not immutable. The PB theory provides specific principles and analyses for considering the way that individual differences can be stable or unstable.

Personality in Behavior Causation

It has been said that the BBR is an independent variable a cause as well as a dependent variable an effect. If the BBR is composed of behavior, how can it be the cause of behavior? The BBR can be a direct cause of behavior in various ways. For example, let us take the case of the child who has learned to attend to what an adult says when requested to do so. This is a part of the verbal-motor repertoire. A child who has this repertoire will attend to what a teacher says in school, will experience the stimuli the teacher presents, and thus learn new things. The child without that aspect of the verbal-motor repertoire will not attend, will not experience the stimuli, and will not learn. The BBR is thus the proximal cause of children's behavior in class, the experience received, and the learning that results.

This conception of the BBR changes one's view of the causation of human behavior and the phenomena of individual differences. We can see that a child with a certain BBR is different from a child lacking that BBR. The two will behave differently, experience things differently, and learn differently. These differences will occur when the children are in the same situation, where the same reinforcers are available, and where the same controlling stimuli are present. That is why non-behavioral psychologists have not accepted radical behaviorism's insistence on considering the cause of human behavior to be the situation that confronts the individual.

Intrinsic to the traditional concept of personality is that it is a cause of behavior. Everyone has personal experience of internal events commonly called thoughts, images, and emotions – that affect one's behavior. That personal experience is supplemented by all the findings that show that people who measure differently on tests like intelligence tests and interest tests and tests like the Minnesota Multiphasic Personality Inventory (MMPI) behave differently. Tests seem to be measuring a cause of human behavior.

The concept of personality causation is thus firmly entrenched in the field of personality and in cognitive psychology. But traditional personality theories have never faced up to the demands of good theory with respect to explaining that causation. If an internal process or structure is said to determine the way the individual behaves, then this statement calls for specification. For one thing, the question of how personality *affects* behavior must then be specified how and according to what principles. For another, the way that personality determines behavior cannot be specified unless personality itself is first specified. It is necessary to define personality before indicating how it acts as a cause. What are interests such that they cause one individual to behave in a successful manner in a particular job, and another person, with different interests, to fail? And how do interests work these effects, by what principles? What is the extroverted personality trait that makes the individual behave in an outgoing manner with people, and how does the trait function to affect behavior? What is intelligence that it makes the individual behave skillfully in various situations?

Traditional personality theories do not answer such questions. Psychological tests do not provide the definition of the personality traits they measure, or the principles of how the personality traits determine the way the individual behaves. Freud's theory, interestingly, provided some specification of this kind. For example, his theory stated that the stage of psychosexual development determined the individual's needs. Those needs determined in what objects the individual would have an emotional investment (cathexis). Cathected objects became goals to be attained, and thus affected behavior. However, despite tidbits here and there, Freud's theory generally contained little specification of his personality concepts (like the *id, ego,* and *superego*), and of the manner in which they determined behavior.

The PB personality theory lends itself to the type of specification required.

Personality is seen to be composed of specified and specifiable BBRs. Some have mistakenly thought that the concept of the BBR is an intervening variable a logical term that connects the experienced environment with behavior. But personality in the PB theory is not an intervening variable. Personality is considered as something real and substantive. Psychological behaviorism's analyses of personality refer to complex language, motor, and emotional repertoires. These are not logical figments; they are actual stimulus response constellations that have to be stipulated; what they are, how they are learned, and how they act upon the individual's behavior. The preceding chapters have aimed to indicate that the BBRs have specific contents. Nevertheless, study is necessary to specify fully the behavioral contents of the BBRs, how the BBRs function, and by what principles. PB has begun this task. But it is a very large task, and there is much to do. Additional specification will be provided in the next chapter.

Environment in Behavior Causation

One of the features of the PB personality theory is how the environment is treated. Systematic separation of the roles of the distal and proximal environments helps provide reasons for introduction of the new concept of the BBR, for one thing. For another, the concept of the two actions of the environment sharpens the way organic conditions can be considered, as indicated in Figure 4.2. The environment separation makes it clear that organic conditions operate on the individual at different times, in three different ways. Organic conditions must be considered as they affect the learning of the BBRs, the later functioning of the BBRs, and the individual's ability to respond to the life situation. The distinctions should help in studying the way behavioral conditions interact with organic conditions in determining behavior.

How about the other behaviorisms? Second-generation behaviorism has lacked systematicity here. There used to be a difference in the manner in which the second-generation behaviorisms considered learning and behavior. A central concept in Hull's theory was habit strength (sHr), which represented learning. And in experimentation, Hull employed situations in which the learning of a response was critical. So Hull thus was interested in learning (as a theoretical concept), and focused on defining his concept of learning and its relationships with other concepts.

But Skinner differed from other behaviorists in this respect. He did not consider himself a learning theorist. His experimental worked ignored learning in favor of the reinforcement variables that affected the organism's *already learned* behavior in the operant chamber. His study was of the effects of reinforcement schedules on *behavior,* not learning, with individual animals subjected to successive variations in reinforcement to see the effects on that behavior. What that represents conceptually is a focus on the effects of the present situation on behavior.

This characteristic is carried by those who employ Skinner's theory for considering human behavior, as in the fields of behavior analysis and behavior therapy. How about the concept of "learning (or conditioning) history"? Although the concept is used widely in behavior analysis, the concept actually proves the point. For there has been little systematic study in radical behaviorism or any other second-generation behaviorism of the learning histories that produce human behavior. The concept is thus scientifically empty. That fact has recently been recognized for the first time in behavior analysis.

Skinner's methods were valuable in the study of animal behavior in stipulating how reinforcement schedules could affect behavior. However, in human behavior *past* learning is centrally important. To illustrate, the stimulus circumstances, including the *potential* reinforcement conditions (schedules), in a classroom are largely the same for all. The behavior the children display in that situation is determined by what they bring to class, that is, their BBRs. *In fact, that behavior will largely determine the reinforcement the children receive.* One child with rich BBR development will behave in a way that harvests reinforcement for achievement behaviors, while the child with sparse BBR development will display disruptive behaviors that harvest the teacher's disapproval. Such characteristics of human behavior underlie the traditional rejection of radical behaviorism's focus on explaining how the environment determines behavior, and the concept that the individual is not responsible.

These are reasons why the position that PB takes is fundamentally different from Skinner's radical behaviorism. The PB framework, in separating the distal and proximal environments, provides for the systematic study of the former (and the latter). The human learning/cognitive and child development levels have been explicitly developed for the study of distal learning, and the BBRs that result. Radical behaviorism has lacked these levels of study. Because PB theory treats both a learning environment and a behaving environment, I have referred to it as a learning-behavior theory, not just one or the other.

Person—Situation Schism, And PB's Interaction Approach

Watsonian behaviorism was seen as a challenge to the conventional conception of personality traits that determine individual differences in behavior, across situations. Moreover, studies were conducted that appeared to support the radical behavioristic idea that it is the situation that determines behavior, not general personality traits. Thus, Hartshorne and May conducted an extensive study of children's "moral" character using a number of different situational tests of honesty. These researchers found a low correlation among the various tests, indicating that a child who was honest in one type of situation might not be in another. Their conclusion was that there are specific habits, elicited by specific situations, but not traits that are general. Newcomb found the same situational variability with indices of the trait of extroversion introversion. The issue died down in the 1930s, only to be revivified by Mischel, who again asserted the situationism position of behaviorism. In response, a number of studies were conducted, some in support of the situationism position and some in support of the person (personality) position.

When such contests occur, a resolution may be offered that says, in effect, that both sides are right. This has occurred in the several cycles of the situation person issue, most recently in what is called interaction psychology.

This interactionist position draws upon studies that suggest there are personality-causal variables and situational-causal variables, as well as an interaction between the two, also considered as a causal variable. For example, Gilmor and Minton found that, under a success situation, internal locus-of-control personalities attributed success to internal factors more than did external locus-of-control subjects, but such attribution was reversed under a failure situation. The statistical interaction, thus, predicted the attributions better than either the personality variable or the situation variable.

However, the PB view is that such interaction is a statistical figment of the analysis of variance experimental designs employed. There is no real "interaction" it is only that people differ in their BBRs and, for that reason, do not respond to situations in the same way. Actually there is consistency in behavior. There are only two types of causal variables in subjects, the personality (BBR) variable and the situation variable. It is suggested that analysis of what internal and external locus of control BBRs actually are would reveal directly why the subjects responded in one way in the success situation and in another way in the failure situation.

Let me exemplify this analytic PB position. Let us say in studying learning ability we select two groups of subjects: one composed of individuals with a highly developed language-cognitive BBR, and a poorly developed sensory-motor BBR, and the other with the opposite BBRs. If we then exposed these two groups to two types of learning one involving language materials and the other involving learning sensory-motor skills we would find one group would be the better learners in one situation, but the other group would be the better learners in the other. An analysis-of-variance treatment of the results would produce a large statistical interaction term. That term, however, only reflects the very direct effect of the different BBRs on learning. There is no "interaction causation." It is only because person situation interaction studies do not analyze the situations, BBRs, and behavior involved that the statistical result is interpreted as some sort of person situation interaction causation. As PB has pointed out, if we wish to explain behavior it is necessary to be analytic. Vaguely specified studies are fertile ground for unresolved issues.

Free Will, Agency and Self-Causation

In traditional views humans are thought to have free will and self-determination. Originally the concept of free will was that the individual's divinely given soul was responsible for the individual's behavior. And this soul was free, not determined like the material, physical things of our world. When psychology became a science its interest was directed toward the study of natural, rather than supernatural events, and the soul was given up as an appropriate subject matter. Concepts, such as personality, which could be studied using scientific means, were substituted. Still, the general reluctance to view humans as automatons, directed by their environment, was satisfied by including a concept of freedom within the concept of personality.

Radical behaviorism, in its eagerness to deny anything else than natural causes of behavior, has rejected the idea of freedom from environmental causation. Watson maintained that the legitimate subject matter of psychology consisted of the observable environment, as the cause, and observable behavior change, as the effect. The deterministic behavioral philosophy of science has had no place for indeterminate, "free," causative events. Skinner set his position forward on this issue in dramatic fashion, stating that "a person does not act upon the world, the world acts upon him", thus subtracting humans' freedom and dignity. Non-behavioral psychologists have considered that behaviorisms, in general, thus make humans passive responders to the environment.

Psychological behaviorism takes the position that the major problem here is the manner in which the issue is posed. Neither position cares what phenomena and issues the other is trying to consider. This is in contrast to the PB approach, which is to examine what is involved in the phenomena that give rise to the original conception. Then PB's approach is to analyze those phenomena behaviorally, in order to create a unified view thereby strengthening the behavioral approach, while satisfying the legitimate interests of traditional psychology. In this particular case it is necessary to consider what it is that prompts so many, including psychologists, to believe in freedom and spontaneity in human behavior.

There are various phenomena that lead to the belief in personal causation. Centrally, the conception of freedom is based on the many experiences we have of doing what we want to do, what we plan and intend to do, what we have reasoned we should do, and such. And it is based on the experience we have that others do the same and that people who want different things, who plan different things, and such, behave differently from one another. We experience these things in our common experience. Radical behaviorism rejects consideration of such experiences. Psychological behaviorism recognizes them and sees the task of analyzing those phenomena in terms of behavioral principles. What we experience are our BBRs. We experience their operation as our *self,* our being. We experience the operation of the BBRs in our thinking, planning, and wanting, and how we behave as a result of these activities. We experience that our thinking, planning, and wanting is different from others', as is our purposive behavior. We experience the way our behavior affects the environment, especially the social environment. And we experience the way that our behavior, as it acts on the social environment, in turn, acts back on us. These are the reasons that all of us are so sure that we have had a hand in our destinies, that we have not just passively responded to the environment, that we are responsible for what has happened to us, that we are purposive.

And we are right. But it is not necessary to go outside of scientific causality to provide an explanatory account. PB, not resting on analysis alone, has conducted experiments to demonstrate the principles of its *behavioral interaction* position. For example, Staats, Gross, Guay, and Carlson showed that individuals who differed in a part of their emotional-motivational repertoire displayed different choice behaviors. Moreover, that choice behavior resulted in the subjects having different experiences that produced different learning in the subjects. Difference in measured interests in this experiment produced an interaction—in the same situation subjects with different personality measures behaved differently and, in doing so, set different causal sequences in motion. The manner in which the individual's behavior is determined by what she feels and thinks can be studied in behavioral research.

The reason that the belief in self-causation and freedom is so strong is because the individual does not know why her thinking, planning, intending, and wanting are the way they are. The extraordinarily complex cumulative- hierarchical learning processes involved are too complex and too removed to be recognized as causes. The BBRs also are too complex to comprehend. It is understandable that the lay person will not recognize these causes; psychology itself does not generally provide the necessary knowledge.

Psychological behaviorism's personality conception, in contrast to Skinner's position, says that the world acts upon the person, *but that the person also acts upon the world and on herself.* That is, the individual learns BBRs which determine how the individual will act in the situations met. But that behavior will affect others, importantly acting upon the world. Moreover, those effects on the world will, in return, act back upon the person. In this way the individual determines the environment she meets, and she determines her own behavior, because that environment will affect her.

A general theory of personality must confront and resolve such issues as this, toward establishing unification of the psychological and the behavioral. The psychological behaviorism conception of interaction, developed in various analyses, such as the PB theory of abnormal behavior, was begun very early. In adopting PB's approach to abnormal behavior as social learning theory, Bandura summarized the PB interaction conception. In further works the social learning position came to be called reciprocal determination. A more detailed comparison of the two related conceptions has been made. It may be added, however, that there are fundamental differences also. As indicated here, the PB conception of the environment/ personality/ behavior/environment interaction is based on detailed, specific analysis, with explicit theoretical and empirical definition. The conception is founded in the basic learning/behavior principles and is tightly constructed, level by level, through the human learning/cognitive, child development, and personality levels. The theory of personality involved includes specification of the content of personality and is unified with psychological testing, as the next chapter will indicate. These are the characteristics that allow such topics as freedom, agency, creativity, self-direction, and self-determination to be dealt with in a manner that unifies the psychological (and cognitive) and the behavioral.

5

Theory of Abnormal Personality and Behavior

Introduction

The PB theory of personality derives from preceding levels of study, on the one hand, but serves itself as a basic theory for application to other more advanced fields, such as personality measurement. In the present view, in constructing a theory of personality, it is as important to characterize its applications as its foundations. This chapter and the next will constitute applications of the PB theory of personality; in the present case to the construction of a theory of abnormal behavior.

First PB Theory of Abnormal Behavior

As indicated already, PB presented the first behavioral theory of abnormal psychology. Abnormal behavior, like normal behavior, was considered to be learned. It had been proposed by Eysenck that the neuroses consisted of surplus conditioned reactions or deficient conditioned reactions. However, the concept was not employed in a theory that analyzed the behavior disorders. The PB theory developed a concept of the deficit or inappropriate dichotomy as a dimension of abnormality, but several basic dimensions of behavior were added in constructing the general theory. One dimension was that, although the behavior itself might not be abnormal, it will be considered as such if the stimulus control of the behavior is deficit or inappropriate. An example of deficit stimulus control occurs in date rape, when a women's pleas to stop have no effect. The sensory-motor behaviors of intercourse are not in themselves abnormal (although they may be if forceful behaviors are involved). Normal behavior will also be considered abnormal when inappropriate stimuli control the behavior, for example, when the sight of someone in pain controls approach behaviors, rather than eliciting behavior that decreases the stimulus.

Aside from how the behavior is controlled by stimuli, behavior can also be deficit or inappropriate in and of itself. For example, the individual may never have learned a reading repertoire a deficit. Conversely, the individual may have learned a repertoire of inappropriately brutal physical aggression. Another category of abnormal behavior was said to involve a deficit or inappropriate reinforcement system. For the person with a deficit reinforcement system stimuli that should be reinforcing are not. In the second case, the individual may have learned inappropriate reinforcers. (The term *reinforcer system* was later changed to *emotional-motivational BBR*, as more appropriate to the theory.)

This early taxonomy and theory of abnormal behavior was set forth when the field of behavior therapy was just beginning and its concepts and principles affected the development of the field and were incorporated into it. The PB account was intended as a framework theory for the field of abnormal psychology, with development planned in several directions. For one thing, the theory was expected to be empirically heuristic, to open new types of research. To illustrate, the theory called for the development of behavioral assessment instruments with which to measure deficits and inappropriacies in the several categories of abnormality. Moreover, the framework theory itself was considered to be a beginning, needing development along various dimensions. One dimension involves taking advantage of the advances in the various levels of study basic to the theory. For example, as PB's personality theory was developed, this provided the basis for advanced construction of the abnormal psychology level of theory.

Basic PB Theory of Abnormal Behavior

At the time of its introduction, there were no other behavioral theories of abnormal behavior in radical behaviorism or social learning theory or the nascent behavior therapy. The first PB theory of abnormal behavior was largely a theoretical projection a derivation from more basic PB theory, PB rese rch, the use of PB analysis in clinical and personal experience, along w th the PB analysis of traditional literature and the few behavioral works of others.

The first PB theory focused on the analysis of behavioral symptoms in the disorders that were addressed. But the PB concept of the individual's reinforcer system actually introduced the first behaviorally defined personality concept. The concept stated that each individual learned a large and different set of stimuli that were positively reinforcing for her, as well as a large set of negative reinforcers. The theory also said that the individual's behavior was affected widely by the nature of her reinforcer system, producing individual differences in the control of behavior, as well as in learning new behaviors. Moreover, abnormal behavior was seen to arise because the individual's reinforcer system was deficit or inappropriate. Although this was a personality concept, its most general implication was not generally understood namely that a behavioral approach to abnormal behavior needed a behavioral theory of personality.

Twelve years later the overarching PB theory had been advanced along various dimensions. One was in the development of an explicit theory of personality. This theory set forth the language-cognitive, emotional-motivational, and sensory-motor BBRs as the constituents of personality, a trichotomy that is widely used today. And the theory was then employed as the foundation for constructing a framework theory of abnormal behavior. In summary form, this PB conception dealt with how behavior disorders result from deficits and inappropriacies in the language-cognitive, emotional-motivational, and sensory-motor BBRs. Table 5.1 is taken from that account.

Table 5.1 characterizes the conception, with its two dimensions composed of deficits and inappropriacies, on the one hand, and the three BBRs on the other. The symptoms of various behavior disorders are then shown to fall into the six cells created by the two dimensions. There are disorders, for example, that involve deficits in the

Table 5.1 The PB Conception of Behavior Disorders

	Symptoms Deficit behavior	Inappropriate behavior
Basic Behavioral (Personality) Repertoires *Emotional-Motivational Repertoire*	Flat emotionality of schizophrenia	Psychosomatic disorders
	Lack of motivation of neurasthenia	Sadistic pleasures
	Lack of achievement motivation of cultural deprivation	Phobias
	Childhood autism deficits in affection for parents	Sexual disturbances involving aberrant sex objects; fetishes
		Autistic children's preoccupation with self-stimulation
Language-Cognitive Repertoire	Mental retardation deficits	Paranoid delusions
	Autism deficits	Defense mechanisms
	Lack of verbal-motor control in psychopaths	Antisocial conceptual systems like racism
	Cultural-deprivation deficits	Stuttering, gesticulation substitutes for language in nonspeaking children
Instrumental Repertoire	Lack of social skills	Violent social behavior (rape, beatings)
	Lack of approach behavior to the opposite sex	Aversive social behavior (arrogance, cruelty, overly demanding, selfishness)
	Lack of work skills	Bizarre actions of psychotics
	Enuretic lack of toilet skills	Self-stimulation, repetitive behavior, self-destructive behavior of autism
	Lack of recreational skills	
	Lack of imitational and observational skills	

emotional-motivational repertoire, as is the case with the flat emotionality in schizophrenic patients, and the autistic child's lack of affection for parents. Deficits in the language-cognitive BBR are characteristic of mentally retarded children, autistic children, schizophrenics, and criminals who display a high incidence of non-reading. Deficits in the sensory-motor repertoire are characteristic of certain schizophrenics, as well as retarded and autistic children.

With respect to inappropriate BBR developments, the anxiety disorders involve inappropriate emotional-motivational characteristics for example, the person with a phobia has an inappropriately extreme negative emotional response to some type of stimulus. On the positive side, a paraphiliac has learned a strong sexual emotional response to an inappropriate sexual object, as in the case with pedophilia, sexual sadism, and masochism. The language-cognitive repertoire can also be inappropriate and result in symptoms of various behavior disorders, as is the case with paranoid delusions, pathological lying, an unrealistically negative self-concept, and such. An inappropriate sensory-motor repertoire is exhibited in cases of rape and other types of assault, the bizarre motor behaviors of some psychotics, and the self-stimulation and repetitive behaviors of some autistic children.

This second-generation formulation of the PB theory of abnormal behavior was a considerable advancement but it was still a beginning framework theory. It presented the principles and concepts of the theory-construction endeavor, and gave examples, but it needed development. Even at that point, as with the first PB theory, the theory had some things traditional theories of abnormal behavior lack. For one thing, although the PB theory of abnormal behavior was only of chapter length it was part of and drew upon the multilevels of a much more elaborate theory. Advancement of the PB theory of abnormal behavior was to come from advancement of the overarching behaviorism. But there were advancements to be made within the abnormal behavior level itself. One was in elaborating and stipulating the PB theory of abnormal behavior. A step in this direction was made in constructing the PB model of abnormal behavior and its causes as shown in Figure 5.1.

In the model shown in Figure 5.1, the basic concept of deficit and inappropriate was developed in several directions. For one thing, the conception is that the individual's past environment, S_1, may be either deficit or inappropriate. That results in deficit or inappropriate learning of the language-cognitive, emotional-motivational, or sensory-motor BBRs. Since the BBRs help determine the individual's behavior, when the BBRs are deficit or inappropriate they will result in a deficit in necessary behavior or in the occurrence of inappropriate behavior, both of which are abnormal.

The model indicates, in addition, that the individual's current environment (life situation), S_2, also helps determine the behavior the individual displays. If the current environment is deficit, other things equal, the behavior the individual displays will be deficit and, hence, abnormal. If the current environment is inappropriate, other things being equal, the behavior the individual displays will be inappropriate and, hence, abnormal. Thus, the various sites of causation of abnormal behavior are specified in the model, with various implications.

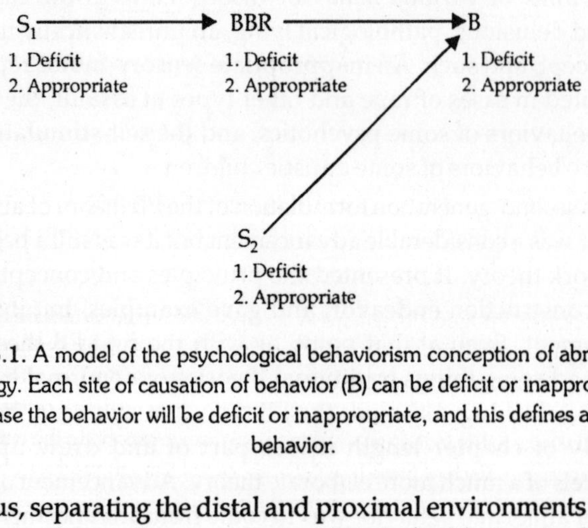

Fig. 5.1. A model of the psychological behaviorism conception of abnormal psychology. Each site of causation of behavior (B) can be deficit or inappropriate, in which case the behavior will be deficit or inappropriate, and this defines abnormal behavior.

Thus, separating the distal and proximal environments made it possible to address the several roles of biological factors in abnormal behavior. The greater stipulation of the theory provided for greater stipulation in this area. As shown in Figure 5.1, giving the environment two separate roles makes explicit that biological conditions can play a role in three different ways in the causal chain. That is, biological conditions can be awry at the time the individual is learning the BBRs (as in cases of microcephaly or Down's syndrome), even though the learning environment is quite normal.

In Figure 5.2 the biological conditions operative at this time are depicted as O_1. Such abnormal biological conditions can result in *learning* abnormal BBRs, either deficit or inappropriate.

In addition, however, after normal BBRs have been learned, abnormal biological conditions (like brain damage, or drugs) can destroy or distort those BBRs, resulting in deficit or inappropriate (abnormal) behavior. Such biological conditions are represented as O_2 in Figure 5.2. Moreover, abnormal biological conditions may distort or create deficits in the individual's ability to sense and respond to the current environment, S_2—even though the individual's BBRs are normal. For example, the individual may lose hearing in old age and the deficit in auditory stimuli may affect behavior. As another example, a man taking drugs for hypertension may be unable to obtain an erection in what would ordinarily be a sexual situation. Such biological conditions are represented as O_3 in Figure 5.2.

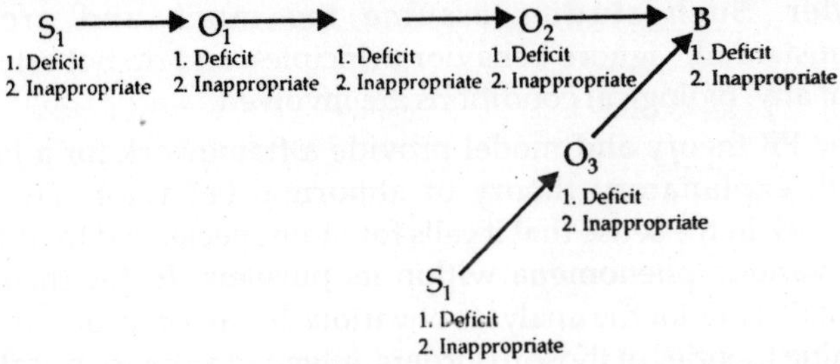

Fig. 5.2. The PB model of abnormal behavior elaborated to include the places where organic conditions can act as a determinant. The biological organism can be deficit or inappropriate when the BBRs are being learned (O_1), or after they have been learned (O_2). Or the biological organism (O_3) can be deficit or inappropriate with respect to the individual's ability to sense and respond to the current life situation (S_2). Each of these biological abnormalities can produce abnormal behavior.

The conception recognizes that biological conditions can result in abnormal behavior. However, PB methodology requires empirical-theoretical specificity in biological as well as learning explanation. Biological factors in causation must be shown directly, not inferred or assumed. *Moreover, the conception requires that specification be made of how the biological condition affects the learning of the BBRs, the functioning of the BBRs, or the ability of the individual to respond to the current situation.* It is not enough to find that a higher percentage than usual of people with some behavior disorder display an overdeveloped or underdeveloped part of their brain, or show greater activity in a part of their brain. *The unusual part or activity of the brain may result from the individual's behavior, rather than cause it.* Such a biological finding, thus, is only the beginning. For it is necessary to indicate how that anatomy has affected the learning of the BBRs, the BBRs after they have been learned, or the ability of the individual to respond to current situations. Until the biological phenomenon has been extended by the necessary behavioral stipulations its meaning and value are unclear. PB states, thus, that research must be done to establish the manner in which environmental events, organic conditions, and behavioral variables interact in the determination of abnormal behavior. This has to be done specifically; generalities are not useful. This applies especially to studies that show the person with abnormal behavior has parents or siblings who have the same disorder. Such studies assume too much and are too "circumstantial," ignore behavior principles, and do not establish what, if any, biological conditions are involved.

The PB theory and model provide a framework for a broad, unified, explanatory theory of abnormal behavior. This is a framework in the sense that it calls for more specialized treatments of the various phenomena within its purview. In the theory of abnormal behavior the analyses of various behavior disorders were beginning theories of those disorders, intended as heuristic calls for more detailed, complete, and profound theories of the different behavior disorders. That program, actually, had begun very early PB's analysis of the developmental disorders (especially reading) introduced this area of study to behavior analysis and behavior therapy and the PB theory of reading disorder constituted one of the foundations of its general theory of abnormal behavior. The rest of this chapter will be focused on presenting several of PB's theories of behavior disorders, beginning with reading disorder, mental retardation, and childhood autism. The adult disorders treated will be limited to depression and the anxiety disorders.

Developmental Disorders

One of the early focuses of PB was on developmental disorders, especially problems in academic performance. The history of this program, and how it provided one of the foundations for the development of behavior therapy (behavior modification, behavioral assessment, and behavior analysis). Here I will be concerned only with the PB theories of developmental disorders, beginning with Learning Disorders, especially reading disorder.

Reading Disorder

In our culture dyslexia, or developmental reading disorder, is a devastating deficit. Its impact can be gauged by the fact that a large proportion of prison inhabitants cannot read.

DSM Description

The *Diagnostic and Statistical Manual of Mental Disorders,* called the *DSM-IV,* refers to reading disorder only when there is interference with academic achievement and daily living.

The essential feature of Reading Disorder is reading achievement (i.e., reading accuracy, speed, or comprehension as measured by standardized tests) that falls substantially below that expected given the individual's chronological age, measured intelligence, and age-appropriate education. If a sensory deficit is present, the reading difficulties are in excess of those usually associated with it. In individuals with Reading Disorder (which has also been called "dyslexia") oral reading is characterized by distortions, substitutions, or omissions.

The *DSM-IV* goes on to describe how reading disorder tends to be associated with various other problems such as dropping out of school, difficulty with employment, Conduct Disorder, Oppositional Defiant Disorder, Attention Deficit/Hyperactivity Disorder, Major Depressive Disorder, and such. With respect to etiology, "There may be underlying abnormalities in cognitive processing (e.g., deficits in visual perception, linguistic processes, attention, or memory, or a combination of these) and genetic predisposition, perinatal injury, and various neurological or other general medical conditions may be associated with the development of Learning Disorders. This coincides with the general belief that there are inherited brain deficiencies other than those thought to cause mental retardation, sensory handicap, or specific neurological defect that can cause specific learning disabilities such as reading disorder. This conception represents a vague theory, however, since it does not indicate the specific organic problem and how the child's learning to read is affected. The theory also does not include specification of what reading is, how reading is learned normally, and what is involved when learning to read has gone awry. What is it that the child with reading disorder cannot do that normal children can do? The fact that a theory of that vagueness can be so widely held indicates the low standards that operate.

Reading

When reading is analyzed in PB's behavioral terms to indicate what repertoires are involved, how they are learned, and how they function in the act of reading then there is a context for considering what reading disorder is and how it comes about. Essential in the psychological behavioral analysis is that reading is a specialized, advanced development of the individual's language repertoires. Let me exemplify the position by taking the verbal labeling repertoire. In the ordinary acquisition of language the child has to learn to label many objects and events that is, to make particular vocal responses to particular stimuli. In learning to read the child must learn to make those same vocal responses to printed or written word stimuli. The child must learn a very large repertoire of speech responses to visual verbal stimuli. The same is true with other repertoires. The child learns motor, image, and emotional responses to different spoken words. To be an expert reader the same words in visual form must elicit those same responses.

Reading Disorder is not Biologically Caused

Even this abbreviated behavioral analysis of reading provides the basis for stating that dyslexia does not have a biological cause. First, a diagnosis of dyslexia is only made when the child's intelligence measure is normal (or above that of the reading level). But in PB terms normal intelligence indicates that the dyslexic child has normal language. And the PB theory of language shows that no different ability is demanded in reading than that which is demanded in spoken language. When we examine language and reading we see that the visual stimuli that elicit verbal-labeling responses in natural language are no different in kind than the visually presented words that elicit reading responses. Whether an *ant* itself elicits the word "ant," or whether the printed word *ant* elicits the response, does not involve any different biological structures. Two small visual stimuli are involved. The same is true for the verbal-image, verbal-motor, verbal-emotional, and other repertoires no different biological structures are required whether the stimulus is an object or an auditory word, as in spoken language, or a printed word, as in reading. There is no biological reason why children with normal language do not learn to read. As will be indicated, children with reading disorder have been successfully treated with PB's training methods, which have been widely used in behavior therapy. What is clear is that the accepted explanation of non-reading in terms of biological (learning ability) deficit is as errant as it is vague.

Reading Learning

Why is it then that children of normal intelligence do not learn how to read? One of the things that leads to the belief that dyslexia involves some *specific* brain dysfunction is that children who learn to read always have language, but not all children with language learn to read. If the same brain development produces reading as produces language, then children who acquire language should acquire reading skill. So a different "ability" is assumed to be involved for reading. The problem with such reasoning is that it looks for explanation in the inner (biological) characteristics of the child rather than in what the different "abilities" consist of and in how those abilities are learned.

To realize why children can display normal language but no reading, based solely on learning, it is necessary to have an analysis of what the two repertoires consist of and how they are learned. And to generally answer questions regarding reading disorder it is necessary to understand what normal language and reading are and how they are learned and function for the individual. The PB theory of language has already been presented. The language BBRs are acquired in a cumulative-hierarchical learning process. As a consequence, different classes of spoken words come to elicit different types of responses in the child, and the child learns also to produce spoken words herself. These repertoires undergo a progressive elaboration, and thereby become very complex.

Reading involves, essentially, learning the same repertoires that are made to life objects (and spoken words) to printed (and written) words. On a simple level we can see how this learning can take place. Let us say the child already has the verbal-labeling response "cat" under the control of a cat as the stimulus. We could print the word on a card and show it to the child and say this is the word for cat, and ask the child to say the word while looking at the cat. If we did this a few times (with reinforcement) the child would come to be able to read the printed word. (Also, the image elicited by the spoken word would be conditioned to the written word.)

While this type of learning is involved in learning to read, the complexity of what must be learned is great, much more than the above training multiplied by the number of words. For one thing, the example has involved having an adult tell the child the name of the word that is to be read. But there are too many words to be learned to have an adult present to give the name in each case. What must be done, therefore, is to teach the child a system by which the child can teach herself. This involves teaching the child to say the names of letters and syllables, as well as the skills of sounding-out the letters and syllables when new, unknown words occurs. (This is called phonics learning.) The child this way can supply herself with the new names of words so they can be learned. Through innumerable learning trials of this kind, in the expert reader a very large number of printed words must come to elicit spoken words, as well as the image responses, motor responses, and emotional responses the spoken words elicit. Various repertoires must be learned in becoming an expert reader and this requires an exceedingly large number of learning trials.

Learning Language Compared to Learning Reading

With this brief analysis in hand it is possible to answer some of the questions concerning reading disorder. First, it is possible to understand why it is that some children with normal IQs (language) nevertheless do not learn to read. Centrally, although reading learning depends upon language, learning language and learning reading have some essentially different characteristics.

For one thing, reading learning is based on already having language, not the reverse. The fact that the first learning has taken place normally does not guarantee the second will also. For example, language training is based on sporadic learning trials. Reading training is done formally in set periods, which means massed learning trials. Massed trials are effortful work demanding attention and active participation. The spaced learning of words in the home requires no such effort. Moreover, and this is important, typically there is a reinforcing event involved. When the parent says "Cookie?" and the child answers "Coog," and is given a cookie, there is immediate, personally delivered, and effective reinforcement.

Those elements spaced training trials, little effort, quick and effective reinforcement are very good, and they pertain during the learning of the basic language repertoire. Centrally also, from the beginning the child learns language responses that have immediate utility, that is, will enable the child to gain reinforcers more generally in social interaction. For example, as soon as the child learns to name the parents and other objects and actions, the child can call for those things much more effectively than using only an undifferentiated cry. And, importantly, there is no "failure." Using the above example, if the child does not respond when the parent says "Cookie?" life simply goes on; there is no admonition, no exhortation, no implication of stupidity.

None of those advantageous conditions are involved in learning to read. The training is not gradual for many children, but begins abruptly in school. There are formal teaching periods during which the child is called upon to attend and to scrutinize and compare stimuli, and to make designated responses. Especially for the unprepared child this is effortful, as can be seen in teaching a young child to read the letters of the alphabet. Without some form of reinforcement a child of four will remain voluntarily in such training for ten or so minutes. Without reinforcement the young child will begin fooling around and not attending. Even if there is reinforcement, but it is not rich enough, attention and participation will deteriorate.

When the child's attention wanders, and the child begins doing other things, the child is no longer participating in the learning task. That the child is in the classroom means nothing; without participation there are no learning trials. When that happens early, and continues, the child will become dyslexic. What is it that ensures that many children do attend, do participate, and do learn, making normal progress toward acquiring the complex and difficult reading repertoire? Let me suggest that, in general, this depends upon two types of condition: (1) that the child is already so well prepared for the task, by having necessary basic repertoires, that the task is sufficiently easy and the indications of learning provide reward; and (2) that the child has learned work habits such that she remains in the task for adequate periods even without strong forms of reinforcement. This can be elaborated.

Why Do Only Some Children Learn to Read?: Etiology

The Learning Prepared Child. Why are there individual differences in learning to read, from not at all to spectacularly well? For one thing, many parents provide training in the home that yields some of the preliminary, basic skills that are foundations for the beginning part of reading instruction. The child is introduced to coloring books and learns to hold a crayon and colored pencils. The child is read to, and individual words and letters are indicated. The child is also trained in easy, but somewhat formal, circumstances to read the letters of the alphabet and to write some of them.

What does the child acquire through this experience? Whether or not the child knows the letters of the alphabet has been considered the best predictor of whether or not the child will succeed in learning to read. Why is that? For one thing, the child who has learned to read the letters of the alphabet has learned that important repertoire. But the child in so doing has learned much more. The child has learned to scrutinize small line drawings (the letters), to make vocal responses to those stimuli, to compare the letters, to distinguish them by their differences, to follow instructions, and to engage in a task demanding these things. There are thus perceptual skills involved. In addition, the various skills help compose another repertoire that has general import, that of "work habits." Staats, Brewer, and Gross showed that children exposed to the task of learning the letters become better and better workers, making more and more responses within a given amount of time.

PB research has also shown that, as children are presented with such training, they progressively become better (quicker) learners. Some children in the home learn the basic repertoires involved, and for them the task of learning to read in school does not require unusual effort.

The Unprepared Child. Some children, whose parents have not tried to teach the children much, will not have learned the repertoires. Thus, they will not respond well when they begin school and, as a result, they will not learn well. Some children will enter school with an even greater handicap. That is, in some cases the parent is not a good trainer. Then the parent may notice the child is not advancing as rapidly as other children, and attempt to more formally train the child to some skill. This is likely to go poorly, since the child has not been prepared properly, and the parent is not a good trainer. As a consequence, the child will then not do well in the learning task and will want to withdraw. Then the parent is likely to attempt to force the child to participate, and the child will learn an inappropriate learning repertoire. That is, the child will learn behaviors to escape the learning situation, and will learn a negative emotional response to learning situations. As a consequence, the child will come to avoid learning situations and, if caught in them, will not attend and not participate as instructed. This child generally will now learn poorly whenever there is formal instruction. Thus, at the time children enter school some will have a good learning repertoire, some will have none, and some will have a negative learning repertoire. The learning ability of the three groups, other things being equal, will vary as a function of the type of learning repertoire the children have.

School as a Learning Situation for the Developing Dyslexic

The child's own learning repertoire is so central because of the nature of the school training situation. The effortfulness of the formal training situation is one drawback. Another thing is that the sources of reinforcement are not good. Children are taught in groups, so response-contingent reinforcement is not possible, and it is also impossible to monitor the child's attention and participation. Whatever reinforcement is administered comes later, by the teacher or the parent, so it does not strengthen the central behavior of attending and participating. Moreover, there is no intrinsic utility of the reading responses the child learns at the early stages. For example, learning to name the letters of the alphabet is a very large and effortful task, but the responses themselves have no utility unlike the case with learning language other than in displaying them to the teacher or the parent. Thus, the traditional expectation that "Learning is its own reward," does not apply for many children.

In beginning school this adds up to effortful learning behavior for long periods when, for many children, there are poor sources of reinforcement, insufficient for maintaining moment-to-moment attention and participation. Under such circumstances, some children do not attend and participate at the very beginning of reading training. When the child falls behind another set of learning circumstances occurs in school. That is, *not learning* does not just produce a deficit. For, in school, how the child learns is the measure of success both for pupil and for teacher. *Not learning* is failure. Blaming the pupil's "learning ability" relieves the teacher, and the parent. The child is aware of such things. Even a child of six has already learned that doing well at anything constitutes a positive emotional stimulus, and doing badly is a negative emotional stimulus. The negative emotional response elicited by doing badly will be conditioned to the learning situation of the school. The learning situation, as it comes to elicit a negative emotional response in the child, will be avoided. There are various types of avoidance behaviors. When I was a clinical student at UCLA I worked with a child whose avoidance response was to disrupt our learning trials by conversational gambits of various kinds. Avoidance behavior can take the form of classroom disruptions, daydreaming, or truancy. In schools where failure to learn is rather general, the avoidance behavior may also involve setting up a student atmosphere that derogates scholastic achievement and esteems rebelliousness, physical prowess, and social domination through that prowess.

Ordinarily, the child who fails in learning to read will become very "sensitive" because of the negative emotional conditioning. Such a child, as soon as she or he does not do well on some item, will have a negative emotional response that will elicit the child's characteristic avoidance behaviors. In one of my reading studies, for example, there was a volunteer trainer (a former teacher) who did not rely on the token reinforcer system. She exhorted the child to do better, but that was an indication of failure. The child's negative emotional response was reflected in the child's behavior. Attending and participating which had been maintained very well by token reinforcement deteriorated, and acting-out behaviors began to appear. The child who has failed in classroom learning will learn inappropriate emotional responses to learning situations, and will be a more difficult learning problem than a child who is yet to begin the learning task. This is a central aspect of dyslexia.

Three PB Concepts Important for the Developmental Disorders

The Learning Repertoire. At this point it is relevant to introduce three of PB's primary concepts in its theory of learning disorder. In addition to BBRs that constitute recognized abilities (like the language repertoire), the child can learn BBRs that constitute a "pro-learning repertoire." This repertoire consists of such things as attending when an instructional situation arises, following instructions, looking at the stimuli as requested, and making the responses requested. The pro-learning repertoire also includes a "work tolerance," which is being able to continue at a task that demands effortful behavior. And it includes having learned a positive emotional response to learning situations, such that such situations are approached, not avoided. A child with a well-developed pro-learning repertoire, other things being equal, will generally learn better in school than a child whose repertoire is weak.

In considering learning disorders there is a counterpart to the pro-learning repertoire that is equally important. The concept is that of the "anti learning repertoire." For children can learn a basic behavioral repertoire that interferes with their learning in instructional situations. Elements of that repertoire have just been described. A central element is the negative emotional response to learning situations, for it produces the avoidance responses the child has learned. The avoidance responses are part of the "anti-learning repertoire," for they interfere with learning, or take the individual out of the learning situation. Like the pro-learning repertoire, the anti-learning repertoire is a BBR, for it helps determine how the individual experiences learning situations, how the individual behaves in those situations, and how the individual learns.

It is important here, however, to add the principle that connects the pro learning and anti-learning BBRs. They are in a competitive relationship. When the individual has a strong anti-learning repertoire it will prevent experiences from occurring that would produce a pro-learning repertoire in the individual. And the converse is also true.

Learning Ability and the Learning Repertoire. A general conception in our culture is that there are individual differences in learning ability. This conception is that some people, by virtue of the quality of their nervous systems, have exceptional learning ability, either in the positive or negative direction. The PB conception is that learning ability is composed of the individual's learning repertoire, either pro- or anti-, as well as the other BBRs that are necessary as a foundation in the specific learning task.

Perceptual Development and the Perceptual Repertoire. Dyslexic children do poorly on tests of visual perception. This is generally taken to prove such children have a biologically determined perceptual deficit. However, tests of visual perception do not measure a biological condition. They measure the perceptual skills the child has learned and the skills are learned *in the process of learning to read.* Collette-Harris and Minke, using PB's training materials, showed that dyslexic children given training in reading improved on their perceptual test scores. PB research with preschool children has shown that all children start with poor perceptual skills they write letters sideways, upside down, of unequal size, backwards, and such.

What improved such skills were additional learning trials in writing letters. Dyslexic children miss the usual learning trials, and thus have poor reading skills as well as poor perceptual skills.

Learning ability, perceptual development, readiness, and other concepts that are inferred to be inner processes of a biological nature are seen in PB to consist of learned repertoires.

Additional Points in the Theory of Reading Disorder and Other Academic Skills Disorders

In the PB view, analyses of what reading consists of, the repertoires on which the learning of reading is based, and the conditions that can go awry in the learning process, produce a true theory of reading disorder. The theory indicates the causes that need to be manipulated to prevent the problem. And the theory indicates how to treat reading disorder. The Sylvan Learning Centers today employ methods that, in some essential features, are like those developed in the PB program of research, with similar results.

Attempts to show that reading disorder is inherited by showing that it runs in families, that more boys have the disorder than girls, and the like, do not constitute the same type of data. It is circumstantial, based on inference. It does not yield a theory that stipulates just what the disorder consists of, and that isolates the causes of the disorder. It does not indicate variables that can be manipulated to prevent the development of the disorder or to treat the disorder after it has arisen. The biological theory of learning disabilities has not even shown that particular brain injuries will subtract specific academic skills, like reading and mathematics, while leaving normal language intact. PB has taken the position that if a child has learned a normal language that child is completely fit neurologically to learn to read. The fact that dyslexic children can be trained to read indicates additionally that there is nothing neurologically wrong with the children in the first place. Now even those in neurobiology are beginning to recognize the logic of this position, as can be seen in the following conclusion, made after finding that children can be successfully treated, through learning, for a particular language deficit. "There may be no fundamental defect in the learning machinery in most of these children, because they so rapidly learn the same skills at which they have been defined to be deficient. For 40 years PB has been developing a learning approach in contrast to the traditional "biological" explanation, and now neurobiology is generally developing a supportive position (see Begley, 1996).

Like reading, writing and arithmetic are BBRs learned in a cumulative hierarchical manner on the basis of the language-cognitive BBR. Deficits in writing and arithmetic are considered learning disorders in children with normal intelligence. PB research has analyzed what basic writing and arithmetic skills consist of and how they are learned. Writing and arithmetic also are additional learned elaborations of the language-cognitive BBR. Such disorders do not reflect disturbances of learning caused by an underlying biologically based condition. For the children's normal intelligence (language) guarantees they have all the abilities that are needed for successful learning.

Traditionally it is thought that skill in mathematics depends on individual differences in a special ability, located in the brain. The psychological behavioral analysis rejects that speculation. No new abilities are necessary for arithmetic-mathematic learning, save a great deal of learning experience. And there are great individual differences in learning opportunity, for the types of reasons that have been described, as well as others. The sex difference that is found in the development of mathematics in the PB view is to be explained by learning factors, not biological differences.

Mental Retardation

Mental retardation is one of the major classifications in the developmental disorders. As the *DSM-IV* description indicates, it is a more severe disorder than those that have been described.

DSM-IV Description

The essential features of Mental Retardation is significantly subaverage general intellectual functioning that is accompanied by significant limitations in adaptive functioning in at least two of the following skill areas: communication, self-care, home living, social/ interpersonal skills, use of community resources, self-direction, functional academic skills, work, leisure, health, and safety.

Another criterion is that the onset must occur before age 18.

PB Theory of Mental Retardation

Various biological problems—O_1, in Figure 5.2—result in mental retardation. The *DSM-IV* lists children with Down's syndrome, Tay-Sachs disease, and other gene and chromosomal abnormalities that are inherited that cause mental retardation. These are said to account for 5% of the cases. Early embryonic changes are said to account for another 30%, and pregnancy and perinatal problems for 10%. Infections, trauma, and toxic conditions account for 5%. In addition to these biologically produced cases of mental retardation, environmental influences and mental disorders are said to account for 15%-20%. But mental disorders are generally thought to involve some type of biological problem. So the proportion of cases of mental retardation that are due to environmental-learning problems is thought to be quite small. "In approximately 30%-40% of the individuals seen in clinical settings, no clear etiology for the Mental Retardation can be determined despite extensive evaluation efforts".

There are several reasons to raise questions in this area. The first is that, while biological causation in mental retardation is very explicit in a certain percentage of cases, in other cases biological causation is only inferred. When a child is mentally retarded, if case histories reveal there have been problems in pregnancy and perinatal conditions, infections, trauma, and toxic conditions, these will be considered to have caused biological damage that is responsible. In such cases, however, this is an assumption, as it is when "extensive evaluation efforts" reveal no biological causation.

In the PB view the general interpretation that mental retardation is caused by biological defect is overdrawn. In addition to the very strong biological orientation in explaining human behavior in our culture, a counterbalancing learning explanation has been weak. There has not been an accepted learning theory of intelligence and of the lack of intelligence. For this reason it is typically difficult to see how cases of mental retardation could have arisen just from lack of learning opportunity, unless the environment is dramatically deficit. And the fact that there are identifiable biological defects that in many cases lead to mental retardation is, in contrast, impressive. For these reasons it is easy to assume that biological causation exists, even when there is no direct evidence to that effect. This is abetted by poor logic. For example, when a mentally retarded child comes from a home where the parents are of below average intelligence, it is assumed that the child has a poor genetic inheritance. On the other hand, when such a child comes from an advantaged home, especially if there are other normal children, this is assumed to be proof that there must be something wrong with the particular child. The *assumptions* that are made erroneously favor the accepted belief, the biological explanation.

In the PB view, any case of mental retardation for which there is not an identifiable biological cause *may* be due to biological cause or it may be due to environmentally caused learning problems. That may involve a majority of the cases of mental retardation. Moreover, a biological explanation of mental retardation is not complete until the biological defect has been identified, as well as how the defect interferes with the learning of the BBRs. For the psychological behaviorism approach states that *mental retardation consists of deficits in the intelligence BBRs that have been described, the language-cognitive BBRs and the sensory-motor BBRs, especially, and, to some extent, aspects of the emotional-motivational BBR.* Having a theory of what intelligence is provides a basis for defining mental retardation. And this stipulation of intelligence must be interwoven with biological study to provide a full theory of mental retardation and its etiology.

The PB position is that the BBRs that constitute intelligence are learned. Biological defects can interfere with that learning. But deficits can occur in the learning conditions necessary for the acquisition of intelligence, and this will result in mental retardation. A theory of mental retardation must indicate the ways the learning process can go awry in childhood to yield retardation. Only with extensive study of this type will the necessary evidence be obtained. In terms of what is known about normal learning of intelligence and the ways that learning can go awry it can be seen that deficits can occur in many different scenarios. There are the dramatic cases of "feral" children, who have been raised in different conditions (sometimes with animals) that provide no or little exposure to language. There are the much more widespread cases of children raised in ghetto conditions by parents with little education with poorly developed language and other skills, exposed to a social group that is similarly lacking. There are cases where the parents' problems criminality, drug and alcohol abuse, depression, and such so seriously interfere with parenting that the child has a severely deficit environment. But, there are also cases where there is nothing clinically deficit in the parents, even where the parents' achievements are high, that nevertheless involve a cumulative-hierarchical learning process for the child that has gone awry and that results in mental retardation. How can deficits in learning conditions occur, in a way that produces devastating deficits, without being noticed? How do those deficits occur in homes that appear normal? What is not understood is that parents can be highly educated and very intelligent, good parents in terms of the care they give and the love they have for their child, and yet things may occur that very early set the cumulative hierarchial learning process on a downward path. The parent, for example, may not provide good training conditions for the child's language learning.

The child who does not develop normal repertoires like the language cognitive repertoires when other children do will soon be faced with abnormal experiences. One case with which I dealt involved a child who had no language at the age of four. The child's speech was delayed due to several circumstances including the fact that the parent herself was not vocal and did not speak much to the child. This was observable in the way she was treating another year-old infant she had who had no language and was very passive. With the older child, when the parent recognized the delay in speech development she began attempting to teach the child to speak by trying to get him to repeat nursery rhymes. However, repeating sequences of unknown words has no function in this case it only produced a few poor echolalic elements. Trying to force the child to endure such training, moreover, is aversive. The most prominent result in this case was to teach the child that learning situations are unpleasant, and to avoid them with anti-learning behaviors.

It should be noted that there may be various types of "skills" in a child's anti-learning repertoire. The child may learn, for example, that passive "dumbness" in the face of learning tasks will be rewarded by the cessation of the effortful and bothersome learning situation. The parent after a number of such interactions simply becomes convinced that the child is unable to learn is retarded and abandons the effort. When this occurs sufficiently the parent no longer presents the needed training to the child. I was once asked to evaluate a child of three years of age who the parents (both trained professionals) thought was retarded. I did so primarily by observations in the home. The little boy was a middle child with a very aggressive brother a year younger and a sister several years older. The aggressive younger child had learned to bully the three-year-old possibly originally because the younger was protected by the parents – and both siblings, in their striving for attention, pushed the "retarded" child away from interacting with the parents. If the "retarded" child did something to attract the attention of the parents, the other two, especially the younger brother, would be aversive to the "retarded" child. The "retarded" child had thus learned to be unresponsive, not to try for the parents' attention but, rather, to spend time alone. In this way he was involved in less rivalry and was picked on less. The other children displayed more skilled behavior, interest, and striving and thus appeared "brighter." The child's behavioral development, including language, was indeed behind the other two. The parents had seen a psychologist, described the behavior of the child, and had him tested, and their concerns had been confirmed. So the parents had come to the conclusion the three-year-old had some biological deficit and was retarded and they had begun treating the child as though he were.

I explained what was happening among the three children and the parents and the effect it was having on the child in question. I also showed the parents how the child could be interested and responsive that is, intelligent in play, when there was no competition from the other two children. I instructed the parents how they must provide for interaction with the child and positive learning experiences, where the child could not be pushed aside by siblings. This analysis and the very capable actions of the parents resulted in a complete turnaround in what otherwise was developing into a downward cycle of learning leading to retardation. The child is now in medical school! Had the downward cumulative-hierarchical learning process continued, the child would have been a retardate in a family of accomplished children and parents.

In general, the parent typically learns how to respond "appropriately" to the child who displays the repertoire of non-responsiveness in the face of a learning situation. There is much research that indicates that parents speak to their children differently depending upon the child's ability. The parent of the child who demonstrates deficits is only a special case. This parent learns not to present learning tasks to the child that will produce awkward and unpleasant experiences for both the child and the parent. The parent does not want the child to experience failure. What that means, however, is that the child has been placed in a "special education class" at home, where the learning opportunities are much less rich than for other children, even for other children in the same home. Pretty soon the whole family, parents, siblings, and other relatives and friends, begin to treat the child as retarded. They are kind and forgiving and undemanding. So the child is happy, is reinforced for the behavior, and continues to develop the "dumb" anti-learning repertoire. That is the child's adjustment. But the result is that, for such a child, learning opportunities are inferior, and that is reflected in the child's "retarded" learning of the BBRs.

This can happen under very benign family circumstances, where everyone has the child's best interests at heart. Deficit learning conditions can also happen in less benign family circumstances, of course, even though the home, on casual examination, appears to be normal. What these examples are intended to indicate is that the human environment is very complex, with an infinite number of variations, and many opportunities for cumulative-hierarchical learning to predominate in developing the anti- learning repertoire that can be central in mental retardation.

Implications of the PB Theory of Mental Retardation

The PB theory of mental retardation may be stated very simply. Mental retardation consists of the absence of the BBRs that are measured on intelligence tests, as well as the absence of the types of repertoires that are measured on tests of adaptive functioning, both of which were analyzed in the preceding chapter. It should be remembered that the intelligence test measures BBRs that are essential to later learning, so the child who is low in intelligence will have difficulty learning "adaptive functioning repertoires." These deficits can occur because of limitations on learning imposed by biological conditions. We need to know much more about these conditions and, especially, how these conditions translate into deviations in the child's learning. At present we do not have a good handle on what takes place biologically during learning. We need to know that. And we need to know how the anatomy of the brain affects complex learning. For example, the brain of a Down's syndrome child is simpler, less convoluted than the brain of a normal child. How does that abnormal condition affect learning? Is it primarily to limit the number of stimulus response elements the child can learn, and thus the richness of learning possible, and even the rapidity of learning when it depends upon the richness of past learning? Does the condition mean that the child is capable of learning the various human characteristics (BBRs), but more slowly and more sparsely? Or, does the biological conditioning affect specific types of learning? Just what are the learning effects of the condition? That is the knowledge that is needed. This type of knowledge, of course, is fundamental when it comes to treatment of the types of deficits we label as mental retardation. Such knowledge, for example, might tell us that we have to provide the same type of learning opportunities for the child, but introduced more gradually, dealing with less complex material. Or, there may be other directives that will result when our knowledge is more complete. Or, it may be that children with Down's syndrome, as one example, vary greatly in brain structure as well as learning possibilities. In that case it would be necessary to establish *behaviorally* just what it is the child can do, for example, by providing excellent and rich learning conditions in order to see what type of progress the child can make.

In any event, it must be emphasized that the deficits in the BBRs can also arise solely from complex learning circumstances involving deficits in learning conditions. Such deficits will produce deficits in the child's learning ability of two types. First, the child will not learn BBRs that are basic to learning more advanced repertoires. A child, for example, who has no or poor language BBRs will not have the wherewithal to learn to read. Second, deficit or inappropriate learning conditions can result in deficits in the pro-learning repertoire, or in acquiring the anti-learning repertoire, both of which will handicap the child in all learning tasks.

Since the deficits in the BBRs that compose mental retardation may result from a biological condition or from poor learning conditions, it is not possible to infer from the deficit behavior and poor learning ability themselves just what the cause is. That realization is fundamental, and it has fundamental implications for working with children who have deficits.

Childhood Autism

The *DSM-IV* presents a classification of Pervasive Developmental Disorders, which includes Autistic Disorder.

DSM-IV Description and the BBRs

The *DSM-IV* criteria of autistic disorder involve disturbances in social interaction, intellective functioning, and in activities and interests. In the first category the child shows lack of awareness of others' feelings, no pleasure in the comfort of others, no or impaired imitation, no or abnormal social play, and gross impairment in making friends. In the second category, the child does not communicate verbally or non-verbally, does not display imaginative ability, such as in taking roles or appreciating stories, speech is absent or disturbed, and even if there is speech, conversation is not sustained. In the third category the child has stereotyped body movements, is preoccupied with parts of objects, is upset by trivial environmental changes, and has a narrow range of interests and preoccupation with only one. These are descriptions of devastating deficit and inappropriate characteristics.

PB Etiology Position

The *DSM III-R* suggests that a wide range of pre-, peri-, and post-natal conditions can cause "brain dysfunction and are thought to predispose to the development of Pervasive Developmental Disorders [that is, autistic disorder]". The *DSM III-R* also says there is no support for the view that autistic disorder can be caused by "parental personality and child-rearing practices". The *DSM-IV* does not include these statements. This change is interesting; the radical behaviorism approach to autism essentially took the position that autism had a biological etiology and has not set forth a theory that autism is learned. Nevertheless, Lovaas went on to apply to the treatment of autistic children some of the same types of language training procedures developed in PB, showing the positive impact of training on the autistic child.

The PB view has always been quite the opposite of the biological position. The PB view recognizes that it is possible that biological conditions could limit the child's ability to profit from environmental experiences and thereby produce deficits in the BBRs. Whether or not that is the case, however, must be shown directly, not accepted on the basis of assumption, or on the basis of the type of "circumstantial" evidence that has been employed in twin studies of intelligence. *The PB theory is that, whatever behavior the autistic child displays, it is learned.* If there are biological conditions that impede or distort learning then just what is involved must be shown. The fact is there is no hard evidence of the biological causes of autism. And, the symptomatology of autism could be produced very straightforwardly by learning conditions inadvertently introduced by parents in homes that are otherwise quite normal.

PB Theory of Autism

In the PB view the definition of autism in the *DSM-IV* is considered to consist of descriptions of the typical behaviors displayed by such children, organized into commonsense categories.

Thus, lack of communication skills, imaginal skills, speech, conversation skills, friends, playing, and so on, all involve deficits in the child's language-cognitive BBR. All of these activities, even social activities, demand the child have acquired the various aspects of language. The child cannot have play interactions with other children, for example, without being able to respond to speech and to produce speech in return. So the autistic child, without language, will have deficits in the learning that comes from peer interaction. This is also true of acquiring interests in different activities. Without language, the child can only use (be interested in) objects on the basis of their primary characteristics. A toy car, for example, in terms of its basic properties is only an object—to mouth, to throw, or to pound. However, if the child can respond to such directions as "Let's play racing cars and see which one rolls down this board faster," then the car can be used, additionally, in a manner that is social and playful. If the child has the words for cars and what they do and what they are used for then the toy car can be used in an "imaginal" way. These types of activities are beyond the autistic child who has not learned normal language repertoires.

Other descriptions of the autistic child involve deficits in the development of the emotional-motivational BBR. Thus, the lack of emotional response to comforting and affection so different from the usual child is a frequent characteristic of autism, supposedly due to the child's biological abnormality. The PB view is that such symptoms simply indicate the child's learning circumstances have not produced a positive emotional response to being comforted and receiving affection. The fact that the child atypically does not make eye contact with the parent, does not approach the parent affectionately and seek the parent, calls for analysis in terms of the child's learning. The same also applies to the sensory-motor BBR. The autistic child typically has not developed repertoires in this area as well. Playing with toys and with other children demands sensory-motor skills. A child deficit in those skills will not engage in those activities. The autistic child typically will also have learned inappropriate sensory-motor repertoires such as repetitive movements, head-banging, and other forms of self-damage. Studies have shown that, when appropriate conditions are imposed, such behaviors can be removed by extinction (non-reinforcement).

"The most severely incapacitated are those who have widespread deficits in those basic behavioral repertoires ordinarily acquired early in life. The autistic child also has learned bizarre and maladjustive repertoires of behavior that further prevent him from learning the necessary repertorial skills". What is being said is that all of the symptoms by which autism is described involve either deficits in behavior or inappropriate behaviors. And, in each case, only the conditions of learning for the child may be the cause, without any biological causation. The PB analysis of autism has been presented in various places, in the context of describing both normal and abnormal basic behavioral repertoires. Important in the etiology of autism is the cumulative-hierarchical process. For example, deficit learning conditions produce repertoire deficits that then produce social treatment that is deficit and inappropriate, in an interactional way. Because the child has deficits the parents try to press the child to learn and that results in the child acquiring negative emotional conditioning (anxiety) to learning situations and to the parent. This then provides the basis for further undesirable learning.

With younger children the behaviors that are learned because they remove the child from anxiety-producing learning situations can vary widely. The child may "escape" the learning situation by insisting to the parent that he be allowed to perform the task himself, even before the parent has finished the instructions. He may run to another activity, or begin another activity. The child may refuse to look at the relevant stimuli, or he may make other irrelevant responses.

The types of behaviors the child will learn will depend upon which of them are successful in getting him out of the situation. These can range from the mild behaviors just described to those that are bizarre enough to be considered "crazy." The author recently encountered a case where the child would become visibly upset whenever the situation took on the appearance of formal training. He would then become hyperactive and move about with increasing rapidity and frenzy as the parent attempted more strongly to bring him into the learning situation. He would not respond to verbal stimuli. He would not attend. This would continue until the attempted learning situation was abandoned. He thus had been learning hyperactive frenzies because through this behavior he avoided the learning situations in which he ordinarily received punishment the parent's impatience and disappointment, not reward. We will then see a child who so successfully avoids situations that he suffers grievous deficits in the acquisition of his basic behavioral repertoires. These deficits will make learning even more trying for the child yielding further punishment in learning situations. A vicious cycle can be developed that hinders normal learning and produces abnormal learning. When such cycles are continued over a period of years they will result in children we term emotionally disturbed, autistic. This may include (1) self-destructive responses such as knocking one's head against the wall, biting oneself, and so on, (2) hyperactivity, (3) crazy behaviors such as monotonous rocking, weird gestures and facial expressions, uttering crazy noises, and so on.

The parent child interaction can come to elicit primarily negative emotional responses in both, and escape from the interaction can in each case be a reinforcer. The PB theory of autism, thus, is that the interaction of parent and child does not provide learning conditions by which the child acquires normal BBRs. Rather, the child begins to acquire undesirable repertoires. And the cumulative-hierarchical learning of the child progressively develops along both paths. Very central is the extensive development of the anti-learning repertoire, including undesirable behaviors of all kinds that protect the child from the learning situations that have made the child uncomfortable. Evidence in support of the PB conception of autism is provided by research showing that autistic children can be trained in the normal BBRs that PB has analyzed and dealt with .In the PB analysis *if these repertoires can be taught to children after they have become autistic, which means they have the anti-learning repertoires that make learning more difficult, then these children could have learned those normal BBRs at the beginning*. This is the position other works are now beginning to support. This suggests there is nothing biologically wrong with the children with respect to their potential for normal learning. The same is true of the "idiot savant" phenomenon, where an autistic child who has pervasive deficits nevertheless has some special skill in music, art, number operations, and such. This is generally taken to mean that such children have generally defective brains but with one "bright" spot. There is no evidence to back this up. In the PB view special skill in one area means the child has the wherewithal to have learned skills to the same level in other areas.

Adult Disorders

Several PB theories of the childhood disorders have been summarized to characterize the PB abnormal psychology. The following sections will do the same for several adult disorders.

Depression

Depression is one of the most common behavior disorders, occurring more with women than men, and frequently accompanying old age. Depression constitutes a widespread problem.

DSM-IV Definition

DSM-IV description of Major Depressive Episode includes such symptoms as dysphoric mood (depression) and loss of interest and pleasure in all or almost all usual activities and pastimes. The disturbance is salient and persisting occurring "for most of the day, nearly every day, for at least 2 consecutive weeks during which there is either depressed mood or the loss of interest or pleasure in nearly all activities" and involves at least four additional symptoms from a list including "changes in appetite or weight, sleep, and psychomotor activity, decreased energy, feelings of worthlessness or guilt, difficulty thinking, concentrating, or making decisions, or recurrent thoughts of death or suicidal ideation, plans, or attempts".

Behaviorizing-Psychologizing the Definition of Depression

Depression was the second behavior disorder to be elaborated into a full theory in PB. In treating this theory I will suggest, first, that the dysphoric mood described in the definition constitutes a negative emotional state in PB. The emotional state is experienced for "most of the day, every day," indicating that much more than ephemeral emotional responses are involved. The negative emotional state is a function of the individual's life situation and emotional-motivational BBR, as shown in Figure 5.3.

Placing depression disorder in the PB framework theory in this manner has various implications. It can be expected, for example, that the negative emotional state will induce other negative behaviors of a language-cognitive as well as a sensory-motor type. In the language-cognitive category are the recurrent thoughts of death and suicide. What is described as feelings of worthlessness and guilt, and it might be added of inadequacy, wrongdoing, and the like, really refer to thoughts of (language behavior with respect to) such things. This is true also of worry, self-blame, self-pity, and negative appraisal of the future. Such verbal-behavior negatively impacts on others.

Other symptoms of depression refer to the characteristics of the emotional state itself. Thus, depressed individuals typically experience little or no pleasure in usual activities, for example, in eating, and in sexual activity. The PB view, following the algebraic sum principle, is that a strong negative emotional state subtracts from experiencing the positive emotional responses usually elicited by food and sexual stimuli.

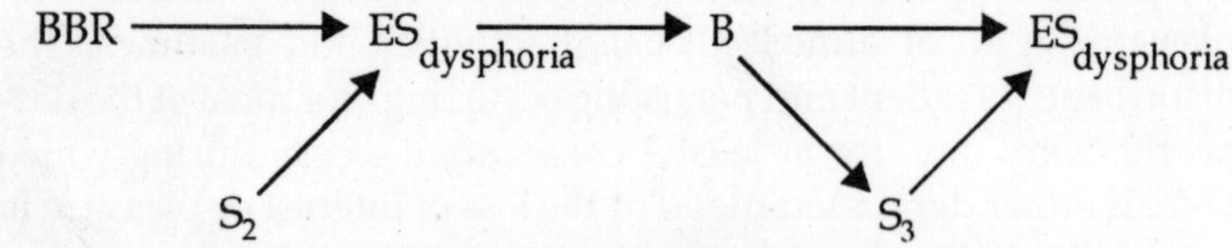

Fig. 5.3. This model depicts the PB concept of the vicious cycle of depression (and other mood disorders). Because of the individual's personality repertoires (BBR) and the life situation (S_2), the individual experiences the negative emotional state (ES) of dysphoria. The dysphoria in turn affects the individual's behavior in undesirable ways. This behavior then affects the individual's social environment (S_3) in negative ways; in this continuing development, that social environment further impacts on the individual to deepen the dysphoria.

The negative emotional state also lowers the extent to which stimuli will serve as positive reinforcers or incentive stimuli for the individual. For example, since food stimuli and sex stimuli no longer elicit such a positive emotional response, they will not strengthen food- and sex-securing behaviors. The depressed person, thus, displays less eating behavior (loss of appetite) which can result in weight loss. This is true also of sexual behavior, which diminishes in frequency. The emotional effects on behavior also involve the incentive function of stimuli. Positive emotional stimuli elicit approach behaviors; anything that diminishes that emotion will lessen their incentive strength. When the individual is depressed the positive emotional response to all stimuli is decreased, resulting in the typical decrease in activity and "energy." For example, the individual will have an attenuated emotional response to the announcement of a movie, and thus be less likely to go.

The negative emotional state will, on the other hand, *add* to stimuli that elicit negative emotional responses. The individual who is depressed, thus, will cry more easily than usual in response to bad news, or any sad event, and become annoyed or irritable more easily. Any stimulus that elicits a negative emotional response will be enhanced by the negative emotional state of the individual. This includes the enhancement of pain, as a new PB theory of pain indicates (Staats, Hekmat, & Staats, in press). The individual, as a consequence of the negative emotional state, is also likely to display sensory-motor characteristics of dejection.

In actuality these events interact. Let us say the negative emotional state begins because of some environmental loss that entails a number of negative emotional stimuli. The emotional state, in turn, affects emotional responding to life's other stimuli and, hence, the incentive and reinforcing value of those stimuli. And the emotional state affects the things the individual says to herself the self-blame, the worry, the negative thinking. But these are powerful and continuing events that themselves elicit negative emotions that contribute to the negative algebraic sum of the negative emotional state. In further interaction the depressed behavior of the subject the negative language behavior, the lack of participation in activities, the dejected motor behavior, and such have an effect on the social environment, which then acts back on the individual. The spouse, for example, disaffected by the depressed person's negative talk, inactivity, dejection, and irritability, may be alienated and complain, threaten reprisals, and generally act negatively, all of which deepen the person's depression. This is schematized in Figure 5.3.

Current Environment in the PB Theory of Depression

Analyses of depression have frequently considered environmental misfortunes such as death of a loved one, losing a job, moving away from family and friends, a failed marriage or rejection by a loved person, retirement, and old age. Some environmental events seem anomalous like attaining a major life objective, receiving a promotion, or the birth of a child. But attaining something, in effect, can remove a life goal, and a promotion or a child may bring threatening responsibility. In PB terms "The environment in which the individual finds himself or herself may be deficient involving losses or inappropriate such as occurs when a new boss who dislikes the individual makes unreasonable demands, withholds usual rewards and recognition, and creates special problems for the individual".

Each misfortune actually consists of a large number of individual stimuli. The individual who loses a job, for example, does not just suffer one negative emotional stimulus. Many negative stimulus circumstances result, such as having to spend life savings, to resist buying needed or desired things, to withdraw from participation in recreations, and the like, all of which will elicit a negative emotional response. There are also a host of social stimuli that result from having lost status as an employed, worthwhile, contributing, successful member of society. These are stimuli that can elicit numerous, continuous, and strong negative emotional responses. Such negative emotional responses begin the continuing emotional state, dysphoria, that defines depression.

One of the things that has been confusing is that, although a good percentage of patients will have experienced a discrete, apparent misfortune before becoming depressed, many will not. Reactive depressions that involve a misfortune can more easily be seen to have a demonstrable cause. Let me suggest, however, that a person's life may involve many stimuli that elicit a negative emotional response even without the occurrence of some specific, dramatic loss. The individual may have a poor or non-existent family life, a non-fulfilling job, few friends and enjoyable activities, and so on. In such a case there may be no dramatic loss that precipitates depression. The precipitating event may occur within, such as the verbal projection this scenario is not going to improve. And, even when external circumstances appear very good, we cannot know what is occurring in the unobservable intimacies of the individual's life, as in marriage, in the discrepancy between a life-dream and reality, in the response to aging, and many others. It is easy to assume in such "unjustifiable" cases as these that the cause must be some biological condition, but the error is in our ability to analyze and apprise ourselves of the causal events. The environmental and behavioral conditions of depressed people need to be studied systematically, so that we can have better knowledge of the variety of circumstances that can be involved. In the PB view the current life environment interacts with the individual's BBRs to produce dysphoria and depressed behavior, which further affect the environment.

Understanding the disorder calls for knowledge of these several sources of causation.

Basic Behavioral Repertoires in the PB Theory of Depression

Not all individuals who experience a great loss in life become depressed. Their mourning does not begin the complex interactions that bring a persisting state with disabling symptoms. In the PB view such individual differences are due to variation in the BBRs. One individual, for example, may learn a very rich positive emotional-motivational repertoire, with positive emotional responses to many people, recreative stimuli, work stimuli, sexual stimuli, family stimuli, social stimuli (friends, relatives), religious stimuli, intellectual stimuli, political stimuli, as well as material things of various kinds. On the other hand, another individual may have learned a much more restricted, sparse positive emotional-motivational BBR. There may also be differences in individuals in the extent to which the *negative* emotional motivational repertoire is learned. An individual may learn a negative emotional response fear, anxiety, annoyance, hate, dislike to many things.

The same is true of the sensory-motor repertoire. Some people have learned a variety of sensory-motor skills, in areas like playing tennis, repairing cars, sewing, cooking, playing an instrument, painting, playing with children, gardening, and love-making, among others. Other individuals will have learned a narrower range of sensory motor skills. Some sensory- motor skills also may affect the individual's physiology in various ways that may be relevant for depression, for example, recreational exercise may help determine the individual's weight and health, as well as physiologically (biochemically) affect the individual's emotion elicitation.

The same is true of the language-cognitive repertoire. One individual may have learned negative language-cognitive characteristics, such as generally labeling events, including those yet to happen, in a negative way. This individual may verbally criticize herself and generally describe herself in what we would call a negative self-concept. As another individual difference variable, some people are very "introspective." That is, they engage in a lot of self-language, whereas others may respond more to external stimulation, such as interacting with others, working on tasks, reading, and listening to television. Moreover, individuals who are introspective may vary in their perseveration and the depth with which they treat a topic. Some individuals who experience something positive or negative will examine the experience in detail, analyzing what happened, thinking of related issues, implications, and the possibilities of further development of the situation involved. Others will do so much less. These various differences will affect the positive and negative emotional responses people experience and, hence, their emotional states.

Depression Vulnerability. These BBR differences are centrally important with respect to how the individual will respond to a negative environmental development. Not everyone who loses ajob, a loved one, one's health, or whatever, becomes depressed. Some people, because of the nature of their BBRs, are more vulnerable to depression than are others (see Carrillo, Rojo, & Staats, in press). As in the above example, a person who describes herself in negative emotional terms will be more vulnerable to depression than a person who describes herself in positive emotional terms. As another example, a person who ruminates excessively over things that happen will be more vulnerable to depression, in contrast to a person who gives each situation its due and then moves on. Thus, characteristics of the individual's language-cognitive repertoire will contribute to vulnerability.

With respect to the emotional-motivational BBR, a person who has a very richly developed emotional-motivational BBR, in which there are many stimuli that elicit a positive emotional response, will be less vulnerable than a person with a less developed BBR. Let us take the example of two mothers, each of whom has lost an only child. The mother who has a happy marriage, rich sex life, a fulfilling career, compatible relatives, close friends, various enjoyed recreations and cultural pursuits will weather that loss much better than a mother with an empty marriage, no sex life, no career, incompatible relatives, no close friends, recreations, or cultural pursuits. Each of these categories is a potential source of multiple positive emotional stimuli. When those sources are few in the individual's environment, or when the individual has not learned a positive emotional response to such stimuli, there is not much to counterbalance the scales when negative emotional stimuli are encountered in life. The individual is then *vulnerable* to depression.

The same is true of the sensory-motor repertoire, for sensory-motor skills are one usual means of "acquiring" positive emotional experience. The individual who has the sensory-motor skills of being a carpenter, a musician, an athlete, a cook, or a lover can gain important positive emotional stimuli through their use. The individual who has multiple repertoires in different areas will not experience a great loss if performance of one becomes impossible. An individual, for example, who has the sensory motor skills involved in being a good tennis player, surfer, musician, socializer, and painter will not feel as much loss with an achilles tendon injury that prevents playing tennis as someone who has few other areas of sensory-motor development. Again, the richness of the development of the sensory-motor BBR will affect vulnerability to depression.

In the above section a person was described who has a poor family, work, recreative, and social life who progressively realizes that her dreams and hopes will never be fulfilled. These "realizations" (self-language) push her into a depression. The person who has rich BBRs that obtain a rich family, work, recreative, and social life, in contrast, will not engage in that type of negative appraisal and thus will be less vulnerable to depression. When considered within the framework of PB theory, it can be seen that the topic of vulnerability to depression, and other behavior disorders, deserves systematic research, including test construction.

Depression and the PB Principle of Compounding

The principle of compounding is actually involved in the above examples, but needs to be stated explicitly. The theory states that, because of the interaction of the various determinants of depression, the individual can experience a more intense negative (or positive) emotional state than external environmental circumstances warrant. The individual, for example, may lose ajob. That event brings many negative emotional stimuli, and consideration of the various negative results of that loss should elicit a negative emotional state.

If, in addition, however, the individual describes what has happened as an indication of personal worthlessness instead of, say, an economic downturn that self-description and its continued elaboration can intensify and continue the negative emotional responding, deepening the negative emotional state. And that, in turn, will have the effect of eliciting further negative self-descriptions, descriptions of others, descriptions of other circumstances. In the person with vulnerable BBRs, losing the job can precipitate a negative "view" of the self and the world, an ample supply of negative emotional response elicitation. Worse, the individual's language behaviors, as well as her other symptoms, which make her ineffective in various settings, will be responded to by others in a negative manner. This will result in additional negative emotional stimulation. The simple job loss has in these various ways been compounded, which means a deepening of the negative emotional state beyond that which the current life situation itself warrants.

Part of the theory task, thus, is the analysis of the various sites of causation of depression and the manner in which they interact to produce an *exaggerated* condition of negativity. Understanding this phenomenon involves understanding the basic PB principle that behavior can play two roles. A behavior may be a dependent variable, induced by a stimulus, but also be an independent variable as well, that induces yet other behavioral symptoms. The behavioral-environmental-BBR interactions in depression are part of the disorder and must be understood.

Biological Conditions and Depression

There are twin studies that suggest depression is inherited. There is also a belief that misfunctioning biological mechanisms are the cause of depression. For example, Schildkraut proposed that depression is caused by a deficiency in norepinephrine in the brain, and mania (inappropriate euphoria) is caused by an excess in this substance, which aids transmission of nervous impulses. There are various studies that support this hypothesis, for example, by showing that depressed people have an excess of norepinephrine (one of the catecholamines) in their urine, and by showing that treating manic patients with lithium carbonate reduces the mania as well as the level of norepinephrine available in the brain. PB analysis, however, advises caution in interpreting such studies. Increases in norepinephrine may *result* from the depression rather than *produce* it.

In the PB view, it is possible that there are brain characteristics, *independent of BBR/environmental events,* that cause depression. The PB position, as has been indicated, is that the emotional response occurs essentially in the brain. Biochemical processes could directly affect the functioning of the brain to produce a negative emotional state. We see such an effect, usually in the opposite direction, when most people consume alcohol. Typically the individual's mood (emotional state) becomes happier. We can see the same effect in drug studies, where patients report being happier when administered antidepressant drugs. In PB terms the drug attenuates the negative emotional state of depression. And, as expected in PB, change in the negative emotional state will change behavior; with drug treatment "Pessimistic worry about future problems showed the greatest change". There is a current controversy concerning whether or not antidepressant drugs change personality. Psychological behaviorism provides a framework for resolving that controversy by specific analysis of what is involved.

It should be emphasized, however, that alcohol or drugs raise or lower (as in drug treatment of manic disorder) the individual's emotional state; however, this *does not mean that the individual's brain was malfunctioning beforehand.* Such results only demonstrate that chemicals can indeed directly affect the emotional mechanisms in the brain. Let me also make another observation in this respect. Maas, Fawcett, and Dekirmenjian showed that the reduced levels of catecholamines in depressed subjects return to normal when they are treated with antidepressant drugs. Such a finding, again, does not show that the depression began when the subjects' brain in and of itself became deficient in the catecholamines. The deficiency could have occurred because of environmental/BBR events that produced a negative emotional state.

Let me elaborate. The emotion mechanisms in the brain have been constructed by evolution so their function is to respond to environmental events. The PB hypothesis is that, when the individual with certain BBRs faces a life situation that elicits a negative emotional state, *this occurs by means of changing the physiology of the brain.* Generally, it is the individual's BBRs and life situation that determine the physiological state, rather than the reverse. Research needs to be conducted to test this theory. It is important to realize that whether the physiological state in the brain is caused behaviorally or by the brain independently, correcting that state will correct the depression. For that reason, studies that use drugs to change emotional states do not isolate just which biological or behavioral—causation was involved in the first place. *An essential point is that pharmacological studies of this type do not provide evidence for the biological causation theory of depression.*

Again, other than the PB position, we have not had a theory framework in which biological and behavioral causation are interrelated. We need the unification of neurobiology and psychological behaviorism, and unified research efforts.

Heuristic Characteristics of the Theory of Depression

In describing the theory of depression examples have been given of research implications. One further example will be described to indicate something about the biological-behavioral interaction contained in the PB approach. The example refers to a recent study that found that the success of treatment of depression with antidepressant drugs is related to the individual's personality. The subjects under treatment suffered from major depression, and about half also received diagnoses of personality disorder (PD). Two thirds of these patients had two or more such diagnoses. Patients diagnosed with no personality disorder did best four months after treatment started, those with one such diagnosis did less well, those with more than one such diagnosis did less well, and those with a diagnosis that included paranoid, schizoid, or schizotypal disorders did the poorest of all. Such results traditionally feed into a biological theory of depression, the relationship of personality disorders to depression enhancing the general suggestion there is some brain defect involved.

In contrast, the PB analysis is that the patients without a personality disorder are more likely to be suffering a depression because of environmentally caused problems. That is why these patients show more remissions; for the life problems pass, or the individual may adjust to them. Moreover, part of the depression in such cases results from the *compounding principle*. When the antidepressant drugs cut off the depression, the individual's unrealistic worries, guilts, and self-recriminations diminish and the individual behaves more positively. As a consequence, others treat the individual better, so a positive cycle is produced that reverses the vicious cycle involved in the depression.

The circumstance with those with personality disorders is not so positive. The behavior (BBR) that is part of their disorder is likely to be generating problems that are the primary cause of the depression. Moreover, as the number of those diagnoses (paranoid, schizoid, and schizotypal) increases, the disturbed behavior is more widespread, and there are thus more negative current life circumstances. These conditions produce the depression. Moreover, those with personality disorders have fewer behavioral resources for adjusting to environmental problems. Personality disorders will ordinarily continue. Even though the antidepressant medication reduces the negative emotional state, the individual with the personality disorder will continue to behave in the same disordered way, thus continuing the negative current life situation. This study should not support a belief in biological determination of depression. The PB theory of abnormal behavior provides a behavioral understanding of the findings. Moreover, there are a host of empirical questions suggested by this analysis. For example, one line of research would investigate the extent to which the patients without personality disorders, in comparison to those with such disorders, are reacting to the occurrence of new life problems. Another study, which presents technical problems, would concern the extent to which the differential effects are the result of the reduction in compounding produced in patients without personality disorders. Another line of research would seek to establish the extent to which the depression of patients with personality disorder diagnoses is caused by the behavior of the patients themselves. This line of research would investigate this effect in relationship to the different diagnoses. This, of course, is a type of research that is important with respect to various disorders, not just depression.

A major point here is that we need to make PB analyses of the manner in which the behavior of patients with different types of disorders contributes to the causes of their disorders, as well as how that behavior is determined by BBR deficits and inappropriacies. In depression, for example, such study is necessary before interpreting just what the role is of drugs, for the drug induced alleviation of the negative emotional state can set in motion behavioral processes that are a large part of the treatment effect.

Anxiety Disorders

The anxiety disorders are generally considered as a class, as indicated in the following succinct description.

DSM-III-R Definition

The characteristic features of this group of disorders are symptoms of anxiety and avoidance behavior. In Panic Disorder and Generalized Anxiety Disorder, anxiety is usually the predominant symptom, and avoidance behavior is almost always present in Panic Disorder with Agoraphobia [phobia for being out of doors]. In Phobic Disorders anxiety is experienced if the person confronts the dreaded object or situation. In Obsessive Compulsive Disorder anxiety is experienced if the person attempts to resist the obsessions or compulsions. Avoidance behavior is almost always present in Phobic Disorders, and frequently present in Obsessive Compulsive Disorder.

Phobias occur to such things (stimuli) as being on an elevator or airplane, seeing a particular animal (dogs, insects, snakes), or being called upon to speak in public. Panic disorder involves an intense, unexpected, repeated fear or discomfort with physiologic concomitants such as shortness of breath, dizziness, palpitations, trembling, and sweating. Obsessive compulsive disorder is divided. As *DSM-IV* indicates, obsessions are considered as "recurrent and persistent thoughts, impulses, or images that are experienced as intrusive and inappropriate and that cause marked anxiety or distress and that the person attempts to ignore or suppress or to neutralize with other thought or action". Compulsions are defined as "repetitive behaviors (e.g., handwashing, ordering, checking) or mental acts (e.g., praying, counting, repeating words silently) that the person feels driven to perform that are aimed at preventing some dreaded event or situation". Generalized anxiety disorder involves unrealistic or excessive anxiety and worry about two or more areas of life, such as one's children's safety or one'sjob or health, for six months or longer, most days, with physiological signs of negative emotion.

PB Emotional State and the Anxiety Disorders

In introducing the concept of the emotional state in the preceding chapter, it was stated there are only two types of emotional response positive and negative. The different negative emotions commonly referred to such as anger, fear, hate are the same with respect to the emotional response itself. The distinctions among such emotions result from differences in the situational stimuli that are involved and in the behavior made to those stimuli. Thus, although a hated person and a feared person both elicit a negative emotional response, there are stimulus differences that elicit different behaviors.

The same thing is true of the emotional state. It can vary in intensity. And it can vary in constancy. And it can vary in direction positive, negative, or neutral. And the emotional state may be produced by stimuli that have different characteristics. For example, the stimuli may be explicit, as with the loss of a loved one. In contrast, the negative emotional responses elicited by one's own life situation or one's behavior may not be so explicit. Moreover, the negative emotional stimuli may be actual or portrayed in language (as in worry) and thus be "potential" or "threatening." For example, a downturn in the economy, an increased mortgage on a new house, an impending restructuring of the individual's employing company, and children who will soon need college tuitions are threatening events. It may turn out, however, that the individual retains her job, continues to have an income, does not have to pay for her childrens' college tuition. Nevertheless, the negative emotional responses can be experienced beforehand through language "anticipations" that produce an anxiety state.

And different circumstances can produce the negative emotional state; for example, it may result from losses of positive emotional stimuli, or the presentation of negative emotional stimuli. Since the emotional state is produced by multiple stimuli, there can be various combinations by which a negative state of a certain intensity can be reached. In one case moderate negative emotional stimuli and the paucity of positive emotional stimuli can produce a negative emotional state. In another case, the same level can be attained where the negative emotional responses are intense, but are counterbalanced to a some extent by strong positive emotional responses elicited by life circumstances. There may be differences in the effects of these states, even though their intensities are equal.

Frequently in life there are positive emotional stimuli mixed with negative emotional stimuli, actual and potential, where the outcome could be positive or negative. Take a career woman with a promotion pending, a new love and relationship that could go either way, the responsibility for the company party, a large project that may succeed or fail and add or subtract from her promotion chances, an upcoming city tennis tournament that will determine her state ranking, and the problem of resisting her parents' request that she move back in with them without alienating them. Worry about losing such strong positive emotional stimuli, and receiving the negative, can both contribute to an anxiety state. Such life stimuli, all calling for time and effort, may also elicit excessive activity, and too little sleep, and thereby add to the negative emotional responses. Moreover, the negative emotional stimuli such as work deadlines and competitions, social demands, and parental demands will elicit negative emotional responses that contribute directly to a negative emotional state. An emotional state produced by such circumstances, where activity remains high, will be labeled as anxiety (or stress). This anxious individual experiences an emotional state that is negative and includes pressure and tension along with sustained activity, which is different than the experience of depression.

Differing emotional states can result from the various arousing stimuli that can occur. We need additional evidence on the emotional states that people can experience. One implication would be to use the PB theory with which to construct an instrument to survey differences in the experience of people with disorders involving negative emotional states. And comparisons should also be made in the physiological symptoms that are displayed for example, by depressed, phobic, GAD, panic disorder, and obsessive compulsive patients (as well as those suffering from stress).

The PB theory is that the emotional state is a function of both the individual's BBRs and current life situation. Only some of the individuals subjected to the same pressurized life situation will experience an anxiety state. But there are also differences in the nature of the complex life situations faced.

Personality (the BBRs) and the Anxiety Disorders

This topic has been dealt with more deeply in the PB theory of the anxiety disorders, but the approach can be illustrated here.

The Emotional-Motivational BBR. The emotional-motivational BBR is defined by all of the stimuli that would elicit either a positive or negative emotional response in the individual. But there are individual differences in the balance that is learned. Thus, some individuals have an emotional motivational BBR that tilts them in the negative direction and others in a positive direction. Let me illustrate, with a mother who has a negative emotional response to many potential things such as dogs, being alone, contagious germs, illness, various failures, being different than others, not keeping up appearances, economic conditions, international tensions, parental censure, sibling competition, loss of sexual attractiveness and performance, loss of husband or his affection, infidelity, loss of friendships, planning trips and social affairs, as well as the uncertainties of children's health and school and social success, and on and on. The mother is concerned that her young child may get chilled, play with the rough boy down the street, eat junk food, get too tired, play too hard, be accosted by strangers, touch contaminated things, not behave properly in the presence of her husband's boss, and on and on.

A mother with such an emotional-motivational repertoire is likely to provide conditioning experience to her children that will produce the same type of emotional-motivational learning. The child need not experience anything unusual raised with an "anxious" parent the child will learn that the world contains many "fearful" stimuli. Other things being equal, an individual raised that way will experience more negative emotional responses and states than an individual raised without that conditioning. And, PB theory states the "anxious" individual will be vulnerable to acquiring an anxiety disorder. Research of a prospective-longitudinal and psychometric nature should be conducted in this context. This would involve constructing a test to measure children's negative emotional-motivational repertoire. Children then measured should be followed, to ascertain who develops an anxiety disorder, as a means of studying the contribution to vulnerability of having a negative emotional-motivational BBR.

The Language-Cognitive Repertoire. In the above example, much of the child's conditioning will be conducted through language. The mother who cautions the child about all the things she has a negative emotional response to will be conditioning the child to have a negative emotional response also to those things. Through language conditioning the child can become conditioned widely and easily, and imperceptibly. The mother who says things like, "I hope you pass the test," "I wonder whether enough of your friends will come to the party," "Dad is really late, I hope he didn't get in an accident," "The flu is going around so don't play touching games," is training her child to negative emotional responses, albeit in a way that will not be noticed.

Moreover, in this process the child will learn also word sequences (modes of thought) that are of a similar nature. For example, let us say that two students face an important test and one describes how little time she has to prepare, how she does not have the right background, how she does not learn or retain material in this field, how tough her competition is, how anxious she becomes in test situations, and how uncertain her performance is likely to be. Let us say the other student describes the same things in positive terms, and a third student does neither, simply going about the business of preparing for the examination. The upcoming test will elicit more anxiety in the first student, and much less in the second two. The important thing here is that these individual differences in language behavior are important in the development of the anxiety disorders. A person who has such a "negative" language-cognitive repertoire, and who employs it widely in response to life events, will experience a great deal of negative emotionality that may contribute to a continuous anxiety state, a basis for one of the anxiety disorders, when the actual events of her life are no different than they are for others who do not display negative language and do not suffer an anxiety disorder.

There are wide differences between people in their language-cognitive repertoires as involved when we describe someone as (1) overly conscientious, feeling anxiety unless they do things just right; (2) negative in outlook, especially about themselves; (3) a worrier who frequently anticipates negative occurrences; (4) believing that what they think is what will happen. These are descriptive of people with anxiety disorders. It is the present view that what we call vulnerability to development of an anxiety disorder involves the individual's personality repertoires, because these repertoires can set the individual up for development of a disorder. It should be possible to study such things prospectively. Thus, it should be the case that if we isolated a group of subjects who displayed a strong tendency to describe events including pending events in terms that elicit negative emotional responses, we would have a group that would display a greater frequency of development of an anxiety disorder than would a group of individuals who describe things neutrally or positively. We need such prospective research. But we must first define the language-cognitive repertoires that make the individual vulnerable to the development of clinical psychopathology.

A supportive PB account of worrying further develops the importance of the language-cognitive BBR in the development of an anxiety disorder.

Worry may be construed as distressing and pervasive thoughts, self-verbalizations, and rumination that are crystallized on domains of prime significance to the worriers. These domains include health, illness, family, financial, academic, environmental, religious, vocational, interpersonal situations, future catastrophes, and personal control-related issues .... Worrisome individuals tend to experience more trait anxiety, state anxiety, social anxiety, self-blame, low thrill seeking, low boredom susceptibility, depression, self-esteem problems, rumination, obsessional symptoms, unpleasant thoughts, public self-consciousness, negative daydreaming, cognitive intrusion, sleep problems, avoidance problems, wishful thinking, attention focusing problems, distractibility, hypervigilance, and health concerns.

Excessive worry is considered the prime symptom of generalized anxiety disorder. The majority of anxiety disorder patients spend 50% or more of a day worrying.

Many contemporary behavior therapy descriptions use a general cognitive behavioral theory-language. Worry is thus treated as an unanalyzed cognitive process. These clinical descriptions support the PB position; but PB provides the principles and concepts by which to treat what worry is and how people learn a "worrying" repertoire (part of the language-cognitive BBR) that produces anxiety.

The Sensory-Motor Repertoire and the Escape-Avoidance BBR. The experience the anxious mother provides the child not only produces negative emotional stimuli, but it also trains the child to be vigilant of the environment with respect to possibly harmful stimuli. Such vigilance may be considered a sensory-motor characteristic of an anxious person.

In addition, although glossed over in the *DSM* definitions, avoidance plays a prominent role, especially in some of the anxiety disorders. For example, escape behavior is central in obsessive–compulsive disorder (OCD). The individual may step on every line on the cement pavement, return again and again to check whether the door is locked, repeatedly wash hands or take showers, or avoid touching door handles by putting on gloves or using a handkerchief as a buffer. These behaviors provide escape from the negative emotional response that would be experienced if the behaviors did not occur. The phobic person, also, is characterized by escape-avoidance behavior with respect to the feared objects. The person with PTSD generally avoids situations that elicit anxiety. In the PB theory there is a sensory-motor personality characteristic that may be called the "escape and avoidance" BBR, which includes language-cognitive escape-avoidance behavior.

Simple phobics characteristically avoid representations of their phobic object or situation. Sometimes these representations may range far and wide across a number of generalization gradients, including images, thoughts, and objects that seem only remotely related to the original phobic object. By all reports the same can be said for PTSD.

Barlow does not analyze what representations are, how they are learned, and how they operate to produce anxiety. Moreover, the behaviorism he employs does not provide such analyses, nor the foundation principles and concepts necessary. Skinner's position does not provide a basic theory for understanding how language (thoughts and images) can produce anxiety, or how anxiety can affect behavior. Psychological behaviorism's basic theory of language provides the necessary principles and concepts.

For example, let us refer to Barlow's description and ask what is happening behaviorially. What are the "representations" that are avoided? In the PB framework representations are constituted of language behavior; for example, worry includes saying implicitly words that elicit negative emotional responses. And avoidance of negative-emotional language behavior constitutes a type of escape-avoidance behavior. The individual may thus occupy herself with alternate language behaviors to blot out the feared responses as in praying or counting silently. Language-cognitive escape-avoidance behaviors will be illustrated further in the context of the disorders described.

Generalized Anxiety: Basic in the Anxiety Disorders

The PB view is that generalized anxiety disorder (GAD) represents the basic anxiety disorder that all cases of clinically relevant anxiety disorders involve a person who generally experiences anxiety to a greater extent than is usual. The person diagnosed solely with the generalized anxiety disorder may not have developed specific phobias, panic disorder symptoms, obsessive compulsive behaviors, or the additional things involved in PTSD. Thus, the other disorders involve elements in addition to those of GAD.

Phobic Disorder

The general anxiety disorder (GAD) may not reach clinical proportions with the person diagnosed as phobic, but this person has a more than usual level of anxiety. Such a person is vulnerable to developing stronger than usual negative emotions to specific things. For example, the individual may be uneasy about flying, in which case, reading about air crashes can provide additional negative language conditioning of emotional responses. The individual may image crashes, worry about what would happen to children, spouse, and career if killed in a crash, and such, all of which will produce additional conditioning. Once this occurs to the level that the individual avoids flying, the phobia becomes more intractable. Additional negative emotional responses are elicited by others pressing one to fly, by being thought of as odd, and such. And the individual's avoidance behavior prevents the individual becoming accustomed (extinguishing negative emotions and learning positive emotions) to flying.

Panic Disorder

The person who develops panic attacks is an anxious person also. The panic attack seems to occur without stimulus elicitation, because the stimuli are largely self-produced and not obvious. To illustrate this, let us use the case of nocturnal panic states. The anxious individual awakens from sleep experiencing a negative emotional response with physiological stimuli (such as a pounding heart and rapid breathing), perhaps a concomitant of dreaming. But what occurs then is that the physiological stimuli themselves elicit a fear response. Let us say the individual worries, "God, am I going to have a stroke?" This maintains and increases the negative emotional responding and the physiological stimuli. This then leads to further ominous descriptions. This compounding can quickly build to the panic state. We can see this in clinical descriptions, for example, "a patient may become alarmed by a decreasing heart rate that occurs during relaxation a cue to which the panic-prone patient is very sensitive, and which may therefore trigger a panic attack. Similarly, a sleeping individual may be oblivious to his or her environment, but may remain attuned to personally significant stimuli". Among panic-disorder individuals the "symptoms reported with the greatest frequency were strong, rapid, or irregular heartbeat; shortness of breath; hot and cold flashes; choking or smothering sensations; trembling; and fear of dying".

Besides the general anxiety these individuals also have specific fears concerning health, are vigilant concerning body sensations and states, and have learned a negative emotional language-cognitive BBR concerning such matters. The occurrence of physiological sensations then triggers the compounding interaction of these various repertoires. Such attacks increase the individual's fear responses generally to health, the individual's self-concept becomes more negative, and the individual becomes a more anxious person, in a vicious cycle development.

Obsessive-Compulsive Disorder

With these descriptions in hand it is possible to deal with obsessive – compulsive disorder (OCD). To begin, in the PB view the terms obsession and compulsion are not clearly used. Let us ask first, thus, what is it that allows us to differentiate obsessions and compulsions and to see their commonalities as well? To begin the clarification, the obsession occurs and the individual struggles to replace it. However, the compulsion occurs before the feared event, thus postponing that event. There is an analogy to be found in animal studies. A negative reinforcer can be applied in different ways to affect learning. Let us say that two animals separately receive experience in which the floor of an operant apparatus is electrified to deliver a sustained shock until a bar is pressed. In one case, let us say, the shock is turned on again after a systematically varied period, until the animal again presses the bar and this is repeated. The animal will be conditioned to press the bar. In the other case, however, let us say the animal learns to press the bar this way, but with an additional contingency. Every time the animal presses the bar this has the effect of lengthening the period slated before the next delivery of shock. Under the first, *escape,* condition, the animal will learn to press the bar as soon as the shock comes on. That is like the obsession. The shock is the feared cognition. In the second, *avoidance,* condition, the animal will learn frequently and continuously to press the bar so that the shock is not experienced. This is like a compulsion.

When analyzing the behaviors involved other aspects are clarified. Actually, both obsessions and compulsions involve feared stimuli, and in both cases those stimuli are self-produced. The individual who is compulsive originally had an image of an unlocked house, or a thought of contamination, as examples. To exemplify an obsession, let us take a mother who has a repetitive image of doing harm to her children. There is no difference, in principle, with respect to the type of stimulus. Obsessive stimuli and compulsive stimuli elicit a negative emotional response.

Typically, however, there is a difference on the escape response end. With obsessions the *escape* behavior is of a language-cognitive type. The mother with an image of throwing her infant out of a window struggles to replace that image with one of caring for the infant or some other response that removes the negative emotional image. However, the *avoidance* behavior in the compulsion is of the sensory-motor variety. The individual originally afraid of the unlocked house returns to the house; the individual who is afraid of disease and dirt must wash her hands.

The behaviors involved in compulsions and obsessions are exhausting, and self-demeaning in their "craziness," bringing on additional negative emotions and increasing the anxiety state. They are non-effective, for they do not get at correcting the problem, which is that of the generalized anxiety the person suffers from her BBRs and life situation. "If one evaluates a patient with unbearably severe generalized anxiety, recurrent panic attacks, debilitating avoidance, and major depression all occurring simultaneously, the diagnosis is probably OCD. For OCD is the devastating culmination of the most intense manifestations of emotional disorders".

In the present conception, what this means is that the OCD patient has learned the inappropriately negative emotional-motivational BBR, the negative emotion-producing language-cognitive BBR, and the escape-and avoidance BBR in full measure. In addition, the OCD patient has developed all the symptomatology that can result from such BBRs – the phobias, GAD, and panic attacks. Centrally, what is involved is a cumulative-hierarchical learning process where the individual learns ways of avoiding phobic objects. But these behaviors in their unreality and ineffectiveness simply produce more negative emotional stimulation, that is, a heightened general anxiety state. That development then yields panic disorders, which increase the individual's fear of what is happening and her inability to cope. Effects on the social environment loss of status and confidence in the disordered individual bring increased anxiety. Fearful thoughts begin and the patient struggles desperately to escape and avoid them, and thereby also to regain her control and confidence in herself. What is involved is a cumulative- hierarchical learning process.

With respect to OCD it is interesting in this context to note that groups have developed general and stylized language-cognitive behaviors for avoiding anxiety-producing stimuli. For example, meditation devices, like the repetition of a mantra, can function as a type of escape mechanism, preventing the individual from verbal and imaginal responses that would elicit negative emotional responses. The individual can remove anxiety producing sexual, violence, or failure images by this means. Various religious rituals have that same function, such as prayer that may be practiced to a furious intensity in order to avoid thinking about other, sinful things. Thus, the avoidance is accomplished by having other behaviors occur that are incompatible and that prevent the negative cognitions from occurring. The added "appeal" of such avoidance behaviors is that they are "group validated," not "crazy," and thus do not themselves elicit anxiety. Are there general "skills" involved in being an avoider of anxiety-producing cognitions? Do those with anxiety disorders have richly developed escape avoidance BBRs including language repertoires? Are such repertoires "causes" in the anxiety disorders? Psychological behaviorism answers yes, but the questions call for research.

Post-Traumatic Stress Disorder (PTSD)

With this disorder there is a specific experience that seems to precipitate the disorder, such as a dreadful war experience, or sexual or violent assault. In PTSD the individual may experience various symptoms, such as disturbed sleep, reliving the experience, phobic responses to stimuli like those in the original experience, as well as general life disturbance (such as job, marital, and social instability).

Ordinarily the focus of interest with respect to PTSD is the traumatic experience. In the PB view, however, longstanding PTSD cases constitute a complex disorder involving deficit BBRs and inappropriate BBRs (such as generalized anxiety and a well-developed escape-avoidance BBR) and a cumulative-hierarchical learning development. Thus, a war veteran with such problems may return and exhibit problems in work and family relations. For example, the individual may experience anxiety in work situations that are challenging, and engage in various avoidance behaviors to those work situations. The failure that results may then be blamed on the original trauma. The blaming is a form of escape from anxiety. Experiencing anxiety to work situations is a general problem that will impact centrally on the individual if he is reduced to seeking unchallenging jobs that elicit a negative emotional response for that reason. When the individual's life failures elicit a negative emotional state, drinking, which reduces that state, may then enter as an additional problem. These various escape-avoidance behaviors that do not deal with the problem and that thus exacerbate life's problems are central in chronic PTSD. It should be remembered that most people who experience traumatic events do not develop PTSD, so the trauma alone is not the cause. A more complete analysis of this disorder is presented in PB.

Current Life Situation and Stress

It has been recognized generally that environmental losses are involved in many cases of depression. And the life situation is important in the consideration of the anxiety disorders. For example, in the case of PTSD, environmental events loom as an important cause, but current life events should be more the focus of attention than they are. In general, how various life situations (sometimes self-caused) can produce an anxiety state in the individual need to be systematically considered and studied.

Interestingly there is another problem area in psychology that has been concerned with anxiety- or dysphoria-producing environmental circumstances. Called *stress* or *stress management*, the tradition of the field is separate from the study of depression and the anxiety disorders in abnormal psychology. More than with depression and the anxiety disorders, the study of stress arose within a conceptual framework concerned with how certain environmental situations can produce medical problems such as hypertension. It is typical of psychology that these very closely related types of phenomena depression, anxiety disorders, and stress-psychosomatic problems are generally studied and considered separately.

The incongruity of this separation can be seen from the fact that the same types of environmental events are considered in the three areas. As an example, let us take the Social Readjustment Rating Scale which was composed to measure the stress amount of readjustment that life events cause. The most stressful events included are death of spouse, divorce, marital separation, death of a close family member, personal injury or illness, marriage, being fired at work, marital reconciliation, retirement, change in the health of a family member, pregnancy, sex difficulties, gain of a new family member, business readjustment, change in financial state, death of a close friend, change to a different line of work, change in number of arguments with spouse, mortgage of $10,000 or more, foreclosure of a mortgage or loan, change in responsibilities at home. Others listed are trouble with in-laws, wife begins or stops work, beginning or ending of school, trouble with boss, change in residence, schools, or social activities. The important point is that most of those events can also be inducers of *depression* and *anxiety*.

The PB position is that the different problem areas should be studied in an interrelated manner. There are various stressing environmental events. The field of stress needs to study them, along with the physiological symptoms that result from them. But they need also to be studied in a broader context. Are stressful environmental events different for depressed people, psychosomatic people, and for those with an anxiety disorder? For example, there are cataclysmic events like the death of a loved one and there are longstanding, day-to-day events like a pressurized, anxiety-producing, threatening work situation. Does the first type of event tend to elicit depression and the second either an anxiety disorder or psychosomatic illness? Are environmental events different for those with different anxiety disorders ? Or are the differences with respect to disorder primarily a function of the individuals' personality (BBRs)? These questions call for systematic consideration and study.

Unified PB Analysis and DSM Classification

The traditional taxonomies of the behavior disorders began with the idea that there are discrete *mental diseases* with symptomatologies that lend themselves to classification, as indicated in the *DSM* series title. Freud's psychoanalytic theory was the basis for attempts to construct a general, unified theory of abnormal behavior. For a time this approach had a general influence, which has diminished in the past few decades. Moreover, the concept of mental disease has not been supported by evidence. With the weakening of such conceptual foundations, the field has become more descriptive, less conceptual and explanatory, lacking interest in analyzing the various disorders within a unified theory. This trend is continued in *DSM-IV*. The grouping of disorders into classes is done on the basis of symptom commonality. The assumed but undeveloped explanatory conception is biologically oriented, with a recognition that the environment can play a role in at least some disorders.

But having an explicit, unified set of principles and concepts that is explanatory is an obvious advantage in understanding phenomena in any science. Analyzing a wide range of behavior disorders within such a unified set of principles and concepts is central in the PB theory of abnormal behavior. One advantage is that of indicating the relationship among the various disorders. As an example, let us take the *DSM-IV* developmental disorders, including the subclassifications of mental retardation, pervasive developmental disorders (autism), and the specific learning disorders (such as reading, writing, and arithmetic disorder). The *DSM-IV* is only descriptive; as a consequence the several disorders appear to be independent and unrelated, with a suggestion of separate brain defects.

Within PB's explanatory theory, however, the relationships of the several disorders can be seen. Centrally, the basic framework is that child development involves the cumulative-hierarchical learning of the BBRs (personality). The various behavior disorders involve problems in that cumulative-hierarchical learning. Where and when the problems arise in that learning is important. In terms of time, for example, the circumstances are very similar for mental retardation and autism. The problems of learning begin early and for this reason are more pervasive. Nevertheless, in *DSM-IV*, Mental Retardation constitutes a different classification category than the Pervasive Develop-mental Disorders such as Autistic Disorder. The fact is, there is important overlap in terms of the central deficits that occur in the two disorders. For example, in severe cases in both, the learning process begins to go awry in the first years in such central areas as language development (learning). Language constitutes a very central BBR for the child's later learning. The deficit in language development brings to a halt much of the child's general cumulative-hierarchical learning, setting the stage for developing further problems of learning in both disorders.

Thus, the deficits may be similar with respect to the language-cognitive and sensory-motor BBRs. What is the difference between the mentally retarded and the autistic child? These children differ in such things as learning of the emotional-motivational repertoire. The mentally retarded child may have language-cognitive deficits that are as severe as those of the autistic child, but nevertheless may learn a positive emotional response to the parents, along with sensory-motor behaviors of seeking and giving affection. That difference can help establish the differential diagnosis, as in the lack of approach behaviors to parents displayed by the autistic child but not the retarded child. The two disorders also differ greatly in their anti-learning repertories. The retarded child can escape learning situations by "acting dumb." The autistic child can learn bizarre behaviors to escape from the training periods the well-intentioned parent attempts to give the child. On the other hand, bizarre troublesome behavior, when there is pressure to learn, leads to unpleasant parent child interactions. For example, when extremely inappropriate behaviors require physical restraint these encounters produce mutually unpleasant experiences. Love is learned, and when the learning experiences are deficit on the positive side and full on the negative side, the balance can be negative. Although a mentally retarded and an autistic child have the same IQ (language-cognitive BBR development) deficits, they typically differ in their emotional-motivational repertoires (to parents and hence others), and in their anti-learning sensory-motor repertoires. The *unified* analysis helps in understanding both disorders, as well as their relationship to each other.

Specific developmental disorders, like reading, writing, and arithmetic disorders, in contrast to the other two disorders, occur at a *later* point in the child's development. The child prior to the development of the disorder may have acquired normal language-cognitive, sensory-motor, and emotional-motivational BBRs. The child's abnormal development may not begin to occur until the child enters school. Starting at a later time in the cumulative-hierarchical learning process the effects on the BBRs are less severe and general than in mental retardation or autism. However, the cumulative-hierarchical learning of language-cognitive academic BBRs may be specifically or generally stopped or hindered at the point the disorder appears. And that may set the cumulative-hierarchical-learning foundation for the other abnormal developments, such as school phobia and child, adolescent, and finally adult antisocial behavior disorder. The important point here is that the learning disorders are to be considered in a related manner to each other and to mental retardation and autism, within the same set of principles and concepts.

The PB theory also provides a means of relating depression, stress-related problems, and the anxiety disorders, including an ordering of the severity of the latter. The same principles apply, and there is overlap in causative variables, the involvement of the three BBRs, and the role of the negative emotional state. There are also differences among the different disorders, especially in the escape-avoidance behaviors that have been learned as a means of reducing immediately experienced negative emotion. It can be expected that important heuristic developments will arise from consideration of the behavior disorders within a general unified theory.

Summary

The knowledge of abnormal psychology the observations of the behavior of clinical patients has been organized into taxonomies of the behavior disorders. These naturalistic observations have not been established via experimental analysis of behavior technology, or even other behavioral methods, and are not accepted in radical behaviorism. In PB the knowledge of the traditional field of abnormal psychology is considered valuable. The PB methodological philosophy, however, holds that the naturalistic observations made in abnormal psychology can only be made *behaviorally* valuable by means of multilevel theory construction, elaborating concepts and principles from the basic laboratory principles in a step-by-step manner until a theory is created that can make the naturalistic observations understandable in objective, empirical, heuristic terms. This chapter shows how a theory of abnormal behavior, and theories of the individual behavior disorders, can be linked to and derived from the multilevel theory-construction program of PB, validating its concepts and principles.

Central in this development is the theory of abnormal behavior presented at the beginning of the chapter. First, as Figure 5.1 indicates, the field of abnormal psychology must systematically research the learning that produces abnormal behavior. But, although it is generally acknowledged that learning plays a role in various behavior disorders, there has been no study of such learning. To know how learning operates demands that it be observed, in a detailed manner, over the cumulative-hierarchical periods involved, which means long years. Such research would be difficult and costly, but until we conduct that study we cannot know the importance learning has in the production of the behavior disorders. That this is not understood is very revealing.

Moreover, according to the PB abnormal psychology, the theory of personality plays the crucial role. For a theory of abnormal behavior must rest on stipulating the BBRs (personality) that typically are the proximal causes of the behavior disorders. The descriptions of abnormal behavior (as in *DSM-IV*) yield some knowledge of the BBRs. But it should be remembered that those descriptions are of behavior. While those behaviors are in the individual's BBRs, they are but a sample; other aspects of the abnormal BBRs will not be revealed by observing behavior. Take reading disorder, as an example, where the *DSM-IV* focuses on the absence of reading. That description, however, does not indicate what the reading BBR is hence what the disorder involves, the learning problems that produce the disorder, or how to treat the disorder. Reading disorder is a personality disorder, and a theory of that disorder demands a personality theory that specifies the reading BBR and how it is or is not learned. More generally, abnormal psychology must have access to a personality theory that stipulates the normal personality repertoires. The abnormal psychology then must work out what has gone wrong that has produced abnormal personality repertoires. This position, again, calls for new directions of research development.

The PB position also calls for new consideration of the abnormal behaviors that are important in classifying the disorders and in diagnosing individuals. In addition to pure description, we need systematic study of the *effects* of abnormal behaviors in the *explanation* of the disorders. For the PB theory of personality is an interactional theory it recognizes that abnormal behavior produces conditions that have causative effects. Sometimes the behavior has effects on others that exacerbate the problem as in the case of the behavior of the depressed person that produces criticisms in family members that have the effect of deepening the person's depression. Sometimes the behavior has effects on the person herself as in compounding where the depressed person's self-condemnatory language behavior elicits negative emotional responses that add to the person's negative emotional state. We need general and systematic research to study how abnormal behavior has a causative effect in the behavior disorders.

And, finally, we need study of the current life situations that exert causative effects in the production and maintenance of behavior disorders. This need has been recognized as in the study of stress but we need systematic and profound study. There has not been a general and unified theory of abnormal behavior since the psychoanalytic attempt. The PB analysis of abnormal behavior and the behavior disorders produces a unified theory. It is suggested that this theory should be used and further developed as the framework for specialized theories of the behavior disorders that have not yet been treated, or those only dealt with incipiently. Moreover, the theory suggests various new directions for empirical development.

6

Features of Obsessive Compulsive Disorder

Introduction

Compulsions refer to repetitive behaviors, such as hand washing, checking, or ordering, or mental acts, such as counting, that the individual feels driven to perform according to specific rules and that are intended to prevent or reduce distress or some dreaded event.

In DSM-IV, obsessive compulsive disorder is defined as obsessions or compulsions that cause marked distress and last more than one hour per day or significantly impair functioning. The specifier "with poor insight" refers to patients who for most of the time do not recognize that their obsessions and compulsions are unreasonable. This specifier was added in part due to a DSM-IV field trial that identified a broad range of insight among 431 obsessive compulsive patients: 13% were certain that their feared consequence (e.g., causing harm to others) would not occur, 27% were mostly certain, 30% were uncertain, 26% were mostly certain that it would occur, and 4% were completely certain that it would occur. Earlier, instances of lack of insight were coined *overvalued ideation,* or "almost unshakable beliefs, which can be acknowledged as potentially unfounded only after considerable discussion". These differ from delusions, which are more firmly held and even less shakable. Initially, the presence of overvalued ideation was thought to predict poor treatment outcome, although recent research suggests otherwise.

Among clinical samples, obsessions most commonly concern fears of contamination, harming oneself or others, and lack of symmetry. A small group of patients are concerned with somatic, religious, or sexual themes and unacceptable urges, such as shouting obscenities in public. The most common compulsive behaviors are checking and cleaning or washing. A smaller number of patients engage in repetitive mental rituals, such as counting, ordering, hoarding, or collecting. In the DSM-IV field trial, patients typically experienced both obsessions and compulsions (91%) only a minority experienced primarily obsessions or primarily compulsions (8.5% and 1.%, respectively). Others report higher estimates for obsessions primarily, especially among community samples. However, these epidemiological estimates vary widely and may not be reliable.

Obsessive compulsive disorder is most likely to begin at 12 to 14 years or 20 to 22 years of age, although a later age of onset (30s) is suggested by epidemiologists. The disorder tends to be chronic. For example, 43 to 68% of adolescents still meet diagnostic criteria 2 to 7 and 9 to 14 years after treatment. Gender tends to be more equally distributed than for most anxiety disorders, although females are slightly more at risk.

The Epidemiological Catchment Area Study reported lifetime prevalence rates of 1.9 to 3.3% (without exclusionary criteria). These estimates were considerably higher than previously thought. Rates tend to be consistent across countries, with the exception of Taiwan, where rates are lower. Obsessive compulsive disorder is relatively common among adolescents as well, for whom estimates range from 0.7% to 4%. Obsessive compulsive disorder is highly comorbid with other syndromes, particularly mood disorders, social phobia, and substance abuse or dependence. In fact, lifetime prevalence rates for major depression or dysthymia among patients with obsessive compulsive disorder range from 30 to 67%, and corresponding figures for comorbid anxiety disorders are 40 to 86%. Links with depression were noted in a rare longitudinal study in which 18-year olds with obsessive compulsive disorder did not differ from age-matched healthy controls or mixed anxiety disorder individuals in neuropsychological performance at age 13 or temper tantrums, nail biting, thumb sucking, stuttering, stammering, worries, or fearfulness at ages 7, 9, and 11. However, they had more depression at those ages than either of the comparison groups. Naturalistic observations also indicate that obsessions worsen during depressed mood states. Rachman suggests that depression may be one pathway through which obsessive compulsive disorder develops, because negative affect elevates the significance of intrusive thoughts. That is, the causal effects of depression are possibly mediated by appraisals of intrusive thoughts. The notion of "appraisals of intrusive thoughts" is described in more detail below.

The connection between obsessive compulsive disorder and personality traits, obsessive compulsive traits in particular, is not clear. Obsessive compulsive personality refers to "preoccupation with orderliness, perfectionism, and mental and interpersonal control, at the expense of flexibility, openness, and efficiency". Most clinical studies fail to find a specific comorbidity between obsessive compulsive disorder and obsessive compulsive personality, although obsessive compulsive patients tend to present with at least one personality disorder. Two recent studies, however, find the expected relationship. That is, after partialling out the effects of anxiety and depression, the only personality trait with which nonclinical obsessive and compulsive features were correlated was obsessive compulsive personality. Tallis, Rosen and Shafran repeated this analytical approach with a clinical sample of 77 obsessive compulsive patients to find essentially the same results. That is, after controlling for the effects of anxiety and depression, obsessive compulsive symptoms correlated with obsessive compulsive and passive-aggressive personality traits. Thus, they suggest that previous clinical studies did not find connections with obsessive compulsive personality traits because of failure to control the effects of anxiety and depression. On the other hand, correlations in their new study were strongest between obsessive compulsive personality traits and the doubting subscale of the Maudsely Obsessive-Compulsive Inventory. The authors themselves acknowledge that the latter may be more of a trait than a symptom measure. Thus, further research is needed of comorbidity with personality traits. As with all anxiety disorders, relations with personality disorders are confounded by poor measures.

Several posit a connection between obsessive compulsive disorder and trichotillomania, or repetitive hair pulling, given the overlap in the repetitive nature of the syndromes and some evidence to suggest that they respond to the same types of medications. However, recent empirical data do not support this contention. For example, Stanley, Swann, Bowers, Davis and Taylor reported substantial differences between small groups of these patients. Patients with trichotillomania reported a sense of pleasure during their repetitive behavior, in contrast to the anxiety experienced by obsessive compulsive patients. Also, the former group reported less interference from and resistance to their symptoms. Furthermore, trichotillomania patients reported lower levels of anxiety and depression than obsessive compulsive patients and had an earlier age of onset. Himle, Bordnick, and Thyer reported similar discrepancies. Tourette's is another syndrome associated with obsessions and compulsions. Tourette's syndrome is characterized by motor and phonic tics. Rates of Tourette's syndrome increase among relatives of probands with obsessive compulsive disorder. Furthermore, the same neurobiological pathways are implicated in each disorder. However, the exact nature of the relationship is unclear.

Since the seminal work by Rachman and colleagues in the late 1970s and early 1980s, numerous studies have documented nonclinical obsessions and compulsions. Subclinical obsessive compulsive disorder, defined as in the absence of significant impairment, is generally found at a higher rate than clinical obsessive compulsive disorder and can be as high as 19%. Particular obsessive compulsive features are very common in the general population. For example, as many as 80 to 90% of community samples experience intrusive thoughts at some time.

The sudden intrusion of unwanted or unwillful thoughts, images, or impulses is a frequent and natural occurrence within our stream of consciousness. In fact at times we seem almost helpless in our efforts to consciously control the content or direction of our thoughts as evidenced by the unwanted intrusion of a variety of mental events from a mundane tune or rhyme to a negative, possibly even disgusting or abhorrent thought or image. This intrusive quality of cognition may be a particularly adaptive aspect of human nature when it involves the spontaneous occurrence of positive cognitions associated with creativity, inspiration, problem solving, and relief from boredom leading to increased motivation for productive work and social interaction.

Also, 55% of the community exhibit some ritualistic behavior and 10 to 27% of the total exhibit significant compulsive behavior. Conservative criteria, however, generally yield lower estimates for nonclinical populations. Burns, Formea, Keortge, and Sternberger note that 20 to 40% of those who initially score high on a measure of obsessiveness or compulsiveness are no longer classified in the high-scoring group at a second evaluation. Hence, in contrast to 10 to 27%, only 4% of 1,877 university students scored within a certain cutoff range for checking behaviors on two separate assessment occasions. Nevertheless, "nonclinical" obsessions and compulsions are clearly common, if not always stable.

Consequently, a continuum may extend from nonclinical to clinical obsessions and compulsions. In support, familial data and patterns of comorbidity in nonclinical samples tend to parallel those found in clinical samples. Also, although subclinical obsessive compulsive features most often do not progress to a clinical level, a higher (albeit slight) percentage of those with subclinical obsessive compulsive features progress to obsessive compulsive disorder in comparison to a group without obsessive compulsive features (e.g., 1.5% versus 0%). In addition, the content of obsessions does not differ between clinical and nonclinical samples. For example, mental health professionals were unable to distinguish obsessions from clinical versus nonclinical samples. On the other hand, clinical obsessions occur more frequently, are more intense and discomforting, are more difficult to dismiss, and are more strongly resisted.

A similar pattern occurs in the comparison between nonclinical and clinical compulsions. Muris found that obsessive compulsive patients engage more frequently in washing, cleaning, and ordering whereas normals engage in more magical protective behaviors. Nevertheless, there was a close correspondence between the content of compulsions across the two groups. As with obsessional thoughts, compulsions in patient samples were associated with more discomfort and resistance and were more often associated with negative thoughts and negative mood than were compulsive behaviors in nonclinical samples.

Intrusive thoughts are more likely under conditions of stress, such as in mothers whose children are about to undergo surgery. They subside relatively quickly as stress dissipates. Those whose intrusive thoughts do not dissipate, but instead become more frequent and distressing (i.e., develop into obsessive compulsive disorder), may react more negatively to their intrusions. The range of reactions to intrusive thoughts is documented by Freeston, Ladouceur, Thibodeau and Gagnon, who found that the most common responses to intrusions among a university sample were "no effortful response" or self-reassurance (26%), attentively thinking about the thought or seeking reassurance from others (34%), and escape/avoidance (40%) the latter referred to attempts to replace the thought with another thought, become distracted by other activities, or say "Stop." Overall, those who employed the latter two strategies were more anxious and reported more difficulty removing the intrusions. Also, the latter strategy was associated with more sadness, worry, guilt, and disapproval in comparison to the "no effortful response" strategy. Furthermore, obsessive compulsive patients react to their intrusive thoughts with more punishment (e.g., "I get angry at myself for having the thought") and worry (e.g., "I dwell on other worries") than controls. Thus, the development from nonclinical to clinical states may be mediated by negative reactions to intrusive thoughts and repetitive behaviors. This possibility is described in more detail below.

Theoretical and Empirical Developments

Autonomic activity is elevated when patients confront their obsessive compulsive stimuli, such as contaminated objects. Some suggest that obsessive compulsive patients are generally hyperaroused and therefore less able to dismiss intrusive thoughts. If so, as Hoehn-Saric, McLeod, and Hipsley note, they should be more autonomically aroused in general and respond more strongly to nonspecific stressors. However, despite earlier positive findings, later studies failed to support this contention. For example, Hollander found no evidence for elevated noradrenergic functioning in general, and Chappell failed to find differences in levels of corticotropin releasing factor, taken from cerebrospinal fluid from lumbar punctures, between patients with obsessive compulsive disorder versus healthy controls. Similarly, Zahn found no heart rate or skin conductance differences under resting and nonspecific stress conditions (innocuous tones and a reaction time task) in 55 youths with obsessive compulsive disorder compared to 58 controls. They conclude that autonomic elevations may be restricted to occasions when feared stimuli are present, as is the case for specific phobias.

In fact, there is even evidence that individuals with obsessive compulsive disorder are less autonomically reactive to nonspecific stressors than controls. Hoehn-Saric compared 23 individuals with obsessive compulsive disorder and no other Axis I disorders except generalized anxiety or simple phobia to 21 noripsychiatric controls. The obsessive compulsive group did not differ from controls at baseline and had *smaller* changes in interbeat interval, skin conductance, and muscle tension than controls in response to mild stressors. Similar findings occur with panic disorder and generalized anxiety. Thus, rather than peripheral hyperarousal, these patients show physiological inflexibility, which may be "the consequence of diminished attention or the lack of emotional involvement in tasks that are unrelated to a person's disease".

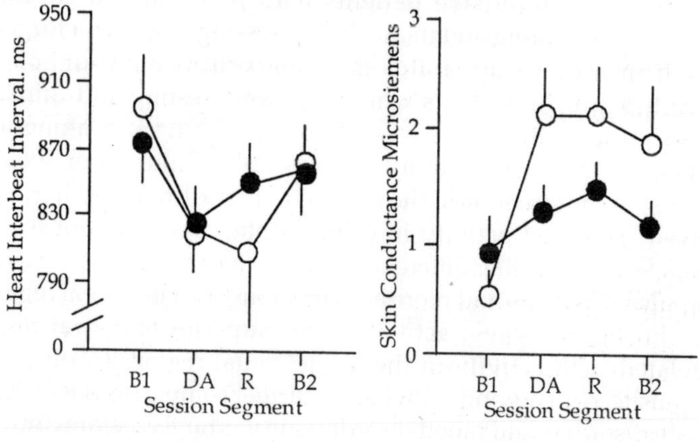

Fig. 6.1. Autonomic measures among patients with obsessive compulsive disorder versus healthy controls during standardized laboratory stressors (Bl=initial baseline, DA=Divided Attention Task, R=Risk-Taking Task, B2=second baseline).

A growing body of evidence from neuroimaging studies shows that certain sections of the brain are associated with obsessive compulsive disorder. The most consistent findings are increased glucose metabolism or other indices of activation in the orbitofrontal cortex and caudate nuclei, which are normalized with successful pharmacological or behavioral treatments. The orbitofrontal cortex, cingulate cortex, and caudate nuclei are part of a circuit that includes the thalamus, which may be involved in regulation of emotional concerns and repetitive thoughts and behaviors. Baxter suggested that the caudate nucleus is underactive in obsessive compulsive disorder, so that thoughts, sensations, and actions generated by the orbitofrontal cortex are not suppressed. A "pass through" of orbital cortical inputs to the globus, pallidus and thalamus may then occur, and increased thalamic input to the orbital cortex results in an abnormal, self-reinforcing circuit. In accord, Robinson found evidence for smaller volumes of the caudate nucleus in 26 obsessive compulsive patients compared to 26 healthy controls, although volume did not correlate with the duration or severity of obsessive compulsive disorder. On the other hand, the fact that others find no such differences raises concerns about methodological artifacts for studies to date. Furthermore, it is not yet clear whether these neurobiological dysregulations (if reliable) are specific to obsessive compulsive disorder. For example, Cottraux compared PET scans of 10 obsessive compulsive patients with predominant checking features while resting and then while obsessing (e.g., "You forget to turn off an electrical apparatus and while you are out your home is set on fire") to 10 normals while they were resting and thinking about normal obsessions (e.g., "You are going out alone and inadvertently you may bully older people, children, or weaker persons on the street or in the crowd"). Interestingly, both groups showed increased activity in orbitofrontal areas with obsessive stimulation. Some other differences were noted: During rest, obsessive compulsive patients had more activity in superior temporal regions, and, during obsessing, activity in the superior temporal region correlated with activity in the orbitofrontal region for obsessive compulsive patients only. Obviously, further comparisons with other anxiety disorders and mood disorders are warranted before drawing strong conclusions about neurobiological pathways of obsessive compulsive disorder. It is also noteworthy that purely biological models are unable to account for the restriction of obsessive compulsive behaviors to specific classes of stimuli. As noted by Rachman (in press), obsessions of causing harm to others always target the helpless the elderly, disabled, and young whereas "there are no Arnold Schwartzenegger obsessions." That is, the fact that there are many stimuli about which patients do not obsess suggests that deficits in cognitive processing, if they do exist, must interact with learning and psychological factors.

Psychosocial Functioning

There is some evidence that parents of nonclinical obsessive compulsive individuals are overprotective. On the other hand, Rheaume, Freeston, Dugas, Letarte, and Ladouceur did not find a relationship between obsessive compulsive features among nonclinical participants and a rating of parental expectations and criticism. Furthermore, in contrast to patients with panic disorder, patients with obsessive compulsive disorder did not score higher than controls on a measure of parental criticism. Thus, in addition to difficulties encountered in retrospective research of this nature, the strength of the relationship and the specificity of the effects to obsessive compulsive disorder are highly questionable. That being said, parental transmission of values and morals may predispose toward catastrophic appraisals of intrusive thoughts.

Learning Theory

Mineka and Zinbarg review animal models of relevance to obsessive compulsive disorder, the major ones of which are summarized here. First, similarities have long been noted between overly trained avoidant responses, which become stereotyped and highly resistant to extinction, and obsessive compulsive disorder. Second, repeated frustration, via insoluble discrimination problems or high stress, for example, produces compulsive ritualistic-like behavior in animals. For example, displacement behaviors in reaction to high arousal or conflict include highly stereotyped behavior, such as grooming and nesting. Displacement behaviors have been hypothesized to give animals time to adjust and make decisions about whether to flee or fight. The parallel is drawn with compulsive behaviors that are brought on by discomforting obsessive thoughts in humans, the latter representing high arousal and conflict.

Ethological models view obsessive compulsive disorder as an inappropriate expression of a complex, fixed action pattern in response to key releasing stimuli. A fixed action pattern refers to innate and adaptive behavioral sequences to specific stimuli, such as acral licking in dogs and compulsive feather picking in birds. Once initiated, a fixed action pattern continues to completion. Individual organisms differ in their responsivity to releasing stimuli, and learning history influences which stimuli are releasers. Fixed action patterns are broader than displacement behaviors because they are not dependent on high arousal or conflict. Also, they have been connected with orbitofrontal and basal ganglia circuits, which, as described previously, may be associated with obsessive compulsive disorder. On the other hand, fixed action patterns fit less well with the usual emotional distress that triggers compulsions in humans, and researchers have not been able to identify the key releasing stimuli for such action patterns. Furthermore, compulsive rituals are not quite as fixed as fixed action patterns.

From the standpoint of preparedness theory, Seligman proposed that rituals of washing' and checking once promoted survival and reproduction and subsequently became genetically coded in the form of prepared learning mechanisms that can be easily triggered. Thus, humans may be biologically prepared to obsess or ruminate about certain stimuli that posed threat to our early ancestors and to perform certain kinds of responses to reduce such distress. In agreement, de Silva, Rachman, and Seligman noted that obsessive compulsive content and behaviors fall predominantly in the range of prepared stimuli.

Finally, much early behavioral theorizing relied on Mowrer's two-process theory of avoidance learning obsessive thoughts elicit anxiety and therefore motivate performance of behavior that becomes a compulsive ritual, which is reinforced and strengthened by its anxiety-reducing effects. Mineka and Zinbarg argue that instrumental anxiety reduction is more relevant to the maintenance than the etiology of obsessive compulsive disorder because there is little evidence of a traumatic conditioning history. However, intense fear due to an unexpected, horrific intrusive thought or image may be viewed as traumatic, in the same way that an unexpected panic attack represents a traumatic conditioning onset for panic disorder.

Cognitive Deficits. The role of cognitive processing in obsessive compulsive disorder has gained much interest of late. As with all anxiety disorders, obsessive compulsive patients tend to allocate more attentional resources toward words that represent their fears, as shown via dichotic listening tasks and inferred from modified Stroop tasks. Dot probe detection tasks show similar patterns. For example, Tata, Leibowitz, Prunty, Cameron, and Pickering compared 13 obsessive compulsive patients, 18 high trait anxious individuals, and 26 low anxious individuals on dot probe detection tasks, to examine attentional effects caused by contamination words (e.g., defecate, perspire, pigsty) and social threat words (e.g., stupid, incompetent, unloved) relative to neutral words. As predicted, obsessive compulsive patients showed more effects from contamination words than social threat words, whereas the converse was found for high trait anxious participants.

Wilhelm, McNally, Baer and Florin raised the possibility that obsessive compulsive patients have difficulty forgetting (in other words, they obsess) due to overelaborative encoding of information. They exposed 36 obsessive compulsive patients and 24 healthy controls to a series of negative (not specific to obsessive compulsive themes), positive, and neutral words. For half of the list of words, participants were instructed to forget, and for the other half of the words, they were instructed to remember. The standard directed forgetting effect was found: Words that participants were instructed to remember were recalled more often than words they were instructed to forget. Obsessive compulsive patients recalled more negative forget-words relative to positive or neutral forget-words, whereas control participants did not show this bias. The authors interpret this as evidence that "obsessive-compulsive patients encode negative words more elaboratively than positive or neutral words irrespective of instructions, and hence remember them especially well". This appears to be at odds with features of cognitive processing in other anxiety disorders, where memory processes appear unchanged or even impeded. Furthermore, it contrasts with evidence for general memory deficits in obsessive compulsive disorder. For example, using scales modified from a standard intelligence battery, Savage found evidence for impaired recall of nonverbal memory in obsessive compulsive patients compared to 20 healthy controls, although this deficit was not apparent with verbal material or with recognition memory.

On the other hand, the directed-forgetting findings are consistent with the work of Enright and Beech, who find that relative to other anxiety disorders, patients with obsessive compulsive disorder are poorer at inhibiting processing. Their paradigm of negative priming involves naming of a target item that was previously presented as a distractor to be ignored; naming is usually slowed under these conditions due to the response cost of having to overcome the inhibition (i.e., the previous instruction to ignore) before further processing is possible. Enright and Beech found less negative priming effects compared to other anxiety disorders, suggesting a fundamental deficit in cognitive inhibition in obsessive compulsive disorder. In fact, they interpret thought suppression effects, described below, as evidence of this deficit, with poor cognitive inhibition causing a greater number of intrusions into consciousness, making deliberate attempts to suppress those intrusions more difficult. More recently, Enright, Beech, and Claridge compared 32 patients with obsessive compulsive disorder to 32 patients with various other anxiety disorders using a Stroop task, in which color naming occurred under various conditions of prior distractors. Again, obsessive compulsive patients showed less negative priming (i.e., less interference caused by distractors) than other anxiety patients, at least with presentations of a fast speed. At slower speeds, the authors conclude that more attended strategies of cognitive processing may mask preattentive deficits in inhibition. Thus, "People who do not inhibit irrelevant information effectively may well be inclined to forget what they are doing or disbelieve what they have just done, leading to repetition and checking behaviours".

Another general cognitive deficit model emphasizes overcomplexity, or overattention to detail. Persons and Foa compared a small group of 7 obsessive compulsive patients to 11 patients with other disorders in a card-sorting categorization task. In support of the overcomplex model, obsessive compulsive patients used more piles to sort both neutral and feared items. Finally, Johnson posited that individuals with obsessive compulsive disorder discriminate poorly between memories for events and memories for images. This is consistent with patient reports of inability to recall whether a behavior was actually performed or not. Brown, Kosslyn, Breiter, Baer and Jenike speculate that such a deficit in reality monitoring is due to either very vivid images and/or very dim percepts (or memory representations for actual stimuli). Alternatively, it may arise from less certainty about the distinction between the two types of memory. In support of the latter, obsessive compulsive patients were less confident than controls about their memories, although the two groups did not differ in actual reality monitoring (actual versus imagined performance of tracing a line-drawn picture or word).

Using a signal detection task, Brown asked 28 patients with obsessive compulsive disorder and 18 controls to compare the heights of the first and last letters of words either written or imagined in lower case, and then later asked them to recall which words had been presented in writing. Similar to McNally and Kohlbeck, Brown did not find support for an actual deficit in reality monitoring. In fact, the patient group tended to discriminate between real and imagined stimuli better than control participants. Constans, Foa, Franklin, and Mathews compared 12 patients with checking compulsions and 7 healthy controls in a series of action sequences, half of which ended with instructions to perform an action and half with instructions to imagine performing an action. Some of the action sequences were relevant to obsessive compulsive fears (e.g., lighting and blowing out a candle, sheathing and unsheathing a knife) whereas others were neutral (e.g., pushing out or pulling in a chair). Later, participants were asked to recall whether the last action for each task was real or imagined. As with previous studies, obsessive compulsive patients were not deficient in reality monitoring with either fear-relevant or neutral stimuli. However, in contrast to previous studies, they were no less confident in their memories either. Thus, the significance of actual reality monitoring and confidence in reality monitoring remains uncertain.

Thought Suppression. Extensive research by Wegner and colleagues shows that attempts to suppress arbitrary thoughts result in the same thoughts becoming more frequent. Thought suppression may, therefore, contribute to persistent recurrence of intrusive thoughts. This ironic process is attributed to several features. First, the suppressed thought becomes the focus of an automatic and unconscious search process, so that when it occurs it can be replaced with a distracter. Second, use of multiple distracters establishes multiple associations with unwanted thoughts, and the distracters become reminders of the unwanted thought at a later point in time.

Furthermore, suppression may enhance emotional reactivity to unwanted thoughts. For example, individuals who chronically suppress thoughts tend to respond with heightened skin conductance to reminders of unwanted thoughts.

Not only does suppression increase thoughts subsequently, but some find an immediate enhancement effect during attempts to suppress. For example, Salkovskis and Campbell assigned nonclinical participants who had recently experienced three or more distressing, intrusive thoughts to conditions of thought suppression, mention control, or three different types of distraction regarding a personal intrusive thought. In the thought suppression condition, participants were informed, "It is very important that you try as hard as you can to suppress the thought 'X,'" although they were also to record the thought if it occurred. The mention control condition entailed recording only. After five minutes, each condition was followed by a period of "think anything." The suppression group experienced more intrusive thoughts during suppression and the subsequent interval of "think anything" in comparison to the mention control group. Distraction only reduced the frequency of intrusions when a specific distracting task was provided. Trinder and Salkovskis conducted a more naturalistic follow-up study. Students who had experienced negative intrusive thoughts in the past month were asked to suppress, simply record, or concentrate on idiosyncratic, personally relevant, negative intrusions over four days. The suppression group reported more intrusive thoughts and more distress over those thoughts during the four days. However, concentrating on thoughts also produced more discomfort than recording only, leading the authors to conclude that neither suppression nor dwelling on unwanted thoughts are therapeutically beneficial. Instead, therapy should focus on changing the meaning attached to such thoughts, as described below.

Thus, several studies indicate that suppression may contribute to the persistence of obsessions. It is noteworthy, however, that studies to date are limited to nonclinical samples. Others have been unable to replicate immediate enhancement or rebound effects from thought suppression. Hence, further evaluation of the role of thought suppression in obsessive compulsive disorder is warranted.

Nevertheless, Oltmanns and Gibbs combine principles from thought suppression and emotional dysregulation in their model of obsessive compulsive disorder. They measured facial indices of emotion in 22 nonclinical individuals selected for obsessive compulsive symptoms, compared to 24 controls, as they watched film clips intended to induce sadness, amusement, and fear. Mates with obsessive compulsive symptoms had a greater number of appropriate (e.g., fright expressions during frightening films) and inappropriate facial expressions (e.g., smiles and laughter during frightening films) relative to controls. They hypothesize that inappropriate facial expressions reflect attempts to suppress exaggerated negative emotion due to its perceived unpleasantness. Suppression of affect is hypothesized to strengthen connections between suppressed affect and accompanying thoughts. Thus, Oltmanns and Gibbs suggest that

> *Certain individuals react strongly to events that trigger an emotional response. These individuals become aware of their exaggerated reactivity and find it unpleasant. In an effort to control their reaction, they attempt to resist or suppress the emotion. As a result of an individual's attempt to suppress strong emotion, a rebound effect occurs, culminating in a vicious cycle. Thoughts that are present during the instigation of such a cycle become robustly associated with the emotion, and may become the content of an obsessive thought.*

Albeit interesting, their interpretation is without direct support and is based on a nonclinical sample.

Appraisals about Intrusive Thoughts. In contrast to cognitive deficit theories that assume obsessional symptoms represent generalized and involuntary disturbances of information processing, appraisal theories emphasize the meaning that is attached to particular thoughts. Originally, Carr and then McFall and Wollersheim proposed that certain appraisals, such as "One should be perfect" or "Magical rituals or obsessing will circumvent feared outcomes," may contribute to obsessive compulsive disorder. More recently, Salkovskis and Rachman propose that obsessions persist because of catastrophic misinterpretations of intrusive thoughts, images, or impulses.

Drawing from Beck's cognitive principles, Salkovskis distinguished between intrusions and negative automatic thoughts (i.e., appraisals) about intrusions. The former are egodystonic (the content is experienced as inconsistent with the individual's belief system and irrational), whereas the latter are relatively autonomous, idiosyncratic, and experienced as reasonable and egosyntonic. Similarly, Wells and Morrison distinguish between obsessions and worries about obsessions. Worry is viewed as "a more strategically driven conceptual activity than obsessions". As alluded to earlier, the element of appraisals may distinguish nonclinical obsessions from obsessive compulsive disorder. That is, those who develop obsessive compulsive disorder are assumed to appraise intrusive thoughts more catastrophically, which serves to transform occasional intrusions into persistent obsessions.

Salkovskis proposed that negative thoughts about intrusions are characterized by an inflated sense of responsibility, which derives from basic assumptions such as that having a thought about an action is equivalent to action (later termed "thought-action" fusion by Rachman and colleagues; e.g., "If I thought I hit someone with my car, then I did hit someone with my car"); failing to prevent or to try to prevent harm to self or others is the same as having caused harm in the first place; responsibility is not attenuated by other factors such as low probability of occurrence; failing to neutralize an intrusion about harming others is similar to seeking or wanting to harm others; and one should and can exercise control over one's thoughts. An overview of Salkovskis's model is presented in Figure 6.3. Others view catastrophic interpretations of intrusive thoughts more broadly, without giving as much emphasis to an inflated sense of responsibility. For example, Rachman (in press) suggests at least three major types of misinterpretations: "I am immoral," "I am dangerous," and "I will lose control and carry out the act I am insane." Evidence for the significance of inflated sense of responsibility is reviewed in more detail later.

As suggested by Salkovskis, thought-action fusion may underlie catastrophic misinterpretations of intrusive thoughts. Thought-action fusion refers to the belief that thinking about an unacceptable event makes that event more probable and the interpretation that obsessional thoughts and forbidden actions are morally equivalent. Examples include beliefs that thinking of causing harm to another increases the likelihood of causing harm to another, and thinking of causing harm to another generates the same moral responsibility as if harm had actually been caused to another. These types of thought-action fusions correlate moderately with obsessive compulsive features. Shafran, Thordarson and Rachman posit that thought-action fusion may arise from cultural factors such as religions that emphasize the sinfulness of having blasphemous, adulterous, or aggressive thoughts or a chance pairing between a thought and a negative event, such as thoughts of wishing one's parent were dead followed shortly by the actual death of the parent. Rachman (in press) posits that obsessional content derives in large part from personal values. For example, intrusive thoughts of harming others will be particularly distressing for the person who values kindness toward others, and intrusive thoughts of sinful actions will be particularly distressing for those with high religious standards. In the terms used throughout this book, such personal value systems are secondary vulnerabilities for the development of obsessive compulsive disorder.

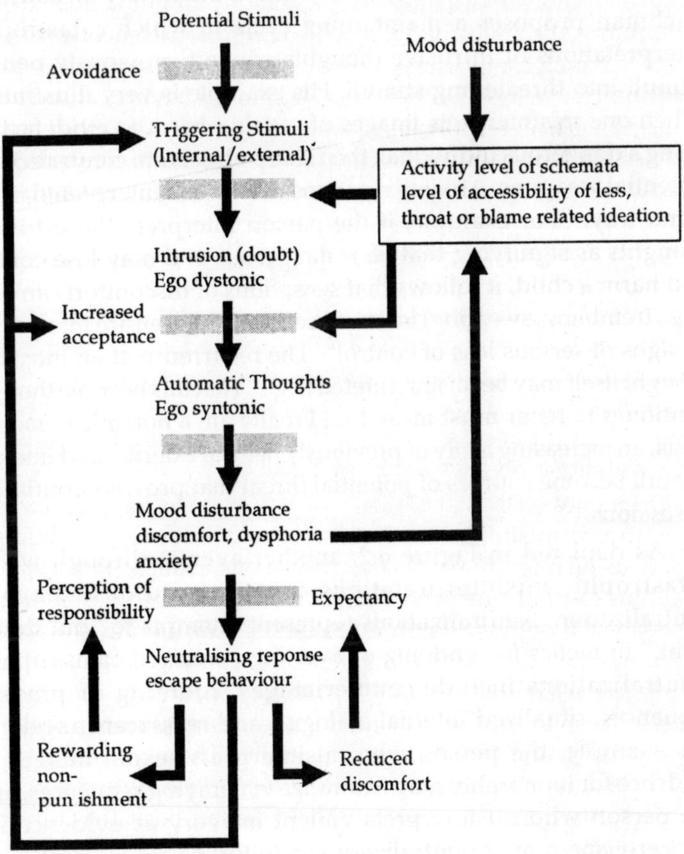

Fig. 6.2. A model of factors that contribute to obsessions and compulsions.

Catastrophic appraisals of intrusive thoughts are presumed to generate obsessions: "Because of pre-existing dysfunctional beliefs about the need to control unacceptable thoughts, and the tendency to misinterpret unwanted intrusive thoughts as an indication that they may be responsible for harm to themselves or others, the intrusions of obsession prone individuals can escalate in frequency and severity to become clinical obsessions". Negative affect that results from such catastrophic appraisals increases the availability of intrusive thoughts. Also, negative appraisals may increase the number of retrieval cues for such intrusions in memory. In addition, Rachman proposes a maintaining cycle in which catastrophic interpretations of intrusive thoughts convert previously neutral stimuli into threatening stimuli. His example is very illustrative: When one misinterprets images of causing harm as evidence for being a dangerous individual, then sharp objects are converted into potential weapons. Anxiety reactions may be misinterpreted in the same way. "For example, if the person interprets the intrusive thoughts as signifying that he is dangerous and may lose control and harm a child, it follows that sensations of discomfort/anxiety (e.g., trembling, sweating) in the presence of children are interpreted as signs of serious loss of control". The recurrence of an intrusive thought itself may be misinterpreted (e.g., "That this horrible thought continues to recur must mean that I really am a horrible person"). Thus, an increasing array of previously neutral external and internal stimuli become sources of potential threat that provoke continued obsessions.

As depicted in Figure 6.2, another avenue through which catastrophic misinterpretations contribute to obsessions is neutralization. Neutralizations represent attempts to "put things right," or tactics for undoing or averting perceived catastrophes. Neutralizations include counterimages, counting or praying sequences, ritualized internal dialogue, and reassurance seeking. For example, the person who misinterprets sexual images as evidence for immorality may neutralize via praying sequences, and the person who misinterprets violent imagery as evidence for dangerousness may neutralize via counterimages of sainthood. Attempts to control intrusive thoughts by neutralizing increases their salience and persistence. That is, neutralizing is a form of suppression, which, as described previously, may cause enhancement or rebound of intrusions. Also, neutralizing is hypothesized to increase preoccupation with intrusions, prevent discovery that feared outcomes do not occur, remove negative affect and therefore become an instrumental reinforcer, and increase the salience of the intrusions and their priority for processing. Similarly, avoidance of stimuli associated with obsessional content (e.g., avoidance of sharp objects for the person who fears harming someone else), like neutralizing, contributes to the maintenance of obsessions by preventing the discovery that feared outcomes do not occur.

To test the effects of neutralization, Salkovskis, Westbrook, Davis, Jeavons, and Gledhill selected individuals who reported frequent intrusive thoughts and tendencies to neutralize. Then, while listening to audio- taped presentations of their intrusive thoughts, they either distracted themselves (i.e., counted backward mentally) or neutralized every time they heard the thought.

Subsequent responses to audiotaped presentations were evaluated. As predicted, the group that neutralized experienced more discomfort when reexposed to the same thought and stronger urges to neutralize and distract themselves during reexposure. In a previous study, Rachman, Shafran, Mitchell, Trant, and Teachman asked healthy controls to think "I hope is in a car accident" (inserting the name of a friend or relative). Then, participants either did whatever they wanted to neutralize or cancel the effects of the sentence, or they were delayed from neutralization for 20 minutes by reading a magazine. Neutralization resulted in prompt anxiety reduction but, importantly for therapeutic purposes, delay also reduced anxiety and urges to neutralize. That is, realizing that anxiety and urges to neutralize eventually subside helps patients to prevent themselves from neutralizing. The same spontaneous decay occurs for urges for compulsive behavior.

In summary, catastrophic misinterpretations of intrusive thoughts, images, or impulses, which derive from preexisting values and assumptions, generate persistent obsessions and attempts to avoid or neutralize, which in turn strengthen obsessional material. As mentioned, Salkovskis emphasizes responsibility, proposing that appraisals of danger without the element of responsibility elicit anxiety or depression rather than obsessive compulsive disorder. That is, he ascribes responsibility a specific role in the development of obsessive compulsive disorder. Rheaume, Ladouceur, Freeston, and Letarte make the same argument. However, evidence for the role of responsibility is mixed. On the positive side, several studies report correlations between measures of responsibility and obsessive compulsive symptoms. Lopatka and Rachman decreased perceived responsibility for 30 obsessive compulsive individuals by having the experimenter assume all responsibility for a situation in which the individual normally engaged in excessive checking and was prevented from doing so. The experimenter informed participants, "I will take on complete responsibility. I will be to blame if anything bad happens or is not perfect. Your name will not be mentioned. I will also take responsibility for any damage that may occur and will pay back or undo any damage or harm that may occur". Urges to check declined under these conditions. Ladouceur, Rheaume conducted a similar study with more behavioral measures of checking behavior. In their second attempt to manipulate sense of responsibility, high responsibility was generated for a manual classification task by informing participants that their responses would be utilized to select colors for packaging different medications for underdeveloped countries. In this study, participants in the high responsibility condition showed more hesitations and checking behaviors, more preoccupation with making errors, and more anxiety than participants who did not believe that their responses would be used in this way. On the negative side, others fail to find substantial correlations between measures of responsibility and obsessive compulsive symptoms. Rachman concluded that perceived responsibility may be situationally specific, because "patients who are tormented by a highly irrational sense of responsibility can describe specific situations in which they welcome responsibility". Situational specificity raises the possibility that inflated responsibility is more a function of than a precursor to obsessions and compulsions.

Another questionable issue is the relationship between perceived negative outcomes and responsibility. Is responsibility only important subsequent to the evaluation of negative outcomes or are negative outcomes perceived because of an inflated sense of responsibility? For example, is the likelihood of harming another elevated by an inflated sense of responsibility or vice versa? Primacy of negative outcomes is suggested by the finding that compulsive washing correlates with estimates of danger after controlling for estimates of responsibility, but not vice versa. However, methods for ascertaining estimates of responsibility seemed limited in this study. Rachman suggests that inflated responsibility elevates estimates of negative outcomes: "When I am responsible, things are more likely to go wrong". Most likely, the concepts of perceived responsibility and negative outcomes are integrally related. Finally, Rachman concludes that the precise mechanism underlying inflated sense of responsibility and obsessions is yet to be established.

The significance of guilt and perfectionism is unclear also. Appraisals of responsibility are hypothesized to evoke guilt. Indeed, nonclinical checkers experience more guilt than noncheckers and obsessive compulsive patients scored higher on a measure of guilt than a comparison group of healthy controls. However, the degree to which guilt is specific to obsessive compulsive features relative to other anxiety disorders is not known. Many studies show a relationship between perfectionism and obsessive compulsive features in nonclinical populations, but Frost and Steketee were the first to examine this relationship in patients. They compared 35 patients with obsessive compulsive disorder to 35 controls and 14 patients with panic disorder and agoraphobia. Although the obsessive compulsive group scored higher on their measure of perfectionism than controls, they did not differ from the panic disorder group, suggesting that perfectionism is not specific to obsessive compulsive disorder.

A Comprehensive Psychosocial Model of Hoarding. Frost and Hartl present a comprehensive model of hoarding behavior that incorporates cognitive deficits and faulty appraisals. They outline three elements. First is deficits in decisionmaking, possibly due to perfectionism and an exaggerated sense of responsibility. Perfectionism, or the tendency to set high standards and employ overly critical self-evaluations, is hypothesized to lead to indecisiveness because the postponement of decisionmaking enables one to avoid mistakes, and such indecisiveness may in turn result in procrastination, hoarding, or compulsive checking. With respect to responsibility, hoarding was associated with a greater sense of responsibility for being prepared and for the well-being of possessions among a nonclinical sample of self-selected hoarders and pack rats. "Each possession is seen as having functional utility under certain circumstances. Although those circumstances may not pertain at present, they may in the future. It is as though they have a solution, but no problem on which to use it. If the solution is discarded and the problem occurs, 'harm' has been done. It is this harm that the compulsive hoarder seeks to avoid". The second element that Frost and Hartl associate with hoarding is deficits in categorization and organization. In particular, overreliance on concepts that are too detailed and category boundaries that are too narrow results in underinclusion in a category. This is similar to the complexity model described earlier. As a result of underinclusiveness, each possession is regarded as unique, rendering discarding it more difficult, and all attributes must be considered before discarding. The third element they associate with hoarding concerns memory, including lack of confidence in memory and overestimation of the importance of remembering or recording information. Consequently, discarding items is difficult because information may be lost.

Conclusion

Intrusive thoughts and compulsive behaviors are common in the population at large, particularly under stress and negative mood states. For some, these thoughts and behaviors become more frequent and more distressing. Etiological pathways for the progression from nonclinical to clinical states include the following. Accumulating evidence implicating the orbitofrontal area and possibly the caudate nuclei suggests a specific neurobiological dysregulation that may underlie repetitive thinking and acting. However, further research is needed to establish its causality and specificity to obsessive compulsive disorder. Moreover, biological models are not able to account for the selective focus of obsessions and compulsions. Why does one person dwell on contamination and another on violence or sexual themes? Or, in Rachman's terms, why are obsessions about harming Arnold Schwartzenegger absent?

Drawing from notions presented throughout this book, I would posit a generalized vulnerability comprising not only biological predispositions but also psychological readiness to perceive threat (i.e., neuroticism). Indeed, Scarrabelotti found that neuroticism was a significant predictor of level of distress over intrusive thoughts, even after controlling for the effects of depressed mood state. A second, separate predictor was sense of responsibility, which I would view as a second-order vulnerability. That is, inflated sense of responsibility is enhanced by the higher-order trait of neuroticism, but is continually modulated by ongoing learning experiences, such as parental modeling or other direct, vicarious, or informational experiences. Consider, for example, the inflated sense of responsibility that may derive from being identified as the causal agent for tragic family events. Thought-action fusion biases may represent yet another second-order vulnerability that derives from learning experiences. Consider, for example, the young girl whose parent repeatedly warned that whatever she teased her siblings about could come true. Other second-order vulnerabilities may include strong values of personal conduct, religiosity, and cleanliness. Cognitive deficits in inhibitory processing or overattention to detail may make up additional second-order vulnerabilities.

All of these second-order vulnerabilities conceivably influence the salience of certain intrusions over others (thus influencing which intrusions become a source of concern). In addition, they conceivably influence intensity of fear in reaction to salient intrusions (thus influencing whether traumatic conditioning takes place or not). Catastrophic appraisals of intrusions and resultant behaviors, such as neutralizations, avoidance, or attempts to suppress intrusions, contribute to a perpetual cycle of obsessions and catastrophic appraisals, along with neutralization, avoidance, and suppression. Finally, these cycles and vulnerabilites may or may not be accompanied by specific neurobiological features that contribute to the repetitive nature of thinking and acting.

Cognitive-Behavioral Treatment of Obsessive Compulsive Disorder

In vivo exposure and response prevention, first developed by Meyer, forms the basis of behavioral treatment for obsessive compulsive disorder. Patients are systematically exposed to their feared stimuli and instructed not to engage in ritualistic behaviors. Foa and colleagues developed a detailed and empirically validated treatment protocol that is outlined in Riggs and Foa. In brief, their protocol involves 2 information-gathering sessions and 15 daily sessions, each lasting two hours. The information-gathering sessions essentially are for performing a functional analysis to identify triggers; characterize situations, images, and thoughts that evoke anxiety; and understand the particulars of obsessions and compulsions. A treatment rationale and description are provided. Hierarchies of fear-provoking situations and thoughts are developed in the first two sessions, including thoughts about harm that might result from not engaging in compulsive behaviors.

Exposure is conducted in vivo and imaginally. In vivo exposure is graduated, beginning with the least anxiety-provoking situation and progresses to the most anxiety-provoking situation within six treatment sessions. The most anxiety-provoking items continue to be practiced for the remainder of treatment. An example of a hierarchy for a compulsive checker is as follows: Turn lights and stove on and off without checking, open doors and windows without checking, send letters without checking, leave house without checking the lock, drive highways without retracing the route, drive over bumpy roads without retracing the route, and drive through a busy parking lot without retracing the route. Hierarchies often end with highly demanding tasks that extend beyond normalcy. For example, a hierarchy for fears of contamination might progress as follows: Touch doorknobs, hold newspapers, touch money, touch sweat under arm, touch sweaty clothing, place hand on door handle of public bathroom, place hand on seat of toilet in public bathroom, hold a paper towel dampened with patient's own urine, and hold a piece of toilet paper lightly soiled with patient's own fecal material. For in vivo exposure to contaminants, patients are encouraged to fully touch hierarchy objects, as well as the rest of their bodies, while minimizing attempts to maintain cleanliness. In addition, patients are informed to "Go ahead and let yourself worry about the harm you are afraid will happen since you won't be washing or cleaning after this exposure." The same instruction is given to checkers as they engage in activities without checking.

Gradually more anxiety-provoking scenes are generated for imaginal exposure. These scenes are intended to be vivid imaginal pictures. Consistent with Lang's bioinformational processing model, the scenes are replete with details of the situation, internal sensations and thoughts, and physiological responses. The following is an example of imaginal exposure for someone who is fearful of glass:

I want you to imagine the following scene as vividly as you can, as if it is actually happening, and to experience the feelings as you imagine. Imagine that you are sitting in a restaurant and you have ordered a drink. Across the room, you see the waitress gradually approaching your table, with a tray full of drinks. The tray topples a bit, and you feel a sudden surge of anxiety as you wonder whether the tray will drop and the glasses break. Your heart rate immediately speeds up and you feel a rush of adrenaline throughout your body. The waitress manages to hold on to the tray, and your anxiety subsides. Now, she is getting closer to your table, and your anxiety rises again. Your stomach feels tense, your hands are sweating, and you want to leave. The waitress is now right behind your chair, and as she leans over to place a drink on your table, the tray of drinks topples and the drinks crash onto the floor. You hear the sound of glass breaking all around you. You see glass everywhere a piece is resting on your shoe and there are many pieces on the floor around you. Your heart is racing very fast, and you feel short of breath and dizzy. You think that the glass is inside your shoe and stuck to your clothing. You want to run out, take off all of your clothes, and throw them away. You feel scratchy feelings all over your skin and think glass is everywhere on your body. You are afraid to move in case the glass spreads even further, but you are afraid to stay where you are. You are stuck in the middle of broken glass.

In the treatment designed by Foa and her colleagues, in vivo and imaginal exposure are practiced with the therapist, from 90 minutes to two hours each session, with repeated checks on self-reported distress levels throughout exposures. As with all anxiety disorders, homework is a large part of treatment. Patients continue practicing exposure for an additional two hours on their own, resulting in four hours of exposure treatment per day. Combined with this, patients are restricted from engaging in all rituals from the start of treatment. For example, "washers" are not permitted to use water on their body during the response prevention period, and supervised showers are restricted to 10 minutes, every three days. Only one check is permitted for checkers (e.g., check one time only that the door is locked before going to bed). Patients are reintroduced to normal rules of behavior in the last few treatment sessions. For example, these may include one 10-minute shower daily and hand washing before meals; after bathroom use; and after handling grimy, greasy, or sticky objects. For a period after reintroduction to normal rules, any washing is followed by immediate reexposure to contaminants.

An initial treatment contract between patient and therapist is essential given the intensity of this treatment. In this contract, patients state that they understand that they will be exposed to things that bother them and will be limited from carrying out their rituals. Patients also agree to cooperate with the therapist, despite the anxiety they will experience during treatment. In addition to the contract, patients are encouraged to obtain support from family or friends for the duration of the treatment, particularly to provide encouragement when they have difficulty controlling their urges to wash or check. This intensive treatment program is usually followed by relapse prevention or booster sessions as patients return to their own environments.

Exposure and response prevention may be conducted over more protracted time intervals, using twice- or once-weekly visits. Clinical lore, however, suggests that severe patients may benefit more from a concentrated treatment effort like the one developed by Foa and colleagues.

Cognitive Therapy Methods

Following from Salkovskis's approach, cognitive therapy for obsessive compulsive disorder means to "concentrate not on modification of intrusions but on automatic thoughts consequent on the intrusions, and on the beliefs which give rise to these. Bland reassurance often involving detailed discussions of tiny probabilities, is notoriously ineffective for obsessional patients probably because it functions as a form of neutralising". For example, an obsession about molesting children is best challenged by correcting misappraisals of oneself as a horrible person for having such a thought as opposed to questioning the details of the molestation. Therefore, results from more traditional cognitive therapy directed at the content of the obsession are not promising. For example, Emmelkamp, van der Helm, van Zanten, and Plochg compared eight participants who received exposure alone with seven who received exposure plus self-instruction training. Overall, the treatments were comparable, suggesting that cognitive therapy did not improve outcomes at posttreatment or six months later. Similarly, rational-emotive therapy did not improve outcomes from exposure. Furthermore, rational-emotive therapy alone was generally less effective than self-controlled in vivo exposure on broad measures of improvement, although very few differences existed on individual outcome measures.

In another earlier cognitive approach, termed thought stopping, obsessions were countered by shouting "Stop" or by flicking an elastic band against the wrist. Rachman notes that thought stopping met with little success, perhaps because it functions as thought suppression. Similarly, he notes that habituation training for obsessions, which involved repeated and prolonged exposure to obsessional material, produced only transitory reductions in distress. Interestingly, however, this type of habituation training is comparable to imaginal exposure, which, as noted earlier, appears to improve outcome from in vivo exposure and response prevention, especially in the long term. Nevertheless, Rachman suggests that thought stopping and habituation training as sole treatment agents fail to deal with the underlying problem -the misappraisals of intrusive thoughts.

Recent cognitive therapies deal specifically with these misappraisals by use of cognitive restructuring techniques in addition to prevention of neutralizations of obsessions. Rachman suggests that therapy begin with education regarding the normalcy of intrusive thoughts and by so doing give reassurance that such thoughts are not signs of deep character flaws. This is followed by discussion of intrusions in a matter-of-fact manner and education about the role of appraisals in transforming intrusive thoughts into clinical obsessions. An illustration may be achieved by describing unwanted intrusions that are regarded as trivial versus unwanted intrusions that are of great personal significance. Similarly, demonstrations of thought suppression and neutralization illustrate why intrusive thoughts persist.

Freeston suggest that cognitive restructuring address the following main areas: overimportance of thoughts and magical thinking, exaggerated responsibility for negative consequences, perfectionistic expectations for control and certainty, and inflated estimates of probability and severity of negative outcomes. To challenge overimportance of thoughts, Freeston suggest explaining the circularity of the reasoning. That is, patients are educated about the illogical nature of their reasoning (e.g., "Because I thought about it, it must be important, or it must mean that I secretly want to do it"). In addition, education about the effects of suppression enables reappraisal of the recurrence of unpleasant thoughts: The thoughts are not important, they are just rebounding from suppression. Freeston tackle thought-action fusion (e.g., "If I think that my child will be kidnapped, and I don't pray for this not to happen, then he will be kidnapped") by behavioral experiments. For example, selecting a household appliance and thinking 100 times each day that it will break down within the next week or simply "Try to kill a goldfish by thought action". For thought-morality fusions (e.g., interpreting sexual arousal in response to intrusive thoughts as a sign of evilness), they suggest education (e.g., the relationship between anxiety and sexual arousal) and clarification of the distinction between thought and actions (e.g., identify thoughts that were acceptable but not acted on and recognize that morality refers to choice of actions versus occurrence of thoughts).

Overestimates of responsibility are challenged with a pie chart in which all possible sources of responsibility are weighted and by questioning perceived consequences of irresponsibility. In addition, responsibility for any harm that may occur may be transferred, by written agreement, to another person, such as the therapist, for a determined amount of time, during which outcomes are monitored. Perfectionistic expectations may be challenged by questioning dichotomous thinking (e.g., "If I didn't understand everything, then I understood nothing"), challenging stated advantages of perfectionism, and behavioral experimentation with imperfect actions (e.g., deliberately read quickly and skip certain sections) to learn that imperfection can be tolerated and disasters do not occur. One way of implementing response prevention with regard to obsessions is a looped audiotape on which intrusive, obsessional material is recorded and later played back continuously. By so doing, the thought or image is kept in mind while neutralization and avoidance are prevented. Again, this latter strategy is very comparable to imaginal exposure, as described by Foa and colleagues. An outline of cognitive-behavioral treatment is presented in Table 6.1.

Table 6.1. Outline of Cognitive-Behavioral Treatment for Obsessive Compulsive Disorder

- ❒ Detailed functional analysis of obsessive and compulsive thoughts and behaviors, conducted in matter-of-fact manner, with education about intrusive thoughts
- ❒ Detailed cognitive-behavioral conceptualization of obsessions and compulsions, e.g., initial intrusive thought that is misappraised and produces distress, followed by attempts to neutralize, reinforced by anxiety reduction
- ❒ Treatment rationale and description and treatment contract
- ❒ Establishment of hierarchies for exposure to obsessive thoughts and situations that elicit anxiety and compulsive behaviors
- ❒ Cognitive restructuring regarding obsessions: overimportance of thoughts and thought action or thought morality fusion, inflated sense of responsibility, perfectionism, and estimates of probability and consequence
- ❒ Cognitive restructuring regarding exposures to situations while preventing compulsive rituals, e.g., harm perceived to occur by not conducting compulsive behavior
- ❒ In vivo exposure to situations and response prevention of compulsive behaviors; exposure to obsessions via looped audiotape and response prevention of neutralizations and thought suppression
- ❒ Relapse prevention

Efficacy of Cognitive-Behavioral Therapy

Stanley and Turner concluded that 63% of obsessive compulsive patients show at least some improvement with exposure and response prevention, in an average of 14 sessions. Earlier studies reported higher rates of success. However, success or improvement is usually defined by 30 to 50% improvement on selected measures, so that symptornatology continues for most patients after treatment. Also, these rates do not include refusers (approximately 12%) or dropouts (approximately 12%), so the final improvement rate is only 50% or less. Finally, although 85% of patients maintain their gains one to three years posttreatment, close to 50% require further therapy.

Nevertheless, in vivo exposure and response prevention is clearly superior to relaxation training. The addition of response prevention is also clearly beneficial (particularly full versus partial response prevention) in comparison to exposure alone. Despite some negative findings, several studies indicate benefit from the addition of imaginal exposure, particularly in the long term. In addition, there appear to be more benefits from therapist-controlled versus selfcontrolled exposure, as well as from more sessions of longer length.

Hiss, Foa and Kozak tested a relapse prevention program after their usual three-week intensive treatment. Relapse prevention (n=8) consisted of identifying possible risk situations for relapse, conceptualizing setbacks as an opportunity to practice skills, inclusion of significant others to identify and consider modification of maladaptive interpersonal relations, cognitive restructuring, and self-exposure. This was conducted over four sessions within a one-week period. In addition, patients received nine follow-up phone contacts over 12 weeks. In comparison, an attention control condition (n=10) consisted of training in relaxation and encouragement to express anything that came to mind about obsessions and compulsions, with involvement of a significant other in the free association. The attention control did not receive follow-up phone contacts. More of the relapse prevention group maintained their treatment gains six months later, according to assessors' ratings (87.5% versus 50%).

In vivo exposure and response prevention were equally effective when conducted in groups, at least when treatment was conducted twice weekly over 12 weeks, in individuals with mild to moderate symptoms who were not suffering major depression or a personality disorder. Behavior therapy may be enhanced by family involvement, such as instructing family members not to participate in rituals with the patient. Family involvement has been advocated especially when treating youths with obsessive compulsive disorder, to provide education, facilitate disengagement, and structure family interactions so that they are not impaired by the disorder. However, the role of family in treatment for obsessive compulsive disorder awaits well-controlled research.

In an early report, Foa noted two features that were predictive of poor treatment outcome from exposure and response prevention for obsessive compulsive disorder: depression and overvalued ideation. However, subsequent research failed to replicate the significance of either feature. Keijsers found that greater initial severity, poorer motivation, dissatisfaction with the therapeutic relationship and longer duration of complaints predicted poorer outcome in a sample of 40 obsessive compulsive patients who received self-directed exposure and response prevention.

Efficacy of Cognitive Therapy

Various case study reports support the efficacy of cognitive therapy for primarily obsessional patients. Ladouceur, Freeston conducted a multiple baseline study with three patients. Their treatment included education regarding obsessional thoughts and the role of neutralization; exposure with response prevention via a looped audiotape; identification and proscription of all activity to control obsessional thoughts; and cognitive restructuring of excessive responsibility, perfectionistic thinking, overestimation of the importance of thoughts, and feared consequences related to each obsession. Each patient ended treatment with none or close to zero obsessicns, although treatment durations were lengthy (158 to 360 days).

Freeston compared the combination of in vivo exposure, response prevention, and cognitive restructuring to a wait-list control for obsessional patients. Treatment lasted on average 41 hours and included relapse prevention and follow-up booster sessions. At the end of treatment, 67% had clinically improved (77% of treatment completers), although this percentage dropped to 53% (59% of completers) by six months later. Van Oppen, de Haan, van Balkom, Spinhoven, Hoogduin and van Dyck compared the newer version of cognitive therapy (n=29) to selfcontrolled in vivo exposure and response prevention (n=29) over 16 sessions for patients with obsessions and compulsions. They found marked improvement in both conditions, with a trend for more improvement in the cognitive condition: 68% and 48%, respectively, improved significantly on three major measures. Unfortunately, van Oppen, de Haan did not include a follow-up assessment. Furthermore, percentages for full recovery were generally low: 39% and 17%, respectively. Thus, as alluded to earlier, although cognitive-behavioral therapies are clearly beneficial for obsessive compulsive disorder, many patients remain symptomatic.

Treatment Summary

In summary, the combination of exposure and response prevention appears to be effective for obsessive compulsive disorder. The response prevention treatment component clearly enhances the efficacy of exposure. Despite the good results with this treatment approach, a substantial number remain symptomatic. Recent cognitive theorizing has led to renewed interest in cognitive therapies that target appraisals about obsessions. Several uncontrolled studies and two randomized studies to date demonstrate that newer cognitive therapies are effective for primarily obsessional as well as obsessive compulsive patients.

Of final note is pharmacological treatment. Clomipramine, a serotonergic tricyclic antidepressant, is effective for obsessive compulsive disorder, as are several other selective serotonin reuptake inhibitors, including fluoxetine, fluvoxamine, sertraline, and paroxetine. A meta-analysis of placebo-controlled trials for obsessive compulsive disorder found that clomipramine was superior to fluoxetine. Similarly, another meta-analysis by Piccinelli, Pini, Bellantuono, and Wilkinson found an increase in improvement rate over placebo of 48.5% for clomipramine, 28.6% for the class of selective serotonin reuptake inhibitors, and 23.1% for nortriptyline. Direct comparisons among serotonergic drugs show few differences. Information regarding relapse upon medication discontinuation is limited, although relapse rates as high as 90% were found following fairly rapid taper from clomipramine.

A relatively recent meta-analysis of pharmacotherapy, behavior therapy, and cognitive therapy concluded that all forms of treatment, with the exception of cognitive therapy, were superior to placebo. In addition, they found no significant differences among these treatment approaches on the basis of independent assessor ratings, whereas effect sizes for behavior therapy were larger compared to serotonergic antidepressants on the basis of patient self-ratings. There is some evidence that behavior therapy and pharmacological therapy have additive effects.

7

Features of Generalized Anxiety Disorder

Introduction

Generalized anxiety appeared as a separate diagnostic entity for the first time in DSM-III, but was delegated to a residual status, assigned only when features of other anxiety disorders were not present. In DSM-III-R, the diagnostic criteria for GAD included excessive or unrealistic worry about two or more life spheres (e.g., finances, health, environment) plus at least 6 of a list of 18 physical symptoms; duration was extended from one to six months, and hierarchical rules of exclusion with respect to other anxiety disorders were removed, although GAD could not be diagnosed if it occurred only during the course of a mood or psychotic disorder. The most recent diagnostic criteria, drawing from more empirical evidence, define generalized anxiety disorder as excessive anxiety and worry about a *number* of events or activities. Factor analyses reveal two major factors for worry in normals social evaluation and physical threat and possibly a third factor of societal problems. Most recently, Roemer, Molina, and Borkovec compared worry content in patients with generalized anxiety disorder, nonclinical generalized anxiety, and healthy controls. Family and interpersonal themes were predominant across all groups. The patient group reported a higher proportion of miscellaneous worries about minor events and a lower proportion of worry about work or school. In addition, DSMIV criteria specify that the individual has difficulty controlling his or her worry and at least three of a list of six physical symptoms. The symptoms reflect motor tension and vigilance scanning (i.e., restlessness or feeling keyed up or on edge, fatigue, difficulty concentrating or mind going blank, irritability, muscle tension, and sleep disturbance). In other words, the autonomic symptom cluster (such as palpitations and sweating) was dropped. Finally, DSM-IV criteria for generalized anxiety disorder subsume the DSM-III-R diagnostic entity of overanxious disorder of childhood.

Overall, lifetime prevalence rates, defined according to DSM-III-R criteria, range from 1.9 to 5.4%. The most recent prevalence estimates from the National Comorbidity Survey are 1.6% for current, 3.1% for one year, and 5.1% for lifetime. These figures place generalized anxiety disorder in the same prevalence range as panic disorder and obsessive compulsive disorder. Prevalence estimates are high for the elderly, ranging from 0.7% to 7.1%. Several researchers are now targeting generalized anxiety in the elderly. Naturally, estimates are even higher in primary care settings, where a current prevalence is estimated at 6.4%. Approximately half of those who seek help for generalized anxiety seek help from primary care. Approximately 40% of high utilizers of medical care are estimated to have a lifetime history of generalized anxiety disorder.

More women than men are afflicted with generalized anxiety disorder and it is a chronic condition. As part of the Harvard/Brown Anxiety Disorders Research Project (HARP), Yonkers, Warshaw, Massion and Keller reported on 164 patients with generalized anxiety disorder who were seeking treatment at 1 of 11 hospitals in the Boston area. The average length of the disorder was 20 years. Remission rates were low only .15 at one year and .25 by two years although relapse after remission was low also (.07 after six months and .15 after one year). Several studies indicate that generalized anxiety disorder often precedes other anxiety disorders. Accordingly, generalized anxiety sufferers frequently report that they have been "that way" almost all of their lives. On the other hand, Breslau found that generalized anxiety disorder preceded other comorbid disorders in only 2 of 23 individuals, and only 53% from the HARP study reported onset before comorbid conditions. Thus, a substantial minority, approximately 35%, report a later age of onset. However, the generally insidious onset for generalized anxiety disorder probably renders exact age of onset somewhat unreliable.

Diagnostic Validity

Generalized anxiety disorder has been conceptualized in several different ways. It has been considered a mild disorder that comes to clinical attention when a comorbid condition such as depression presents. Alternately, it has been viewed as a nonspecific indicator of distress; a characterological disorder; or a prodrome to, or incomplete remission of, other major disorders. Barlow and colleagues consider generalized anxiety disorder to be a basic anxiety disorder because its defining features of worry and physical tension reflect fundamental processes of anxiety that are present to some degree in all of the anxiety disorders. The wide array of views is illustrative of the continuing debate regarding retention of generalized anxiety disorder as a separate diagnostic entity.

Specifically, two arguments have been put forth to suggest that generalized anxiety disorder is neither a reliable nor a valid diagnosis. First, interrater reliability kappa coefficients (i.e., a coefficient of interrater agreement beyond chance agreement) are relatively poor, particularly for current generalized anxiety disorder, using DSM-III-R criteria (.27 to .54). Lifetime diagnoses have fair interrater reliability (.50 to .60). Second, 75 to 90% of patients with generalized anxiety disorder have at least one other disorder. When generalized anxiety disorder is the principal diagnosis, it has the highest rate of comorbidity among the anxiety disorders. The most commonly occurring codiagnoses are dysthymia or major depression, panic disorder and agoraphobia, social phobia and simple phobia. Furthermore, generalized anxiety disorder is the most frequently assigned additional diagnosis in patients with a principal anxiety or mood disorder.

These diagnostic patterns suggest that generalized anxiety disorder may be more parsimoniously viewed as a subset of other anxiety and mood disorders as opposed to a separate diagnostic entity. However, other data support the notion of an independent diagnostic entity. For example, the most common reason for interrater disagreements is relative severity of generalized anxiety disorder and assignment as either principal or secondary diagnosis, as opposed to the presence or absence of the constellation of generalized anxiety features. In other words, raters generally agree on the presentation of generalized anxiety disorder but disagree on its relative importance in an individual's entire diagnostic profile.

In addition, the diagnostic feature of excessive worry can be identified reliably. Earlier data suggested poor reliability for the physical symptoms. More recently, Marten, Brown, Barlow, Borkovec, Shear, and Lydiard collapsed data from several sites to find that most of the 18 DSM-III-R generalized anxiety disorder symptoms could be established reliably, particularly motor tension and vigilance-scanning symptoms (i.e., those retained in DSM-IV). Furthermore, all six DSM-IV somatic symptoms distinguish generalized anxiety disorder patients from controls and from other anxiety disorders. Patients with generalized anxiety disorder were distinguishable from other anxiety disorders on the basis of autonomic scores as well, but here the variance was small and attributable to comorbid panic disorder. Brown, Marten, and Barlow conclude that "a potentially unique feature of GAD relative to other anxiety disorders is that its presentation is associated with a predominance of a certain set of symptoms (e.g., muscle tension, irritability, fatigability) other than symptoms of autonomic arousal (e.g., accelerated heart rate, sweating)". This pattern is important in recent theorizing about generalized anxiety disorder, presented below. Finally, although muscle tension and vigilance type of symptoms do not differentiate generalized anxiety disorder patients from patients with either dysthymia or major depression, other symptoms, such as depressed mood, suicidality, hopelessness and helplessness, and impairment in functioning, differentiate these groups. Thus, limitation of current diagnostic criteria to the vigilance-scanning and motor tension cluster of symptoms, plus other modifications outlined earlier, may raise interrater reliability kappa coefficients for the diagnosis of generalized anxiety disorder.

A second argument for the validity of the generalized anxiety disorder diagnosis derives from a relatively new worry scale. The Penn State Worry Questionnaire measures the tendency to worry to excess or uncontrollably. Examples of items include, "I am always worrying about something," "Once I start worrying, I can't stop," and "My worries overwhelm me." Consequently, the scale is a quantitative, norm-based measure of the cognitive feature of generalized anxiety disorder. Individuals with generalized anxiety disorder score higher on this questionnaire than individuals with panic disorder, agoraphobia, social phobia, simple phobia, or obsessive compulsive disorder, who in turn score higher than healthy controls. That is, excessive worry appears to be characteristic of all anxiety disorders and is probably representative of a general neuroticism or anxiousness, but the element of uncontrollability or excessiveness of this worry seems to be particularly strong in generalized anxiety disorder.

Third, although comorbidity rates are high for generalized anxiety disorder, high comorbidity is not unique to this syndrome. In addition, diagnoses that co-occur most frequently with generalized anxiety disorder (e.g., social phobia) share fewer features in common with generalized anxiety disorder than diagnoses with which it is not highly comorbid (e.g., obsessive compulsive disorder). As noted by Brown, Barlow, and Liebowitz, the comorbidity argument against generalized anxiety disorder is only valid to the degree that the diagnoses with which it is comorbid represent dual diagnostic classification of shared symptomatology (as may occur in the dual diagnosis of social phobia and avoidant personality disorder).

Worry and Stressful Life Events

As reported above, the majority of individuals with generalized anxiety disorder report a lifetime duration. However, there is a subset of persons who exhibit a clearly demarked and later age of onset (36-37%). Conceivably, earlier onset generalized anxiety disorder entails stronger vulnerabilities, rendering these persons more reactive to stressful events, whereas later onset entails weaker vulnerabilities, requiring more stressful events for manifestation of excessive worry. In accord, HoehnSaric, Hazlett, and McLeod found that persons with early-onset generalized anxiety disorder were more likely to develop generalized anxiety without a precipitating stressful event. Several studies report more indicators of overall distress in early-onset generalized anxiety disorder, such as more difficulties in marital sexual relations, past history of psychiatric illness, disturbed home environments in childhood, anxiety symptoms and inhibited or avoidant behavior in childhood, history of interpersonal sensitivity and depression, and developmental and academic difficulties, elevated trait anxiety or neuroticism and current symptornatology. However, the fact that Brown, O'Leary did not find more current clinical symptomatology or comorbidity in early-onset cases illustrates the equivocal nature of these findings.

The interaction of cognitive vulnerabilities and stressful events may account for differences between pure and comorbid generalized anxiety disorder as well. As noted earlier, although the majority of individuals have comorbid conditions, approximately 18 to 23% present with pure generalized anxiety disorder. According to a model of vulnerability and stressful life events, pure generalized anxiety disorder most likely reflects weaker cognitive vulnerability and a later age of onset with more stress precipitants than does the comorbid type. Although individuals with pure and comorbid generalized anxiety disorder did not differ in age, sex, marital status, age of first symptom and treatment, duration, substance abuse, or Hamilton anxiety and depression scale scores, comorbid individuals were more likely to have been treated with medications and more frequently had a history of major depression in a study by Shores. Related are data by Nisita, Petracca, Akiskal, Galli, Gepponi, and Cassano, who compared a group with pure generalized anxiety disorder to panic disorder/agoraphobia samples. In contrast to the usual pattern of results with comorbid types, their pure sample did not have an earlier age of onset and were more likely to relate onset to specific life events than their panic disorder/agoraphobia sample. Thus, there is some evidence that an interaction between vulnerabilities and stressors may account for differences between early versus late onset and pure versus comorbid generalized anxiety disorder. However, conclusions remain tentative given the limited number of studies and reliance on retrospective descriptive data that are subject to poor reliability and validity.

Theoretical and Empirical Developments

The nature of excessive or pathological worry is addressed in this chapter. Borkovec attributes the origins of excessive worry to a tendency to misperceive future events as catastrophic and to misperceive future catastrophes as having a high likelihood of occurrence. Similarly, Eysenck attributes dysfunctional worry, which he calls hypervigilance, to tendencies to overestimate probabilities of aversive events, their imminence, their aversiveness, and a perceived inability to control them. These cognitive biases are believed to derive from high trait anxiousness or neuroticism.

Extensive research demonstrates the existence of such information-processing biases and suggests that overreadiness to perceive threat is a core characteristic of general anxiety. For example, high trait anxious individuals and persons diagnosed with generalized anxiety disorder show an attentional bias toward threatening information. This is gauged via slowed response latency to color naming of threat words in modified Stroop paradigms, faster reaction times to detect probes that follow threat words versus neutral words in visual probe detection tasks and impaired tracking of a neutral stimulus when threatening information is conveyed auditorally in dichotic listening tasks. Thus, various cognitive tests suggest that anxiousness is associated with diversion of attention toward threatening material, even when the material is not consciously perceived. Furthermore, attentional bias is exacerbated by state anxiety. In contrast, low trait anxious or nonanxious controls tend to divert their attention away from threatening information under state anxious conditions. There remains some debate as to whether trait anxiety underlies such attentional biases or vice versa, but most agree on a reciprocating cycle between trait anxiety and attentional biases toward threat.

A second information-processing bias occurs in judgments of likelihood and meaning of negative events. High trait anxious individuals tend to inflate the risk of negative events, particularly under state anxious conditions and to interpret ambiguous stimuli (e.g., homophones) as threatening. Chronic worriers perceive events as more catastrophic; generate significantly more catastrophizing scenarios for potential problems, even hypothetical ones; and generate more reasons for negative events. This is consistent with their tendencies to worry about more minor matters than healthy controls. Vasey and Borkovec suggest that chronic worriers possess elaborated memory stores for answers to catastrophic questions, and being able to retrieve an answer to "What if" questions serves to prolong the catastrophic worry sequence.

Worry to Avoid Fear

Borkovec and colleagues elaborate on factors that maintain the process of excessive worry. Worry is viewed as an abstract reasoning attempt to control unwanted future environmental threats (such as job loss and ill health) as well as immediate somatic responses to perceived threat (such as accelerated heart rate and sweating).

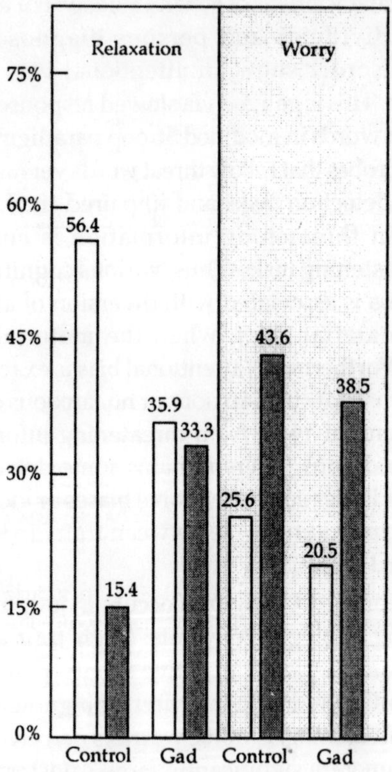

Fig. 7.1. Patients with generalized anxiety disorder (GAD) and healthy controls (Control) rated whether their mental activity was imagery or thoughts while relaxing and while worrying. Under relaxing conditions (left panel), GAD patients endorsed proportionately more thoughts relative to images than control participants.

The abstract reasoning quality of worry is supported by evidence, reviewed in Chapter 1, showing that worriers report proportionately less visual and more verbal cognitive processing than nonworriers under relaxing, baseline conditions. The act of worrying is associated with proportionate increases in the amount of verbalizing. Although there are limitations to this research, such as the problems associated with retrospective measurement of time spent worrying or imagining, the predominance of verbalizing is detected by more behavioral indices of cognitive activity as well.

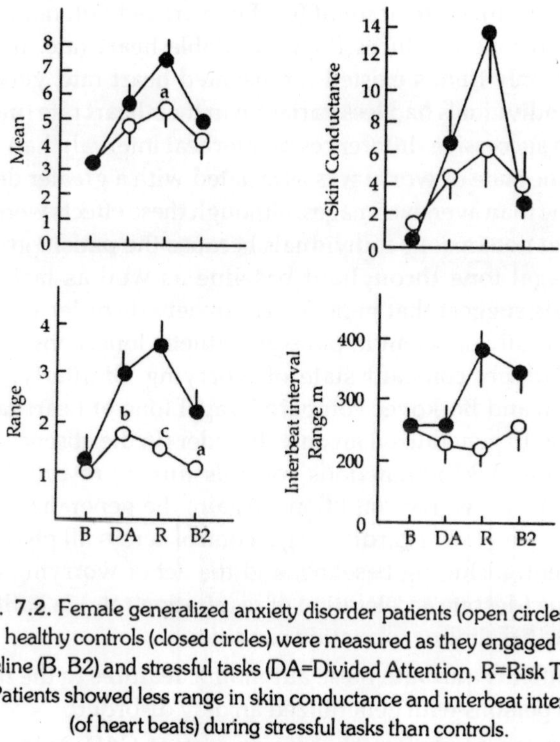

Fig. 7.2. Female generalized anxiety disorder patients (open circles) and healthy controls (closed circles) were measured as they engaged in baseline (B, B2) and stressful tasks (DA=Divided Attention, R=Risk Taking). Patients showed less range in skin conductance and interbeat interval (of heart beats) during stressful tasks than controls.

The possible competition between worry and conceptual reasoning, on the one hand, and fear imagery and arousal. In brief, this proposition stems in large part from experimental work by Lang and colleagues, in which imagery of fearful stimuli increases autonomic responding in comparison to a relative absence of autonomic responding to verbal descriptions of the same material.

The persons with generalized anxiety disorder show less skin conductance and cardiac reactivity to nonspecific stressors than controls, and a preceding interval of worry dampens subsequent physiological responding to fearful stimuli relative to prior intervals of relaxation.

Closer examination of the nature of autonomic dysregulation shows that worry in generalized anxiety disorder is associated with low levels of vagal tone (or parasympathetic activity) in particular, which is presumed to account for the restricted autonomic range. Low vagal tone produces high but stable heart rate. In accord, although only trends existed for elevated heart rate, generalized anxiety individuals had less variation in their heart rate (measured via mean successive differences of interbeat interval) than controls at rest. The state of worry was associated with a greater decline in vagal tone than aversive images, although these effects were mostly evident in nonanxious individuals because the patient group had lower vagal tone throughout baseline as well as tasks. Thus, Lyonfields suggest that generalized anxiety disorder individuals are chronically deficient in parasympathetic tone, consistent with their relatively constant state of worrying. Similarly, Thayer, Friedman, and Borkovec compared vagal tone of heart rate in 34 patients with generalized anxiety disorder (in the absence of panic disorder) and 32 nonanxious controls during resting baseline, relaxation, and worry conditions. Again, the generalized anxiety group showed lower cardiac vagal control across all phases of the experiment, including baseline, and the act of worrying reduced vagal tone (despite acceleration of respiration rate) in both groups relative to baseline or relaxation conditions.

Lyonfields attribute these autonomic features to the nature of worry in persons with generalized anxiety disorder:

> *Given the psychological characteristics of GAD, autonomic inflexibility would be an understandable physiological consequence. The activation of sympathetically based fight-or-flight responses to threat has no effective role. For threats related to nonexistent future events, there is no one to fight and no place to flee. Thus, the reasonable consequences of such a circumstance are the inhibition of motor behavior (analogous to the freezing response of animals whose escape from threat is prevented), increased muscle tension, a shift to mental attempts to search for ways of removing the threat (i.e., worry), and autonomic rigidity.*

However, autonomic inflexibility is also present in panic disorder and obsessive compulsive disorder. That is, inflexibility is not specific to generalized anxiety disorder, but may be characteristic of all chronic anxiety and worry. As reviewed elsewhere in this book, HoehnSaric interpret these findings to mean that persons with anxiety disorders in general are preoccupied with personal stressors and therefore show limited reactivity to nonspecific laboratory stressors. This conclusion follows directly from their methodology; they do not measure the effects of worry but simply reactivity to nonspecific stressors (e.g., number tracking under divided attention conditions). Their interpretation is discounted by the finding that worry about personally relevant topics also lowers vagal tone and causes inflexibility in cardiac responding, even in persons who do not worry chronically. Thus, worrying per se appears to be responsible for restriction of autonomic reactivity in persons with generalized anxiety disorder, other anxiety disorders, or no disorder at all and in relation to nonspecific laboratory stressors or personal stressors.

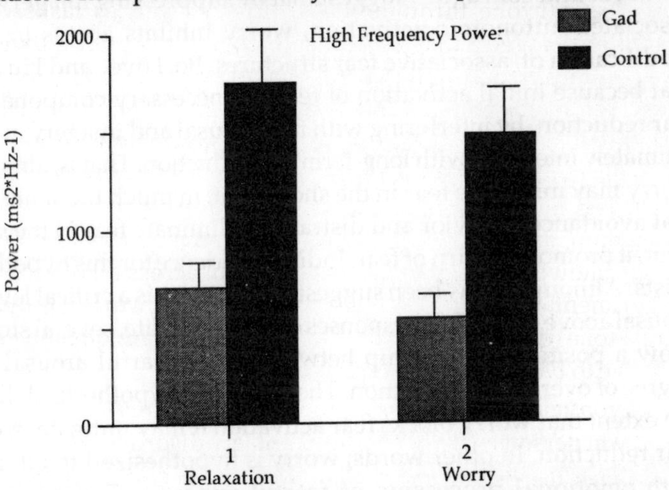

Fig 7.3. Power in the high-frequency component of heart period variability is an index of vagal tone. The higher the power, the more vagal tone. Patients with generalized anxiety disorder (GAD) had lower power and therefore lower vagal tone, during relaxation and during worry, than controls. Also, worry evoked lower power than relaxation overall.

According to this latter hypothesis, vagal tone should be lowered when persons with panic disorder worry about the possibility of panicking or when persons with obsessions and compulsions ruminate about potential contaminants. Unfortunately, extant data regarding autonomic inflexibility for these two disorders are limited to Hoehn-Saric's paradigm of nonspecific stress reactivity.

A final possibility raised by Hoehn-Saric and colleagues is that deficits in autonomic flexibility either represent predispositional factors that contribute to the development of anxiety disorders or are the result of chronic anxiety, as if the autonomic system is being "worn down." Similarly, Thayer note that lowered vagal tone is more characteristic of the elderly, and perhaps chronic worriers are worrying themselves to death.

However, longitudinal data and comparisons between different age cohorts are required to test these hypotheses. Whatever the mechanism, the evidence reviewed indicates that imagery and autonomic arousal are restricted during active worry.

Following the premises of emotional-processing theorizing, Borkovec and colleagues suggest that by suppressing imagery and associated autonomic activation, worry inhibits access to, and modification of, associative fear structures. Borkovec and Hu state that because initial activation of fear is a necessary component of fear reduction, by interfering with fear arousal and imagery, worry ultimately interferes with long-term fear reduction. That is, although worry may minimize fear in the short term, in much the same way that avoidance behavior and distraction eliminate fear in the short term, it promotes return of fear. Indirect evidence for this hypothesis exists. Although it has been suggested that there is a critical level of arousal above which fear responses do not habituate, several studies show a positive relationship between initial fearful arousal and degree of overall fear reduction. Therefore, it is hypothesized that to the extent that worry blocks fear activation it may mitigate overall fear reduction. In other words, worry is hypothesized to interfere with emotional processing of fearful imagery. Consequently, catastrophic images continue to emerge periodically and in turn motivate continued cognitive avoidance in the form of worry. At the same time, blockage of fearful imagery and arousal negatively reinforces worry activity. As a result of this negative reinforcement cycle, preattentive biases toward threat and further catastrophic images, with the associated drive to shift to worry to avoid them, are reinforced. In summary, worry is assumed to preclude emotional processing so that catastrophic images and worry to avoid such images and associated fear arousal are maintained. Additional reinforcement is ascribed to superstitious beliefs about the value of worry, described in more detail below.

Some limited support exists for the worry-imagery reinforcement cycle. For example, Freeston, Dugas, and Ladouceur site a study by Butler, Wells and Dewick in which participants were shown distressing films about industrial accidents. In comparison to instructions to form images, worrying about the film reduced anxiety immediately afterward but increased intrusive images in the following three days. Wells and Papageorgiou exposed students to a gruesome film of an accident, followed by one of five conditions: worry about the film and its implications in verbal form, image the film and its implications, distraction, worry about usual topics of worry, and "settle-down" time. The first condition resulted in the most intrusive images about the film over the next three days.

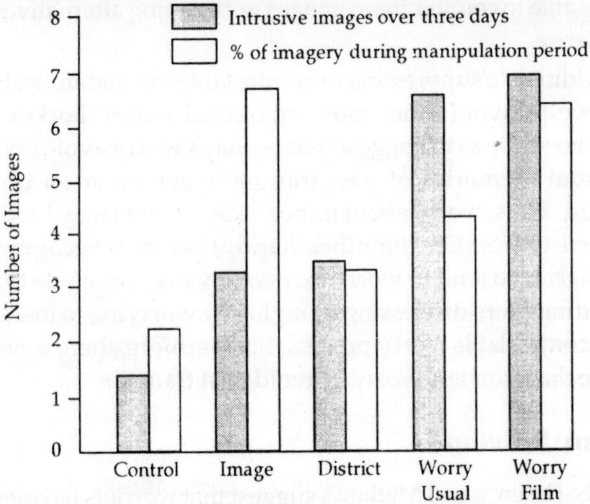

Fig. 7.4. After watching an eight-minute gruesome film, students either worried about the film and its implications (Worry Film), imaged the film and its implications (Image), were distracted (Distract), worried about usual topics of worry (Worry Usual), or were given no instructions about how to respond, for four minutes. Worrying about the film induced the most intrusive imagery over the subsequent three days.

The fact that imaging the film resulted in less subsequent intrusive images was interpreted as more successful emotional processing. However, instructions to imagine the film still yielded more subsequent intrusions than the control condition of "settling down," presumably because the former condition tagged threat-related material with other material in memory, which stimulated more retrieval of threat-related material at a later time. However, the key premise of Borkovec's model is yet to be tested: Does suppression of catastrophic imagery and associated autonomic arousal by the act of worrying generate further worry?

One potential implication from this model is that nonworriers bypass the worry-avoidance cycle by "processing" catastrophic images. That is, by "not avoiding" catastrophic images, nonworriers succeed in quickly reducing the emotionality of such images and hence their likelihood of recurrence. However, a more likely scenario is that nonworriers have fewer catastrophic images to contend with, given that they are less likely to perceive threat in the first place, and are more able to counter these images with coping alternatives when they do arise.

In addition to suppressing uncomfortable somatic arousal, worry may serve to avoid other more emotional issues. Borkovec and Roemer go so far as to suggest that perhaps worry avoids negative affect from memories of past traumatic events or an unhappy childhood. Thus, worry about minor daily matters may block more emotional topics. On the other hand, they also recognize that individuals who tend to worry excessively may conclude that they are avoiding more distressing thoughts by worrying to make sense of an uncontrollable worry process. Furthermore, there is no direct evidence that worriers worry to avoid past traumas.

Problem Solving

Tallis, Eysenck and Mathews suggest that worriers have elevated evidence requirements for making decisions. Consequently, when faced with uncertain threat, such individuals experience delays in problem-solving decisions, resulting in preservation of the worry state. The evidence to date rests on findings that induced worry slows response times to ambiguous concept categorization tasks and delays decisionmaking in stimulus categorization but does not effect performance when the task is unambiguous. Pratt, Tallis and Eysenck attributed elevated evidence requirements to need for perfection. Alternatively, Ladouceur emphasize intolerance of uncertainty, which they posit leads to more focus on uncertain events as dangerous and impedance of problem-solving skills. Their measure of uncertainty predicted poorer performance, indexed by requiring more cues before reaching a decision, mostly in moderately ambiguous situations.

Furthermore, lack of confidence in problem solving may be more critical than actual deficits in problem solving. Indirect evidence derives from questionnaire results showing that the combination of high trait anxiety and a tendency to worry excessively is associated with lack of confidence in problem solving and avoidance coping. Related is the notion that chronic worry reflects a sense of personal incompetence.

Previously, Davey attributed poor problem-solving confidence to high trait anxiety, given that without the influence of high anxiety, worry per se is not directly linked to poor problem solving, at least in nonclinical samples. Thus, Davey speculated that high trait anxiety prevents acceptance of solutions generated by the act of worrying. That is, high trait anxiety generates poor problemsolving confidence, perceived lack of control over problem solving, and catastrophizing tendencies. In accord, negative affect facilitates access to mood-congruent information that is counterproductive to problem solving but instead contributes to catastrophizing. Furthermore, exposure to negative news reports increases negative mood and personal catastrophizing relative to neutral or positive news reports.

More recently, these authors conclude that poor problem-solving confidence may have an independent effect on worrying, separate from anxiety or negative affect. This conclusion derives from a study in which student participants were given false feedback regarding proposed solutions to real-life problem scenarios. Those whose feedback suggested poor performance had increased anxiety and stronger tendencies to catastrophize a personal worry, where catastrophizing was defined as generating bad outcomes and defining a problem as progressively worsening, in comparison to those whose feedback bolstered confidence in problem solving. Multiple regression analyses indicated that these results were more attributable to confidence than anxiety. Thus, the authors concluded that "whereas negative mood may enhance catastrophizing by increasing the individual's ability to access memory stores containing answers to the catastrophic "What if?" question, poor problem-solving confidence may independently facilitate catastrophizing by preventing effective closure of the catastrophizing process". However, we await further evaluation of problem-solving confidence in chronic worriers or persons with generalized anxiety disorder.

Appraisal of Worry

Davey isolated five factors for perceived consequences of worrying: three negative (worry disrupts effective performance, exaggerates the problem, and causes emotional distress) and two positive (worry motivates and helps analytical thinking). Interestingly, both negative and positive factors contributed to measures of psychopathology. That is, dysfunctional beliefs about the positive consequences of worrying, such as superstitious beliefs ("Worrying about an event makes it less likely that it will occur") or beliefs that worry anticipates future events ("Worrying makes me reflect on life by asking questions that I might not usually ask when happy"), may contribute to excessiveness of worry. Like Borkovec and Roemer, Wells and Mathews suggest that meta-cognitions about the positive value of worry are superstitiously reinforced. For example, "Since I have been worrying about losing my job, and I have not lost my job, then worrying must be preventing me from losing my job." That is, the eventual nonoccurrence of anticipated catastrophes is misattributed by the worrier to his or her worry activity.

Another meta-cognition is "worry about worry". Beliefs about the dangers of worry, such as "Worrying could make me go crazy" or "Worrying is abnormal," give rise to worry about worry and may contribute to its excessiveness. For example, worry about worry may lead to attempts to suppress worrying that in turn increase the salience of worry-related activity and prevent disconfirmation of beliefs concerning the dangers of worrying. A newly developed scale incorporates these metacognitions, some of which overlap with the factors identified by Davey: positive beliefs about worry (e.g., "Worrying helps me to plan for the future more effectively"), negative beliefs about the uncontrollability of worry and corresponding danger (e.g., "I find it difficult to control my thoughts"), cognitive confidence in one's memory and attention skills (e.g., "I am easily distracted"), negative beliefs about thoughts in general (e.g., "Not being able to control my thoughts is a sign of weakness"), and cognitive self-consciousness (e.g., "I am constantly aware of my thinking"). However, small samples of patients with generalized anxiety disorder were not distinguishable from patients with obsessive compulsive disorder on these dimensions, and comparisons with other anxiety disorders were limited to a mixed group with "other emotional disorders." Thus, the specificity of these meta-cognitions to generalized anxiety disorder remains to be demonstrated.

Conclusion

In summary, as part of general neuroticism, an overreadiness to perceive threat may increase the frequency with which catastrophic images come to mind and portend the occurrence of catastrophic events. Factors that may maintain excessive worry include negative reinforcement cycles, whereby worry alleviates unpleasant arousal and fear associated with catastrophic images in the short term but at the same time ensures the reoccurrence of such arousal and affect and continuation of worry to avoid them in the long term. This possibility awaits further empirical validation. Furthermore, intolerance of uncertainty or poor confidence in problem solving, and perhaps poor self-concept in general, in addition to appraisals that inflate the value of worry as well as its perceived dangerousness, may contribute to excessive worry. However, the degree to which these features are specific to generalized anxiety disorder has not been clearly established.

Autonomic rigidity, perhaps due to lowered vagal tone, during active worrying is expected given that the purpose of worry is to plan and prepare for potential threats. Autonomic suppression combined with elaborative cognitive processing is most adaptive when threat is a potential (i.e., when worrying). Thus, those who are chronically worried show signs of autonomic rigidity even when not acutely challenged; to date, this is apparent in persons with generalized anxiety disorder, panic disorder, and obsessive compulsive disorder.

The fact that generalized anxiety disorder entails more motor tension and vigilance symptoms than other anxiety disorders may represent the more extreme nature of worry in the former group that persons with generalized anxiety disorder are more persistently worried or worried about a wider array of outcomes. In fact, it is not yet known why the focus of threat in generalized anxiety disorder remains broad as opposed to the more focused threat that characterizes other anxiety disorders (e.g., social rejection in social phobia, loss of control in panic disorder). Is it simply that individuals with generalized anxiety disorder possess stronger "neurotic" predispositions that lead them to perceive threat in a wider variety of situations? Consistent with this possibility is the comorbidity data presented earlier. That is, of all the anxiety disorders, generalized anxiety disorder has the highest rates of comorbidity with other anxiety disorders as well as other Axis I conditions. In other words, broad tendencies to perceive threat are naturally accompanied by specific threat foci as well. In fact, the stronger the predisposition to perceive threat in a variety of situations, the more likely one may be to develop specific foci of threat and additional anxiety disorders.

Cognitive-Behavioral Treatment for Generalized Anxiety Disorder

The cognitive-behavioral treatment for generalized anxiety disorder was relatively nonspecific, given the absence of a unifying theory. Treatments involved relaxation training, cognitive restructuring, problemsolving, and assertiveness training, and their efficacy, as described next, was relatively modest. In contrast to other chapters in this book, treatment outcome data will be presented before outlining a cognitive-behavioral treatment approach. This is done because the most recent treatment approach, which is based on theoretical developments described in the preceding sections, has yet to be empirically validated.

Efficacy of Cognitive-Behavioral Therapy

Treatment outcome research has been hampered by lack of reliable defining characteristics for generalized anxiety disorder, at least up until now,

> *and by the fact that patients with this disorder often present to medical care settings with somatic manifestations while ignoring or denying symptoms of anxiety. Therefore, outcome data are relatively limited in comparison to most other anxiety disorders. Earlier studies employed relaxation training for the most part, with only modest*

success. Later studies incorporated cognitive restructuring and some behavior modification. Percentage improvement is reported by a total of seven independently conducted and controlled studies to date. Improvement was defined as at least 20% improvement on at least three of four measures, including overall severity rating, Hamilton Anxiety scale scores, average daily anxiety and interference with functioning and assessors' ratings of improvement. High end state functioning was defined as scoring within the normal range on anxiety measures and scoring mild or no anxiety on three of five measures, including overall severity rating, Hamilton Anxiety scale, daily anxiety, self-rated anxiety and depression scales, and interference with functioning. (The most effective treatment condition was used for the following statistics when comparisons yielded superiority of one version of cognitive-behavioral therapy over another.) Using these criteria for participants who completed treatment, the average percentages who improve (57%) and achieve high end state (47%) are moderate immediately after treatment and tend to increase slightly an average of 8.6 months following treatment completion (61% and 54%, respectively). These rates of change occur following 13 therapy hours, on average, with an attrition rate of 12%. Despite general improvements and reductions in medications, many remain symptomatic. For example, average percent of the day spent worrying remained at 40% after treatment in the study by Barlow.

Thus, although these treatments are more effective than the passage of time alone, they are only modestly effective and sometimes no more effective than nondirective therapies. Other studies, however, establish efficacy beyond nondirective or placebo controls. Comparisons generally favor cognitively oriented therapy over behaviorally oriented therapy, although Barlow, Rapee, and Brown failed to find significant differences between applied relaxation, cognitive therapy, and their combination.

None of these studies incorporate methods derived from recent theoretical developments, such as emotional processing of catastrophic images or cognitive restructuring of meta-cognitions about worry. A possible exception was coping desensitization, which was employed by Borkovec and Costello. In this strategy, a hierarchy of anxiety-producing situations was developed and, after deep relaxation, patients were instructed to imagine these situations and associated cognitive and physiological responses while also imagining implementing relaxation skills in the situation. Each scene was repeated until it no longer induced anxiety. This strategy may reduce fear that is induced by catastrophic images, which, according to Borkovec's theory, should in turn reduce motivation to worry. However, it is unclear whether catastrophic images were fully targeted by the hierarchy of anxiety-producing situations, and relaxation may serve as a distraction that impedes emotional processing. The strategy called "imagery exposure," described below, attempts to reduce fear of catastrophic images through direct and uninterrupted exposure.

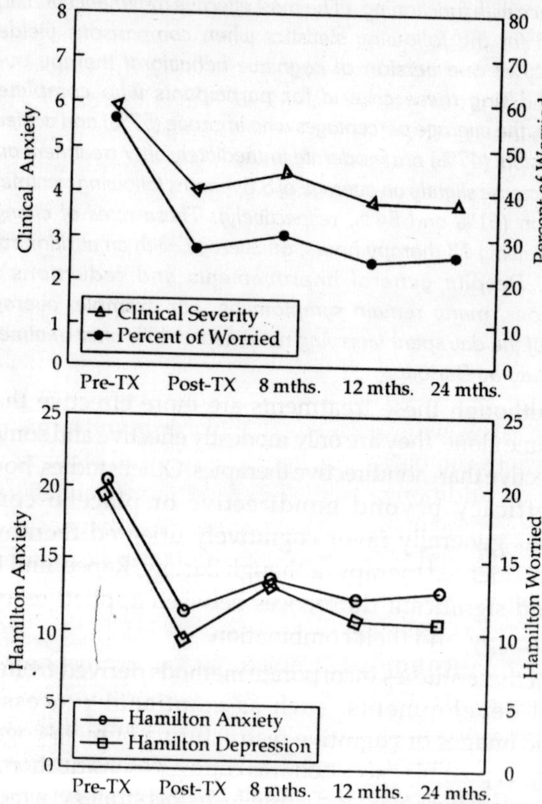

Fig. 7.5. Changes in clinical severity (0-8), percent day worried, and Hamilton Anxiety and Depression ratings in generalized anxiety disorder patients treated with cognitive-behavioral therapy. Note that the average percent day worried remained close to 40%.

Recent developments for treatment of children with anxiety disorders are relevant here, as child samples are usually composed mostly of overanxious disorder. Kendall treated children with overanxious disorder, separation anxiety, or avoidant disorder by teaching them how to recognize anxious feelings and somatic reactions, the role of cognition and self-talk in exacerbating anxious situations, problem-solving and coping skills to manage anxiety, self-evaluation and self-reinforcement strategies to facilitate the maintenance of coping, and planning for dealing with fear. The treatment group was superior to a waitlist control at posttreatment and 12 months later, and therapeutic effects were largely maintained from two to five years later. However, as with adults, the results are not dramatic. For example, only 53% no longer met criteria for their primary anxiety disorder after such treatment in a recent replication study. Although, these rates are improved by family involvement. Specifically, parents were taught how to reward courageous behavior and extinguish excessive anxiety in the child, using verbal praise, privileges, and tangible rewards contingent on facing up to feared situations. Planned ignoring was used in response to excessive complaining and anxious behavior. Also, parents were taught how to manage their own anxiety and skills of communication and problem solving for team development and relapse prevention, including ways of cutting off an escalating conflict cycle, planning and implementing daily discussions combined with listening skills, and problem-solving skills. With the addition of family involvement to Kendall's type of cognitive-behavioral therapy, 84% no longer met diagnostic criteria at posttreatment, and 95% did not meet criteria 12 months later. Corresponding figures for cognitive-behavioral therapy without family involvement were considerably lower: 57% and 70%.

Finally, medication treatments are generally ineffective. Benzodiazepines are used widely for generalized anxiety, but the results are short lived. For example, Lindsay found that although benzodiazepines were effective initially, their efficacy diminished as treatment progressed. Schweizer and Rickels note that approximately two thirds of patients suffer a return of generalized anxiety symptoms within one year of treatment with benzodiazepines. Pourmotabbed found that diazepam attenuated symptoms of generalized anxiety disorder with a peak efficacy during the first three weeks. Thereafter, however, differences from a placebo disappeared due to continued improvement in the latter group. In fact, Barlow concludes from his review that benzodiazepines are no more effective than placebo medications. Thus, there is clearly a strong need for more treatment development from both pharmacological and psychological perspectives. The following cognitive-behavioral treatment incorporates principles from recent theorizing. However, as noted earlier, controlled investigation of this treatment is lacking.

Theory-Driven Cognitive-Behavioral Treatment for Generalized Anxiety Disorder

The treatment involves several components. First is cognitive restructuring to address tendencies to overreadily perceive threat and catastrophize as well as meta-cognitions regarding the value of worry. Next is relaxation training, given the evidence for elevated muscle tension in generalized anxiety. In the third component, termed *imagery exposure,* drawing directly from Borkovec's model, catastrophic images are "emotionally processed" to decrease the motivation to worry. Another component is behavior modification to change safety and cautious behaviors that inadvertently reinforce perceptions of threat. Finally, various problem-solving strategies are taught, such as time management, goal setting, and brainstorming, to address actual and perceived lack of problem-solving skills. Treatment is conducted individually or in groups, generally lasting 12 to 13 sessions. An outline of these procedures is presented in Table 7.1.

Table 7.1. Outline of Cognitive-Behavioral Treatment for Generalized Anxiety Disorder

Session 1	Education regarding the nature and conceptualization of generalized anxiety Three-systems model for describing anxiety
Session 2	Factors that maintain generalized anxiety
Session 3	16 muscle group relaxation Introduction to cognitive restructuring
Session 4	Discrimination training for relaxation Probability overestimation – identifying and challenging
Session 5	8 muscle group relaxation Catastrophizing – identifying and challenging

Session 6	4 muscle group relaxation Review of cognitive restructuring
Session 7	Relaxation by recall Imagery exposure
Session 8	Cue-controlled relaxation Imagery exposure
Session 9	Imagery exposure Worry behavior prevention
Session 10	Imagery exposure Worry behavior prevention
Session 11	Imagery exposure Worry behavior prevention Problem solving
Session 12	Imagery exposure Worry behavior prevention Problem solving
Session 13	Review and planning for future

Cognitive Restructuring

Treatment begins with a three-response system model, in which anxiety is described in terms of thoughts, behaviors, and physical feelings, and a general description and conceptualization of generalized anxiety. Introduction to the role of cognitions in anxiety is much the same as described in previous chapters for other anxiety disorders. Careful attention is given to as detailed monitoring as possible to identify all assumptions and catastrophes in each chain of worrisome thoughts. For example, a chain may extend from negative evaluation from a boss to being fired, or from upsetting someone else by an inappropriate comment to being rejected by everyone.

The therapist coaches ways of countering thoughts, helping to guide the patient to alternative ways of thinking by questioning and prompting. General principles include treating thoughts as hypotheses rather than fact and evaluating the evidence to support or disconfirm thinking. The specific content of worries as well as tendencies to inflate the value of worry is targeted by these means. As with treatment of panic disorder, typical errors in thinking are categorized as overestimation of the probability of a negative event (e.g., "I will fail this exam") and catastrophizing the meaning of an event (e.g., "It will be horrible if I am five minutes late"). Drawing from Beck and Emery, Borkovec and Costello identify the following types of distorted thinking. *Filtering*, or tunnel vision, occurs when only one element of a situation is focused on to the exclusion of everything else (such as remembering the week as horrible despite at least one good day). *Polarized thinking* refers to thinking in terms of dichotomies instead of continuums, such as "If I'm not perfect, then I'm a total loss." *Overgeneralization* refers to making conclusions on a single incident or piece of evidence, such as interpreting one negative evaluation as an indication of failure despite generally good work evaluations. *Personalizations* refer to tendencies to relate everything to oneself, accompanied by comparing oneself to others, thereby assuming that one's underlying worth is questionable and that every experience, conversation, or look is a clue to one's own worth and value. Finally, "shoulds" refers to inflexible lists of rules about behavior, which are considered "right," so that any deviation is wrong. Consequently, "should" statements generate frequent judging of oneself and finding fault with self and others.

In the treatment model my colleagues and I developed, questioning of the odds or probabilities is conducted for examples of probability overestimation, and consideration of ways of coping is conducted to counteract tendencies to catastrophize (the "so what" strategy). Concrete visualizations of negative events and ways of coping are helpful for decatastrophizing. By so doing, therapists aim to generate a sense that negative events are manageable and time limited. In most cases, a worry is handled by a combination of questioning the probabilities and decatastrophizing. For example, restructuring of worries about being fired from work may incorporate "What is the likelihood of my boss realizing that I made a mistake?" "What is the likelihood that my boss would fire me if I did make a mistake?" "What is the worst that can happen if I do make a mistake?" and "What steps would I take to cope with loss of my job?"

Cognitive restructuring also targets meta-cognitions, such as believing that worry prevents projected negative events from happening, or, because future catastrophes can be projected, believing that it is one's responsibility to be concerned and if at all possible prevent their occurrence, because failure to do so means neglect of responsibilities. The effect of worry on future events is questioned, and responsibility is emphasized as only important to the extent that the event being predicted is of high probability most of the events about which chronic worriers are concerned are of low probability. Elements in a situation are categorized as either controllable or not to combat tendencies to assume responsibility for all events. Meta-cognitions about the dangers of worry (e.g., "I will go crazy from worrying") are similarly addressed via questioning of probabilities and generation of alternative outcomes. Cognitive restructuring is emphasized in Sessions 1 through 5, but continued throughout the entire treatment. Thus, each session begins with a review of self-monitoring of anxious thoughts and restructuring for each episode of anxiety between treatment sessions.

Relaxation

Progressive muscle relaxation training is taught following the format developed by Bernstein and Borkovec. This is introduced in Session 3 and emphasized through the eighth session. Training begins with 16 muscle groups that are progressively tensed and relaxed, culminating in a final deepening of relaxation via slow breathing and repetition of the word "relax" on each exhale. Next, discrimination training is incorporated to help patients distinguish sensations of tension from relaxation. Discrimination training entails comparisons between one quarter, one half, three quarters, and maximum tensing capacity. Consequently, patients learn to detect building tension throughout the day so that relaxation can be instituted at the earliest signs of tension.

This set of exercises, which lasts approximately 30 minutes, is practiced daily, usually with initial aid of an audiotape of in-session instructions. Then, the number of muscle groups is gradually reduced to arrive eventually at a more portable technique. Thus, 16 muscle groups is reduced to 8 and then 4, usually those that represent areas of the body that are typically most tense (e.g., stomach, shoulders, neck, and forehead). Next, relaxation by recall is introduced. This involves concentrating on specific body areas and inducing the state of relaxation while consciously letting go of tension, recalling the feelings of relaxation, maintaining slow breathing, and repeating the word "relax" with each exhale.

Daily practice is encouraged, starting in relaxing and nondistracting environments and then generalizing to distracting environments (e.g., at work, while watching television). Finally, cue-controlled relaxation is introduced, in which relaxation is induced by simply repeating the word "relax" and letting all tension dissipate with a few slow breaths. Previous pairings of the word "relax" with feelings of relaxation is assumed to develop conditional properties that facilitate the onset of a relaxed state. Cue-controlled relaxation is intended to be used as needed in response to symptoms of tension or anxiety.

Imagery Exposure

Imagery exposure (also referred to as *cognitive or worry exposure*) is introduced at Session 7 and continues for the remainder of treatment. The goal is to reduce fear associated with catastrophic images that are assumed to underlie chains of worry. In turn, fear reduction is assumed to reduce the motivation for excessive worry. Specific steps include identification of catastrophic imagery for each principal sphere of worry, imagery training practice, and prolonged imagining of worst-possible feared outcomes, followed by generation of as many alternatives as possible.

Direct provocation of catastrophic images provides opportunities to practice anxiety management strategies (relaxing, questioning the evidence, considering alternatives) as weli as habituation to fearful images. The latter parallels habituation to obsessive imagery in obsessive compulsive disorder. Imagery practice can be conducted with the following types of scenarios before repeated exposure to catastrophic images. Imagery practice is intended to enhance vividness of imagery, which may be especially valuable for persons who have learned to avoid emotionally laden images. As advocated by bioinformational theory, images are most emotionally provocative when they contain response elements, and hence the practice imagery scenarios are heavily sensate oriented.

You are sitting by a window. The window is square, with one unbroken pale of glass. There are yellow and white checkered curtains on the sides. You are sitting on a soft chair and feel comfortable and relaxed. Your elbows are on the windowsill, and your hands are clasped under your chin. The sun is streaming in through the window, onto your face and arms. You feel warm, and the light is bright. You close your eyes and feel the warm sun.

Or,

You walk into a square, blue room. The walls and ceiling are all a deep blue. On the floor is a blue carpet. The carpet is soft under your feet. There is nothing in the room except for a plain wooden table in the middle. On the table are a clear glass pitcher filled with water and a tall, clear glass. You are thirsty, and you are glad to see the water. Your mouth is very dry. You walk over to the table and pick up the pitcher in one hand and the glass in the other. You fill the glass with water. Your hand holding the glass feels cool as the glass fills with water. You put the pitcher back down on the table, swallow some water, and then drink some more.

After vivid imagery can be evoked with these neutral scenarios, catastrophic images are recorded on audiotape, incorporating stimulus, response, and meaning elements. For example,

> *Imagine that you are sitting here in the chair and the phone rings. You pick up the phone and it is your daughter. She sounds strained her voice is quiet and tense. You feel your muscles tighten and a gnawing feeling in the pit of your stomach. Your legs feel weak so you grab the desk for support. Your daughter says that something terrible has happened. A rush of fear comes over your body and you wish this were not happening. You feel as if this is the moment you have been dreading for so long. You don't say anything except to murmur, "What?" It does not seem real — things are spinning around you. You hear your daughter sobbing, and you feel sick to your stomach. You ask frantically, "What has happened?" You want to leave but you know you cannot -you have to face the news. Slowly, she tells you that the police called there had been an accident your husband was driving home and was hit by another vehicle he is in critical condition at Harbor Hospital he may not live. You feel as if you might faint so you sit down you feel shaky all over and you don't know what to do. You cannot believe this is happening to you.*

Patients begin with images associated with their least anxiety-inducing worry sphere, rating the vividness of their imagery and maximum level of anxiety (using 0-8 point scales or the like) after listening to their audiotaped descriptions. Assuming the vividness of the imagery is adequate, concentrated imagery then continues for some time, 15 to 20 minutes, possibly interspersed with brief rests (the maximal format for exposure is yet to be empirically tested). Next, management strategies are implemented, including cue-controlled relaxation, questioning the evidence, rating the real odds, and consideration of ways of managing the negative event if it were to happen or alternative solutions to the situation. Notably, anxiety management is delayed until after imagery exposure has ended, given the possibility that cognitive restructuring throughout the imagery may inadvertently reinstitute a verbalizing style that impedes emotional processing of the imagery. This procedure is repeated the number of times necessary for maximum anxiety to reduce to mild levels, or 2 or less on a 0-8 point scale. The next set of catastrophic images from the hierarchy is then practiced in the same way.

Worry Behavior Prevention

We found that over half of our group of generalized anxiety patients were engaging in some kind of corrective, preventative, or ritualistic behavior associated with their worries, such as frequent telephone calls to loved ones to check on their safety and early arrivals at appointments to avoid being late. These behaviors reinforce perceptions of risk-in other words, they prevent disconfirmation of perceived negative outcomes. Worry behavior prevention aims to prevent such safety or cautious behaviors and facilitate evidence gathering that disconfirms perceptions of threat.

A list of behaviors is generated in relation to each major worry sphere. A set of tasks is generated from this list. These tasks essentially replace the overly cautious or avoidant behavior with "normal" behavior. Examples of such tasks include leaving the house without tidying every room, purposefully leaving one room untidy for visitors, limiting checks on the safety of others, leaving work before someone else and not completing every task before leaving, and leaving for an appointment several minutes later than usual.

A hierarchy is established from the least to the most anxiety-provoking task, and then each item on the hierarchy is practiced between sessions the number of times necessary for anxiety to reduce to a mild level. Before, during, and after each practice, anxiety is countered by cue-controlled relaxation, questioning the real odds, considering ways of coping with negative events, and generating alternative solutions. Thus, unlike imagery exposure, management strategies are incorporated as the task of behavioral modification is ongoing. Assignments of this kind are introduced around Session 9 and continued throughout the remainder of treatment.

Problem Solving

Problem-solving skills are incorporated toward the end of treatment. This portion of the treatment draws very much from standard stress management protocols. Time management involves identification of problems concerning task completion, assignment of priorities to tasks, and scheduling. To identify problem areas with respect to task completion, activities completed on a given day, at work and at home, big and small, are listed. Next, planned but not completed activities are listed. Third, highly desired activities for which there was no time are listed. Lengthy second and third lists reflects poor time management. Also, items on the first list are evaluated for signs of unnecessary activities, or poor time management. Ways of reducing unnecessary activities include delegation of responsibility to others, which is usually combined with cognitive restructuring over worries that tasks will not be accomplished by others as well as they would be accomplished personally. Other strategies for reducing unnecessary activities include assertiveness, saying "no" to requests by others, sticking to agendas rather than being waylaid by other tasks, and changing expectations for perfection that only serve to lead to procrastination or excessively lengthy times to complete tasks.

Goal setting can be short term (daily) or longer term. For a given day, a list is made of all tasks planned for the day. Then, the importance of each one is rated. "A" tasks are top-priority tasks. These are the tasks that absolutely have to get done that day. "B" tasks are important but do not absolutely have to get done that day. These are the most common, and if not done, they will eventually become A tasks. "C" tasks need to be done some day but are not really important at the moment. Then, to organize their day, patients are instructed to record the tasks that have to be done at specific times, such as meetings. Next, A tasks are slotted into the times during which they can probably be accomplished. The remaining time slots are filled in with B and finally C tasks.

Finally, brainstorming begins with precise identification of objective details of a given problem, as opposed to thoughts or feelings about the situation. For example, if the problem is to do with a child's rebellious behavior, describing the problem as "Kathy is being very rude" is too vague, whereas describing it as "Kathy doesn't care about my feelings and doesn't appreciate everything I have done for her over the years" is too emotional. However, describing it as "Kathy doesn't do her chores around the house and doesn't tell me what time she will be home" is more descriptive and detailed. Brainstorming means generating every possible solution, no matter how unreasonable it may seem initially. By so doing, potentially good solutions that were not considered previously may be realized. These solutions are then ranked in terms of feasibility, and plans of action are generated for the most feasible solutions. The probability of each plan working is then rated, and the plan with the highest probability is put into action.

Treatment Summary

In summary, cognitive-behavioral therapies to date have yielded only modest effects for generalized anxiety disorder. Exceptions are the recent successes obtained with children with overanxious disorder, as well as other anxiety disorders, especially when treatment incorporates parental training. The modest effects for adults may be attributable to the nonspecific nature of the cognitive-behavioral therapies. Recent theoretical developments summarized in this chapter, and the treatment methods based on those developments, may produce more successful outcomes. Clearly, these "theory-driven" cognitive-behavioral approaches for generalized anxiety disorder require empirical validation.

8

Multiple Personality Disorder

Introduction

MPD is characterised by a lack of integration of different aspects of consciousness, which means that the individual demonstrates several different sub-personalities or identities (known as 'alters ') at different times. Cases have been reported with as few as 2 identities and as many as 4500, the average number being 15 for women and 8 for men. These identities will vary in terms of their names, personality characteristics, age and even gender from the primary personality (that by which the individual is most commonly known). They may switch gradually, but the changeover is often abrupt, and the personalities may interrupt one another. Stress may prompt a change from one identity to another. Some identities will be aware of the others, but they do not all have this awareness. The primary identity is often guilt-ridden, passive, depressed and dependent, while the others may be aggressive and outgoing.Amnesia for personal activities, both long and short term, is common. Thus one identity may not remember something that happened when another identity was in control. In some cases, amnesia may cover an extended period of childhood, and may be linked with physical and/or sexual abuse. Flashbacks and self-mutilation may occur, and present relationships may be abusive ones. The diagnostic criteria from DSM IV are given in Box 8.1.

Box 8.1. Diagnostic criteria for multiple personality disorder

1. Presence of two or more personalities, each with a different way of perceiving, relating to and thinking about the self and the environment.
2. Behaviour is controlled on different occasions by at least two of these personalities.
3. Extensive forgetting of important personal information.
4. Cannot be explained by effects of substance abuse, medical conditions or (in the case of children) fantasy play.

Measurement

In 1986 Bernstein and Putnam produced the first test to measure MPD, called the Dissociative Experiences Scale; this was revised in 1993. More recent scales include the questionnaire of Experiences of Dissociation and the Dissociative Questionnaire. These are all based on the client's response to a set of questions (the DES contains 28, for example) and can be used for routine screening or initial tentative diagnoses. The client is asked to decide what percentage of the time they have certain experiences, when not under the influence of drugs or alcohol. Experiences include finding unfamiliar things among their belongings, suddenly realising that they cannot remember part of a journey they have just made, failing to recognise people they know, and being shown that they have done something that they have no memory of at all. Other questions involve feelings of depersonalisation - feeling that their bodies are not their own, or that they are standing outside and observing themselves. Out of a possible final score of 100, Carlson and Putnam found that normal adults score about 4, schizophrenics 20, post-traumatic stress patients 31 and MPD patients 57. College students, incidentally, score about 14 - often attributed to regular daydreaming! Carlson and Putnam suggested that the cut-off point should be a score of 30, on the grounds that 80% of diagnosed multiples score over 30, and 80% of non-multiples score under 30.

The existence of measurement instruments is an important requirement for further research into this area, but two problems should be noted with these scales. First, results are easy to fake.

Gilbertson found that after instructing groups of student nurses to answer in different ways (normally, faking problems, faking good or faking MPD), they were easily able to produce the required results. Second, questionnaire scores have been subjected to factor analysis. This is a statistical technique that aims to show how many different factors (or clusters of behaviours) underlie responses to questions. In this case, factor analysis of scores from the various different questionnaires available has been shown to yield anything from 3 to 7 factors. Since those found in different studies are not always the same, it has been concluded that there may be as many as 11 factors being measured on the scales. To quote Hacking: 'a problem arises when it seems to many observers that "dissociative experiences" is used to refer to a great many experiences that have singularly little in common with one another'.

History

Bearing in mind the problems of assessment, we can turn next to look at historical changes in the frequency of multiple personality disorder. The prevalence of the disorder has been assessed at different times and in different parts of the world. Perhaps the earliest case was described by Ellenberger, a German physician, in 1791. In 1816, Mary Reynolds was described as a case of 'double consciousness', but it was not until 1876 that the first systematic study was undertaken. This was of Felida X, whose case was identified by the researcher, Azam, as a case of 'dedoublement de la personnalité' (double or split personality). Felida was reported to have two personalities, as the term implies; in 1885, the case of Louis Vivet, who had eight distinct personalities, was reported in France. When this was published in England, he was described as being a 'multiple personality'.

In general, little evidence of MPD was found in the early 20th century. There was also a loss of interest in hysteria, with which it had been associated. Early multiples tended to show hysterical symptoms such as paralysis, and somatic symptoms, and MPD was viewed as a subtype of hysteria. Freud contributed significantly to this lack of interest when he abandoned his seduction theory the idea that hysteria was caused by childhood sexual abuse on the basis that the reports he obtained from patients were fantasies rather than reality. In the literature up to 1944, just 76 cases were reported in the medical literature. Between 1944 and 1969, 14 cases were reported. By 1970 only 100 cases had been reported in professional journals. However, by 1986 around 6000 patients had been diagnosed and it was being described as an epidemic of multiple personality. By 1990 there were thousands in America and Canada. Acocella reports that there were almost 40,000 new cases between 1985 and 1995. Ross estimated that 2% of the North American population may be affected and the prevalence certainly appears to be on the increase. There is now an International Society for the Study of Multiple Personality and Dissociation.

There is also considerable cultural variation in prevalence of MPD. The rate of occurrence of MPD is very much higher in North America than in Britain. Ross. screened 299 psychiatric patients in Canada and found a 3.3% prevalence in that group. Modestin in Switzerland calculated from a survey of psychiatrists that 0.05-0.1% of patients were affected. MPD has been reported as virtually unknown in Czechoslovakia, New Zealand, Australia and India. In India, however, 'possession syndrome' (being taken over by the spirit of a dead relative) is quite common, and could be seen as a cultural variation of MPD, as could 'Zar', a similar syndrome found in the Sudan.

Evaluation: Reasons for Variations in Prevalence

How can these historical and cultural variations be explained? There are four possibilities that we will consider here:

- changes and biases in the diagnostic system;
- changes and biases in clinicians;
- cultural causation;
- social constructionism.

The first two explanations relate to the concept of MPD as an iatrogenic disorder, meaning that it is induced in the patient by the psychiatric system itself. The third suggests that it is spontaneous or genuine. The fourth argues that it may well be a combination of these, a collusion between the system and the person in difficulties.

Changes and Biases in the Diagnostic System

It is clear that MPD has not always been recognised as a disorder in the past, not even in previous versions of DSM. It was not until

1980 that it was officially recognised in DSM IV. As DSM has become more specific in its description of MPD, it might be expected that clinicians might become more confident in diagnosing it, leading to an apparent increase in general prevalence compared with that observed in the past. There may also be variability between cultures according to the training given to clinicians. However, it may also be the case that cultural variation is the result of behaviours shown by MPD patients being an accepted part of everyday life in some cultures and hence not being regarded as requiring psychiatric help, or not being given the same label 'possession syndrome' being a good example of this. Many culturally accepted healing rituals and religious practices in other cultures involve trance states. Lewis-Fernandez argues that these have not been differentiated in the present version of DSM from pathological states. MPD may be a genuine 'culture-bound syndrome' or it may simply be that it is only viewed as a problem in some Western countries.

It may also be possible to query the validity of MPD as a diagnostic category. Most MPD patients also meet the criteria for other disorders at least 3-4 according to North and 11 according to Ross. These include depression (90%), substance abuse (57%), antisocial personality and borderline personality disorder (64%). Boon and Draijer, in Holland, found that many of their sample of 71 had had other diagnoses before; for example, they may have been diagnosed as schizophrenic because they reported hearing voices. In a survey of psychiatrists, Pope found that only 20% felt that there was good evidence for MPD's validity as a category. Most felt that it rarely occurs spontaneously without prompting.

Changes and Biases in Clinicians

The second proposal is that MPD may be the result of clinical bias. Increasing awareness of the syndrome through the development of clear clinical criteria may have had the effect of oversensitising clinicians, in this view. A change of mood, clothing or hairstyle could then be misinterpreted by the clinician as the emergence of an alter. When provided with suggestible patients, it may be possible for clinicians to encourage patients to show behaviours appropriate to MPD. In fact such patients have been found to be more hypnotisable than most, and may be able to go into trances spontaneously without the use of hypnosis (e.g. through the use of guided imagery, a technique in which patients are guided through a fantasy by the clinician). In such states they may be more open to leading questions and suggestions from the clinician. Spanos has pointed out that the diagnostic interviews (described in a later section of the chapter) carried out for MPD contain all the information needed by the patient in order to produce the basic signs of the disorder. Interestingly, Ross found that of 236 cases they surveyed, the mean number of alters was 16 exactly the number shown by the most famous case, Sybil. Patients may also be generally vulnerable people, as shown by the fact that many have other disorders as well (comorbidity). For example, Acocella found that 61% have attempted suicide, 20% have worked as prostitutes and 12% have criminal records.

The high prevalence of the disorder in some countries, such as Holland for example, has been attributed to the frequent visits of North American experts to that country in the past. It is argued that within a culture, a relatively small number of clinicians may be responsible for a large number of diagnoses. Thigpen and Cleckley, who originally reported the well-known case of Eve (see later) have stated that they very rarely see such cases. In Modestin's study of Swiss psychiatrists, it was noted that the patients were not evenly distributed: 3 of the 770 psychiatrists surveyed saw a lot more MPD patients than the others. In Baltimore, America, Ross (1992) found that the numbers of MPD patients at one centre rose by 900% after an MPD expert joined the staff. Thus Acocella concludes, 'Just as some exotic syndromes are confined to Japan, or certain South Sea Islands, [MPD] is a syndrome geographically related to high concentration zones of therapists who identify with the beliefs of a particular psychological sub-culture.' In other words, clinical bias may be responsible for the observed variations in prevalence.Further evidence pertaining to this view can be derived from an examination of what happens when patients refuse to accept that they have MPD. That some therapists are reluctant to accept that the patient does *not* have MPD is evident in some of the terms they use. 'Stonewalling', for example, is the term for a patient's refusal to accept the diagnosis, and it is generally regarded as a poor prognostic sign (i.e. an indication that they will not make good progress in treatment). Claims by patients that they made up all the information given are viewed as 'resistance' to treatment. Acocella provides the following example: 'One patient reports that when she finally told Ault [the therapist] that she had never been abused, that the memories were false, he replied "Which personality am I talking to now?".'

Cultural Causation

This explanation for cultural differences in prevalence argues that the observed cases of MPD are genuine (or 'spontaneous'), and that the characteristics of certain cultures are such that they bring about the disorder. It has been suggested for example that there are four aspects of modern living that make traumatic neuroses of all kinds more likely, because they induce a state of chronic trauma and uncertainty. These are:

- lack of clear moral guidelines;
- lack of control over life;
- sensory overload;
- being disconnected from other people.

Similarly, Martinez-Taboas argues that MPD is more likely in societies in which the individual is viewed as a separate self (individualistic societies), rather than community-based or collectivist societies. Kluft describes MPD as perhaps more properly termed 'multiple *reality* disorder', to emphasise that it may be the result of such confusions. Such theories, however, are difficult to test empirically.

Social Constructionism

The final explanation is that proposed by the social constructionists. In this view, the problem is neither spontaneous nor iatrogenic. Hartocollis argues that it is not iatrogenic in the sense of being artificially manufactured by the suggestions of the therapist, or the result of a false diagnosis, nor is the suffering of the patient in doubt. What is 'manufactured' is the way that experience is dissected by Western culture, and in particular psychiatrists. This could account for historical changes in the way the disorder is expressed. For example, Kenny has pointed out that the early cases had just two personalities, corresponding to the Christian dualism of good and evil. Modern cases have many confused selves, corresponding to the variety of possibilities offered by modern life.

In this view, developments in psychology, as well as developments in society, have gone hand-in-hand to create the epidemic. Among other things, the development of the media in Western society has led to an interest in role-playing, as well as an awareness of different possible identities. According to Acocella 'we are exposed to illusory representations far more vivid than our own lives'. Acocella notes that the increase in MPD parallels the increase in availability of TV remote controls, and suggests that the multiples are 'channel-surfing'. The internet allows people to adopt an on-line persona, and there are web sites for multiples that provide plenty of information about the problem. Television, too, provides models, and following revelations in the Oprah Winfrey show (a well-known American chat show), Kluft has suggested that MPD could also be regarded as 'Oprahgenic' in its origins.

In psychology, there has been a revival of interest in hypnosis in recent years, and in some parts of the world increasing disposable income has facilitated the development of the private psychotherapy business. As cognitive-behavioural therapies have grown in popularity, so the lengthier, psychodynamically oriented therapies have suffered. MPD could be seen as offering them some scope for development, because psychodynamic explanations and treatments, as we shall see later, have proved to be the most popular way of dealing with MPD. The standard treatment, according to Acocella, would cost around 17,000 dollars a year, even after the contribution from insurance companies. This would make such therapists into good money-spinners. The group that mostly patronises such therapists, in fact, consists of white North American females precisely those who are most likely to be diagnosed with MPD.

Other developments in society in recent times that are relevant here are the rise of feminism and the increasing awareness of child abuse that accompanied it. These will be discussed in later sections when we look at explanations and treatments for the disorder. To conclude, a quote from Hacking: 'The fact that a certain type of mental illness appears only in specific historical or geographical contexts does not imply that it is manufactured, artificial, or in any other way not real.' Even if the disorder turns out to be an accepted, even fashionable, way of expressing distress, it is still important to deal with it in an appropriate manner. In the following sections we will look at how it has been dealt with to date. This will give us further clues as to its nature.

Case Studies

Three cases will be discussed in this section: the case of Eve; the case of Sybil; and that of Billy Milligan. They have been selected because they all raise different, important issues about the nature of MPD.

Eve

Eve White was a 25-year-old married woman referred to a psychiatrist for treatment because she suffered from blinding headaches for which no physical cause could be found. On interview, marital conflicts, personal frustrations, blackouts and loss of memory were all revealed as well. Following a hypnosis session, her psychiatrist received a letter from her, with a note added that appeared to be from someone else the handwriting was completely different. She subsequently denied sending the letter at all, but admitted to having heard voices. Her personality seemed to change at this point in the interview, and she announced herself as Eve Black ('Black' was Eve White's maiden name). This personality, in contrast to the serious, conventional, considerate and retiring Eve White, was carefree, mischievous, irresponsible, pleasure-seeking and lacking in depth of feeling. As Acocella puts it she was a 'vivacious party girl leaving her host personality with unexplanied hangovers and a reputation in local bars'. This good-bad split is a common feature of MPD cases.

Following the first spontaneous change, hypnosis had to be used to elicit Eve Black, but it became easier and easier for Eve Black to take over. While Eve Black was fully aware of, and rather despised, Eve White, Eve White had no knowledge of Eve Black (except for that gained during therapy) and no access to her consciousness. This is known as asymmetrical amnesia. Thus during childhood Eve Black would be disobedient, leaving Eve White to get the blame for something that she could not remember doing. Although her parents and husband had observed these changes, they did not interpret them as anything other than inconsistent behaviour. The skills shown by one (such as driving or sewing) could not be carried out by the other. One relative reported that Eve had been married prior to her present marriage. Eve White was unaware of this, but Eve Black eventually admitted it was true, and that her 'husband' had physically abused her. At such times she would allow Eve White to take over so that she would not suffer any pain, and then erase Eve White's memory for the beatings.

After 8 months of treatment, Eve White seemed to be gaining more control, at least in the work environment, but this began to change and blackouts became common again. Eve Black denied responsibility for these, and finally a third personality, known as Jane, emerged. Jane spoke with a different voice, and was considered to be more mature and capable than the other two. She was aware of both Eves, but could not displace Eve Black.

Psychometric and physiological tests were also given to the different personalities. Eve White obtained a higher score on the WAIS than Eve Black, but Eve Black's Rorschach results were considered to be psychologically healthier, indicating regression rather than repression. On the Semantic Differential, which is a test of attitudes, there were clear differences between the three personalities. Eve White came out as socialised, with a normal view of the world but a negative view of self. Eve Black showed less stability over time, saw herself as perfect and the world as abnormal. Jane had the most healthy perception of both the world and herself. On the EEG, Eve White and Jane showed normal records, indistinguishable from one another; Eve Black, however, showed more signs of tension, with a slightly fast trace of a type sometimes associated with psychopathic personality. A later analysis of film footage found that each personality showed a different pattern of eye movements. These pieces of evidence from objective tests indicate that there was a genuine difference in Eve's behaviour when different alters were in control. Such behavioural differences would be difficult to simulate.

Thigpen and Cleckley interpreted Eve's problems as being due to her feelings of rejection as a child, and anxiety about her role as a wife and mother. To escape from these problems, she took on the role of Eve Black to take her back to the period before she was married and allow her an opportunity to be free of responsibilities. Their aim in therapy was to develop Jane's personality so that she would be dominant, as her personality was felt to be better adjusted. However, a fourth personality, Evelyn, appeared some months later. She knew all about the other three, and was felt to be a more complete personality.

This is where the book and the film (*The Three Faces of Eve*) left the story. In 1975, a woman called Chris Sizemore revealed that she was the real 'Eve' and that she had in fact had 22 personalities over the years, the first occurring when she was just 2 years old. In 1989 in her book *A Mind of My Own*, she claimed that some of her alters had been present from birth because they were alters from a past life. When she was 46 years old, they spontaneously integrated into one personality.

Evaluation

Thigpen and Cleckley were not entirely convinced themselves that Eve was a geniune MPD case rather than a skilled actress, and they reported that in the 30 years that had elapsed since their study they had only come across one other case. Although the objective tests would seem to provide convincing evidence of her genuineness, they have been criticised by Orne. In many cases, for example, there were no control conditions employing people who had been asked to fake MPD. The extent to which the people assessing test results may have been biased by being told that they were from different people is also unclear.

According to Arrigo and Pezdek, textbook versions have misrepresented the case by ignoring what they describe as 'the wretchedness of her condition' as regards her early experiences. At the age of 15, Eve eloped with a sexual sadist, and consequently suffered from frigidity and an eating disorder. She had attempted to strangle her own daughter, and subsequently faked integration of her personalities. Her later career as a lecturer, which earned her an award for public service in 1982, has also been ignored.

Sybil

Probably the best-known case of MPD, as a result of the Hollywood film of the same name, Sybil was actually studied by Cornelia Wilbur, an orthodox Freudian, but the case was rejected by scientific journals of the time and eventually written up as book by Schreiber, a journalist. Wilbur, a psychoanalyst, was interested in childhood trauma as the basis of MPD. Sybil Dorsett was referred for treatment in 1954 at the age of 31, because she was unable to account for substantial periods of time. Her problems began at the age of 22, with memory lapses and severe headaches. She also suffered from fugues, a condition in which the sufferer finds themselves in a strange place with no idea how they got there. Wilbur's treatment of Sybil took 2534 sessions over a period of 11 years, and involved sharing a house with her client at one stage. She claimed that Sybil had an IQ of 170. Wilbur used hypnosis and the drug sodium amytal (which increases hypnotic suggestibility) to access her client's early memories.

This eventually revealed no fewer than 16 alters, some of whom were children (including a baby called Ruthie who split off after watching her parents have sex) and two who were the opposite sex (called Mike and Sid). They all had different images of how they looked, as well as different tastes in friends, food and music, and different skills (e.g. one could play the piano). It also revealed that Sybil had been sexually abused by her mother, who had administered cold water enemas which Sybil was prevented from expelling by being bound and hung upside down, She had also had various sharp objects stuck into her anus and vagina. The alters had been created, it was said, in order to cope with the abuse. They would take over, and Sybil would not remember what had happened. What was unusual about Sybil was not only the number of alters, but the fact that some were transsexual, i.e. alters of the opposite sex. The history of abuse also differentiated her from Eve who, although she had had childhood traumas, was never sexually assaulted. Because the case appeared at a time when child abuse was in the public consciousness, it found what Hartocollis describes as a 'cultural fit' in a way that Eve did not, and became the best-known case of MPD.

Evaluation

This case, unlike that of Eve, was never written up in the professional journals where it could be subjected to peer review from other therapists. Wilbur, Schreiber and Sybil are all now dead, and cannot be questioned, but there are some criticisms available from those who worked with them. For example, Spiegel took over from Wilbur during a period of absence. He found that she had originally diagnosed Sybil as schizophrenic, but Schreiber wanted to write about a case of MPD. In fact Spiegel felt that Sybil was a case of hysteria. He also noticed that she was unusually hypnotisable, to the extent that she entered trances spontaneously. When she was in trances, Wilbur gave her different names, and the multiples developed from there. Spiegel narrates an interview with Sybil in which she asks if he wants her to be Helen, adding that Wilbur would have wanted that when talking about the issue under consideration. When Spiegel says that she can be Sybil if she would prefer, she agrees; 'Fine, I'd prefer it that way'.

Another critic is Rieber who obtained 2 hours of taped conversations between Schreiber and Wilbur about Sybil. In the course of the conversations, Wilbur mentioned that she had to list the names of alters for Sybil to get her to respond appropriately. She also used hypnotic suggestions and powerful drugs such as sodium pentothal. Schreiber mentions at one point a letter from Sybil in which she denies everything that she claimed had happened to her. Even before this, in 1987, Miller commented that 'Sybil's life was made up by Sybil, her doctor, when she became a case, and again, when she became a book, by her author. Sixteen selves were imagined, but it is not even entirely certain that there were as many as two.'

Billy Milligan

This is another case that has been written up by a non-academic; Keyes was a novelist and teacher of English. Known as 'the Campus Rapist', Milligan came to the public attention because he was arrested after a series of three rapes carried out in 1977 in Ohio State University. The evidence against him was overwhelming - handcuffs and weapons were found at his flat, as well as the credit cards of victims, and he was identified from fingerprints and mugshots. Initially, he was diagnosed as a schizophrenic with an IQ of 68 and considered unfit to stand trial. Cornelia Wilbur was called in, however, and diagnosed him as a case of MPD. Milligan entered a plea of not guilty on the grounds that one of his alters had committed the crimes. He reported 24 personalities, three of whom were female, with nationalities that included British, Australian and Yugoslavian, and backgrounds ranging from criminal to weapons experts and lesbian poets. More details are given in Box 3.2 of some of the alters. Others were felt to be undesirable and were suppressed by Arthur, the dominant alter who decided who should be allowed to 'hold the spot'.

Box 8.2 Some of Billy Milligan's alters

- BILLY (26): the core personality, a high school dropout.
- ARTHUR (22): English, rational, emotionless, wore glasses and read Arabic. A capitalist and an atheist. He dominated the others (except when the situation was dangerous) and decided who will 'come out'.
- RAGAN (23): Yugoslavian, could speak English only with a Slavic accent, and had a drooping moustache. Read Serbo-Croatian, did drawings, was a karate and munitions expert with a criminal record. He was a communist and an atheist. His role was to protect the others, and he was predominant when there was danger.
- ALLEN (18): the only right-handed alter, smoked cigarettes and parted his hair on the side. Played the drums and was a manipulative con man.
- TOMMY (16): played the saxophone, painted and was knowledgeable about electronics. Generally antisocial. An escapologist who demonstrated his ability to escape from straitjackets while on remand.
- CHRISTENE (3): an English girl who drew butterflies and flowers.
- ADALANA (19): a shy lesbian who wrote poetry and liked cooking and housework.
- DAVID (8): small, highly sensitive. His job was to absorb all the pain felt by the others. Some of these personalities consented to take IQ tests, making it possible to compare their scores. These ranged from 69 (David) to 120 (Allen). Milligan claimed to have been abused as a child by his stepfather, who threatened to bury him alive if he talked about it to anyone else. As a demonstration, he was buried with a pipe over his face for air. At one stage of the trial, his brother was able to partially corroborate the allegations of abuse.Pre-trial treatment was given for a period of 3 months to partially fuse the personalities, so that he would be fit to stand trial. He was in fact found not guilty of rape and kidnapping by reason of insanity, though many who had contact with him thought that he was just a liar. He was admitted to a psychiatric unit, and eventually released in 1988 with his personality allegedly fused. Subsequently, he

was arrested for another crime (not sexual), but there was no claim of MPD.

Evaluation

The importance of Milligan's case lies in the fact that not only does it raise the issue of the legal implications of MPD; it also provides a good example of the relatively rare male multiple. According to Putnam, and Ross, 90% of diagnosed multiples are female. Hacking offers four explanations for this:

- Male multiples are more likely than females to commit crimes and therefore end up in the criminal justice system rather than the psychiatric system.
- Dissociation is a more culturally acceptable way for women to express their distress than it is for men.
- MPD is the result of child abuse, especially sexual, and women are more likely to suffer from this than men.
- Women are more suggestible than men, and therefore more open to suggestions made by therapists.

In terms of the legal implications, Milligan was the first person in America to be acquitted of a major crime because of an insanity plea based on MPD. Initially considered a neurosis, rather than a psychosis, MPD had not previously been regarded as severe enough to warrant a judgement of insanity being made. Since then there have been other such cases. Coons reported that there had been 19 cases in America from 1977 to 1991. Of these, two were found not guilty by reason of insanity, two were incompetent to stand trial and one was found guilty but mentally ill. Slovenko reported a case of murder in which the defendant claimed the crime had been committed by her 9-year-old alter. MPD has also been used as the basis of successful insanity pleas in forgery cases. In England and Wales, MPD has not been used as a defence in court to date, although case studies have been reported in legal journals, as Box 3.3 demonstrates.

Box 8.3 MPD and the courts

A case was reported of a 33-year-old American arrested for stealing antiques when visiting Britain. Four personalities were detected: K, a cool antiques thief; D, an obsessive-compulsive character; R, a 7-year-old child; and another irritable adult. The man satisfied the criteria for MPD, but also for obsessive-compulsive disorder, borderline personality disorder and antisocial personality disorder. He was advised to plead guilty in the light of the weight of evidence against him, given a suspended sentence and allowed to leave the country. At the time of the trial, the 7-year-old was in charge. That caused legal problems because he would then be a minor, below the age of criminal responsibility, as well as being too young to instruct a solicitor. It was considered that he was fit to plead when in the adult state, but there was concern that in court he might revert to the child, leading to a plea of unfit to plead not guilty by reason of insanity.

According to Lewis and Bard, there are four major defences that can be presented in MPD cases:

- The individual has no control over the secondary personalities, and is therefore not responsible for them.
- The individual cannot remember what the alters did, and therefore cannot defend them.
- The individual does not know right from wrong because of suffering from MPD.
- The individual is not accountable because she or he is unconscious of the alters' behaviours.

Alters, however, pose considerable legal problems. For example, it is not clear what would happen if, in America, a child alter were to take over from someone facing the death penalty.

Another problem is that until the primary personality is established, each alter should have separate representation. The courts have also recognised alters as being separate for testimony purposes. Saks reported a case where 6 of the supposed 47 alters of a female witness were sworn in separately. Sarah alleged that two of her personalities had been raped by a man who had sex with one of her other alters. When she switched personalitites, she had to retake the oath. The man was found guilty of second degree sexual assault because he knowingly had intercourse with someone suffering from mental disorder that made her unable to appraise her conduct. In theory, one alter could presumably be called on to give testimony against another, if they are all treated as responsible for their own behaviour. It is difficult to see how this can be sustained, however, as they do not have an independent existence. Dawson argues that in law, the person who carries out an act is considered to be the agent of the whole person, and that person is responsible for the act. Therefore, the insanity defence is inappropriate in this instance, since legally, if not psychologically, the person is still a single entity.

Progress exerciseConsidering these cases, and any others with which you are familiar, note down any similarities and differences that you can think of between the symptoms of MPD and those of:

(a) schizophrenia,

(b) depression,

(c) antisocial personality disorder.

Origins of MPD

Five major theories exist about the origins of MPD; you will see that they are broadly derived from the different models of mental disorder.

The Biological Approach

The finding in the case of Eve that there were physiological differences between the personalities suggests that there may be a biological basis for the disorder. Note, however, that any observed differences may be the cause or the effect of the problems. Putnam measured the Visual Evoked Potentials (records of activity in the cortex) of the alters of MPD patients and compared them with controls who were asked to simulate alters. The real alters showed more variability than the simulated alters, indicating physiological differences. This study could also be used to support the argument that the condition is real, rather than faked.

Tsai carried out a study of a 47-year-old woman patient called Marnie, using fMRI scanners to observe what happened in the brain when she switched personalities. They found that the hippocampus, an area of the brain involved in memory, was shrunken to about half the normal size. This feature has been documented before, in other cases of people who have suffered repeated trauma (such as PTSD and child abuse cases). Changes in hippocampal and temporal lobe function were also observed during the switching process. Since the hippocampus seems to be the brain's centre for 'printing' memories, and memories could be regarded as crucial to our sense of self (our knowledge of our own personality), such damage could well lead to, or be associated with, the observed problems.

The Psychodynamic Approach

Janet was the first to claim that what he called double consciousness was caused by childhood trauma that had become buried in the unconscious. His theory was that the mind is made up of 'psychological automatisms', which are clusters of perceptions and thoughts that are available to conscious awareness. Following an unbearable trauma, one or more of these may become split off or dissociated, so that it is no longer under the control of the conscious mind.

According to later psychodynamic views, MPD is regarded as an extreme case of the use of repression as an ego defence mechanism. Painful memories or, in this case, entire identities are repressed from consciousness. Where childhood involved extreme trauma, such as the abuse suffered by Sybil, the memory for the abuse may be more effectively repressed if the entire personality that experienced it is also repressed. The child imagines that the abuse is happening to another 'self'. The primary personality is typically very inhibited, which supports this idea.

More recent formulations of this idea have postulated a trauma-dissociation model of MPD. This has taken up Janet's original concept of dissociation and linked it with Hilgard's neo-dissociation theory of hypnosis. Hilgard argued that during hypnosis, some cognitive systems can be separated off from consciousness by an amnestic barrier, so that two dissociated streams of thought can exist alongside one another. In this model, then, a child who is so constitutionally predisposed can split off (or dissociate) painful memories from consciousness as a protective device. These then become the alter, separated from consciousness by an amnestic barrier.

Evidence for this explanation can be derived from the child abuse reported in many cases. However, not all cases do report abuse, and not all cases of abuse develop MPD. It is also difficult to explain why the reports of abuse appeared to increase in cases reported after 1980, compared to those reported prior to that date. The prevalence in different countries does not fit well with this explanation, either, since the countries where it is most common are not those where trauma might be most common; compare trauma-ridden Africa with peaceful Canada, for example. It has also been reported that the recovery of such memories does not appear to be associated with therapeutic gain, as the psychodynamic theorists would expect.

Self-hypnosis Approach

In this view, MPD is a form of self-hypnosis used by sufferers to help them to forget unpleasant events. They are able to separate themselves mentally from both their bodies and their surroundings. In support of this idea, MPD is considered to begin around 4-6 years of age, which is when children are at their most susceptible to hypnotic suggestion. Further support can be derived from the finding that most MPD patients appear to be highly suggestible. Sybil, for example, was reported to be able to enter a trance spontaneously.

The Behavioural Approach

The focus here is also on the traumatic experiences associated with MPD. The difference is that according to this view forgetting is seen as a rewarding experience because it reduces anxiety. According to operant conditioning theory, it will therefore become a learned response, because of its reinforcing properties. Another theory based on learning principles is that of state-dependent learning. It has repeatedly been shown that information that is learned while in one state (e.g. mood) is best recalled when the individual is in the same state. MPD sufferers may simply have very selective memories, which means that their recall will depend on them being in exactly the same physiological state when recalling as when the memories were laid down.

Socio-cultural Approach

According to this view, some features of our culture may promote MPD. For example, Varma point out that modern Western culture has placed an emphasis on role playing, particularly through the entertainment industry. Some theories of hypnosis. The fact that there is considerable cultural variation in prevalence and that 90% of cases are women could also fit in with this explanation. The socio-cultural explanations of MPD, whether emphasising spontaneous or iatrogenic origins for the disorder.

MPD and Child Abuse

Here we will concentrate on the major theoretical explanation for MPD, the trauma-dissociation model that links predisposition with a history of abuse. Behavioural and self-hypnosis explanations also depend on the existence of previous trauma or abuse, so the investigation of such patients for memories of abuse is a key issue. Has research confirmed that abuse is commonplace during the childhood of MPD sufferers? The reliability and validity of the evidence on this issue depends crucially on the methods used to obtain the information; this in turn depends on the techniques used in the course of therapy, so we must consider these next.

Treatment

The first true multiple, Louis Vivet, was subjected to a wide variety of strange treatments, including the application of magnets to his body, morphine and emetics. The presence of gold bromide was found to be capable of inducing a personality change. There were only two things that could halt an attack of hysterical symptoms: one was pressure on either the Achilles tendon or the tendon below the kneecap; the other was having his testicles tightly squeezed by his doctors. Treatment has moved on since those days, but given the lack of knowledge about origins of the disorder, it is no less speculative.Spontaneous recovery is rare and treatment often includes the administration of anti-anxiety or antidepressant drugs initially. Psychotherapy usually involves three processes:

- *Recognising the disorder* This is largely an educational exercise for both patients and their families. Videotapes may be shown of

  other cases of MPD, and of the alters, and hypnosis may be used to make the sub-personalities aware of one another. The patient may be asked if she or he ever feels that there is another part of the personality they wish to reveal. Once out, this alter will be named.
- *Recovering memories* Using psychodynamic therapy, hypnosis or drugs, the aim is to help the patients to recall their missing memories. At this stage, they may become aggressive towards themselves and others. Re-enactments called abreactions are used to get the alters to reveal their

memories. These can go on for as long as 9 hours although about 3 hours is typical. Guided imagery or visualisation may also be used, in which the patient is talked through an imaginary scene to help to awaken memories. 'Screen techniques' involve the visualisation of a cinema screen on which abuse or other memories are being replayed. Another technique is the use of 'journaling' - keeping a journal to help pick out recurrent thoughts.

- *Integrating sub-personalities into one* Again a range of approaches can be used, such as assertiveness training for the primary personality, or group discussions between the sub-personalities. Coping skills need to be consolidated to reduce the risk of future dissociation. Psychodynamic therapists may concentrate on the achievement of insight, so that the patient can deal with the memories in a more constructive way than by dissociation in the future.

Progress exerciseBefore you read on, consider carefully whether any of the techniques outlined above, used to help patients recognise the disorder and recover memories, may be conducive to the development of MPD as an iatrogenic disorder. Could they make the patient more susceptible to influence from the therapist? There are three questions to ask about the treatment of MPD:

- Does the treatment work? If it does, this would go some way towards supporting the trauma model.
- Are there generally recovered memories of child abuse? If there are, again the trauma model has some support.
- Are the memories accurate? This must be established as well, before the model can be accepted.

Does the Treatment Work?

The relatively small number of cases reported means that it is difficult to assess the effectiveness of these treatments. Most case studies that are reported indicate that integration can be achieved, but we have already seen that many of these cases are suspect for one reason or another, and that problems of various sorts do persist after treatment has been terminated. Ross has argued that 75% of patients can be treated to integration in less than 2½ years, but there is no evidence to support this claim.

Mair has argued that therapy may do more harm than good. Taking into account initial variations in severity, she found an inverse relationship between future well-being and number of treatment sessions received with more treatment being associated with worse outcomes. She also notes that none of her sample showed 'overall evidence of benefit', especially since there were serious risks attached to the treatment. The risks she referred to included self-harm, suicide attempts, and horrific new (recovered) memories that had seriously disrupted family relationships in many cases.

How Frequent are Recovered Memories of Child Abuse?

Are there in fact reports of child abuse in a significant number of patients seen? Since most MPD cases are female, and more females than males suffer abuse (Bentovim & Tranter 1994, for example, reported a ratio of 4:1), it may be expected that there would be. Taylor and Martin found no allegations of abuse in any of the cases they looked at prior to that date. Since then, however, most patients do claim to have suffered abuse. Early surveys showed that 83% reported sexual abuse, but these have not been objectively verified. According to Ross in a study of 100 patients, 95.1% had a history of abuse. A review of the literature showed that 68-86% reported child or adolescent sexual abuse, and 60-82% physical abuse. A significant number, then, do report abuse.

Are the Recovered Memories Accurate?

The next question is whether those reports are accurate. Freud himself was very sceptical about the abuse reported by his patients, and eventually decided that the reports were sexual fantasies. This led him to abandon his seduction theory. His critics have rejected this view and have produced evidence that the memories may have been genuine. In many modern cases it has been suggested that the memories are elicited from patients during the course of treatment procedures that may not produce reliable memories. Simpson considers that the examination methods used by therapists resemble interrogation techniques. The use of powerful drugs, as in the case of Sybil, leading questions and hypnosis have all been criticised. For example, Acocella has noted that high doses of benzodiazepines may be given to combat anxiety, since MPD patients are considered to be resistant to their effects. Ross admitted in a court case that the patient concerned had been given a dose that was 100 times the maximum.

Leading questions that have been shown by Loftus to be in common use include 'has anything like that ever happened to you?'. Sanders found that mere exposure to stories about the childhood experiences of others altered the memories of participants in experiments, leading many to report that the events had actually happened to them. Guided imagery can also be used to make direct suggestions to patients, and hypnotic recall may also be susceptible to suggestion.

The use of Hypnosis

Hypnotic recall has been regarded with suspicion for some time. McDougall, commenting on the case of Miss Beauchamp, noted that the use of hypnosis 'may have moulded the course of its development to a degree that cannot be determined'. The American Medical Association in 1985 stated that 'recollections obtained during hypnosis appear to be less reliable than nonhypnotic recall'. This is because patients can be cued more easily by the therapist, and because their confidence in the memories produced is increased (without justification). Kline has noted that if the appropriate suggestion is made, patients can be made to recall former lives as chimps, for example. According to Laurence, 'hypnosis increases productivity rather than accuracy of recall this productivity is not real but guided by the verbal and nonverbal cues of the recall setting'. On the other hand, Kluft argues that provided it is not accompanied by leading questions, hypnosis is useful. He found that memories recovered during hypnosis are often able to be confirmed by independent sources.

Independent Verification

What is needed is independent corroboration of the reports to decide if this is in fact the case. In 1991, Hornstein and Tyson reported that 61/66 cases they investigated had reported independently documentable trauma. Coons found corroborated abuse in 17/20 patients, although in some cases the abuse was simply spanking. In 1994 Coons found corroborated abuse histories in 21/22 patients and Kluft found that 56% of abuse memories were corroborated in his sample of 34 carefully screened patients. He accepted the corroboration only if it involved a witness (usually a sibling) or a confession from the perpetrator (usually a parent or sibling). Lewis found objective evidence of severe abuse and early dissociation in a study of 12 murderers suffering from MPD. The murderers themselves had partial or total amnesia for the abuse, but it was reported by others. Clearly then, some, but not all, reports of abuse can be confirmed independently.

False Memory Syndrome

Despite this, there is sufficient concern about the reliability of these reports for the term 'false memory syndrome' to have been coined. This refers to 'a condition in which a person's identity and interpersonal relationships are centred around a memory of traumatic experience which is objectively false but which the person strongly believes'. The False Memory Syndrome Foundation has been set up to defend accused parents, and the British Psychological Society has issued a set of guidelines for practitioners working with clients in situations where recovered memories may arise. These guidelines are shown in Box 3.4. In America, insurance companies now issue policies for therapists containing a clause that voids the cover if hypnosis is used to obtain memories of child abuse. This is because legal proceedings for negligence, malpractice and insurance fraud have become commonplace; therapists usually lose the case, and claims of up to 10.6 million dollars have been awarded against them. Thus the reliability of these reports is not generally considered to be high.

Box 8.4 Guidelines for psychologists working with clients in contexts in which issues related to recovered memories may arise

Preamble The following guidelines are intended to apply to psychologists working in all professional contexts in which such issues may arise. It is clearly part of the professional duty of such psychologists to seek to maintain an awareness of this debate and to develop an empirical and professional perspective on false memory/recovered memories, and base their practice on sound psychological principles and evidence as a counter-balance to the polarised beliefs that abound in this emotive area. As the result of extensive review by the Society and other bodies there can be no doubt for psychologists of the existence of child sexual abuse (CSA) as a serious social and individual problem commonly with long-lasting effects. In addition there can be little doubt that at least some recovered memories of CSA are recollections of historical events. However, there is genuine cause for concern that some interventions can lead clients to develop illusory memories or may foster false beliefs concerning CSA.Members seeking discussion of terms and background material on these issues are referred to the Society's earlier document *Recovered Memories: Report of the BPS Working Party*.

Guidelines

1. The welfare and interests of clients are the primary concern of psychologists working with them. This concern includes the requirement to maintain respect for the client's autonomy and confidentiality the extent of which should ideally be clarified and agreed at the outset of the professional engagement.
2. It may be necessary for psychologists in caring, assessment and therapeutic roles to be open to the emergence of memories of trauma which were not previously available to the client's awareness.
3. It is important always to take the client who recovers memories seriously. The first response of the psychologist should be to accept that what the client tells them reflects their reality and respect their feelings. Nevertheless the psychologist should avoid drawing premature conclusions about the historical truth of a recovered memory.
4. Psychologists must be aware that the question of whether traumatic memory is processed, stored and recalled differently from normal memory is currently unresolved. Unusual, dramatic, powerful or vivid memories, and 'flashback' bodily sensations cannot be relied upon as evidence of the historical truth or falsity of the recovered memories.

5. Psychologists need to tolerate, and help their client tolerate, uncertainty and ambiguity regarding the clients early experience as eventually they may both have to accept that the historical truth cannot be known, and that helping the client to make reasonable sense of their lives is not the same as discovering objective facts.
6. Psychologists should be alert to a range of possibilities; for example that a recovered memory may be literally/ historically true or false, or may be partly true, thematically true or metaphorically true, or may derive from fantasy or dream material. Discovering that some aspects of a 'memory' are displaced, metaphorical, or part of a construction or narrative derived from the therapeutic relationship should not lead psychologists to immediately discount the rest of that memory. Likewise, the discovery that some aspects of a memory are factually accurate does not imply that the whole content of the memory is factual. It is not really possible to establish whether a memory represents factual events without external corroboration.
7. Whilst it may be part of a psychologist's work to help clients to think about their early experiences they should avoid imposing their own conclusions about what took place in childhood.
8. Child sexual abuse should not be deduced on the basis of presenting symptoms such as eating disorders alone. There is a high probability of false positives in such deductions as there are other possible explanations for psychological problems. The construction of syndromes and the use of symptom check-lists in diagnosis in relation to past sexual abuse are currently available.
9. Psychologists should avoid being drawn into a search for memories of abuse, as abused clients (and non-abused clients who are psychologically disturbed) are vulnerable and may be traumatised or overwhelmed by material that has not arisen spontaneously in the course of their psychological work. Psychologists should avoid engaging in activities and techniques which are intended to reveal indications of past sexual abuse of which the client has no memory. When psychologists use such techniques (e.g. hypnosis) for other purposes they must be aware that these

techniques may make memory more confident but less reliable.

10. Psychologists must be alert to the dangers of suggestion. Potential sources of suggestion include subtle cues about the psychologist's attitudes and beliefs that may be inferred from the therapeutic context (e.g. particular books on the shelf) or client contact with 'survivor literature' and subcultures of abuse. Psychologists must be aware that there may be situations in which clients are motivated to recall memories of abuse for a variety of ends.
11. Psychologists working therapeutically must be aware of their inevitable engagement in the client's narrative. Whilst taking care about the implications of active investigation and suggestion, they should not seek to manage these risks simply by refusing to deal with past events and 'work in the present', since this actively denies the client's experience and is unlikely to meet their needs.
12. Psychologists working therapeutically should be aware of the likely impact of their work on their clients' families and wider social network and should not rule out renegotiating the contract with their clients to enable them to meet with relevant family members. However the boundaries of a client's autonomy and confidentiality should only be breached in rare circumstances, ideally as agreed at the outset of the professional engagement.
13. Psychologists should be clear about the circumstances in which they would feel ethically or legally obliged to breach confidentiality. They should carefully assess the risk of self-harm and the risk of abuse to minors. Psychologists working in the public services should be aware of their child protection guidelines and procedures and abide by them. Psychologists working independently should also be aware of their ethical responsibilities to protect others from significant harm.
14. If the role of the psychologist is to obtain evidence that is reliable in forensic terms, they need to restrict themselves to procedures that enhance reliability and avoid techniques, which are known to reduce reliability, such as hypnosis or

suggestion and leading questions. The same care should be taken whenever action (e.g. informing other agencies, legal action, family confrontation) outside the consulting room is being considered.

15. The psychologist has a responsibility to help the client to consider carefully any action to be taken outside the consulting room. The client may wish to take independent legal advice with a view to prosecution of or litigation against an alleged abuser. It is inappropriate to make the continuation of treatment/ consultation contingent on such decisions/ actions. Psychologists must be prepared to accept that it may not be the client's choice to deal with these matters therapeutically or through family confrontation or legal process.
16. Psychologists are reminded of their guidelines for good practice. These may be particularly important when working with clients who disclose memories of childhood abuse. The guidelines will include sections on keeping and preserving appropriate records and seeking appropriate consultation and supervision.

9

Panic Disorder and Agoraphobia in Psychology

Introduction

Panic disorder is characterized by recurrent panic attacks, or sudden rushes of intense fear or discomfort. A panic attack is defined by a cluster of physical and cognitive symptoms, including palpitations; shortness of breath; derealization; paresthesias; trembling; and fears of dying, going crazy, or losing control. It is noteworthy that DSM-IV does not require measures of actual arousal to define panic attacks but rather relies on patient reports of arousal. As described in previous chapters, such perceived or reported autonomic arousal may have little to do with actual arousal. Panic attacks are common to all anxiety disorders. Panic disorder is distinguished by unexpected attacks, or attacks that occur without an obvious trigger, and at least one month of persistent apprehension about the recurrence of panic or its consequences or a significant behavioral change.

The most recent prevalence estimates for panic disorder are 2.3% in the last 12 months, and 3.5% lifetime. Conservative estimates suggest an additional 3.3 to 4.6% experience nonclinical panic, or occasional panic attacks. Degree of anxiety about the recurrence of panic and catastrophic cognitions during panic seem to differentiate nonclinical panic from panic disorder. Agoraphobia refers to avoidance or endurance with dread of situations from which escape might be difficult or help unavailable in the event of a panic attack or paniclike symptoms, such as loss of bowel control. Typical agoraphobic situations include shopping malls, waiting in lines, movie theaters, traveling by car or bus, crowded restaurants and stores, and being alone.

The relationship between panic and agoraphobia is subject to much debate. Epidemiological studies report relatively high rates for agoraphobia without a history of panic disorder: 2.8% in the last 12 months and 5.3% lifetime. In contrast, individuals with agoraphobia who seek treatment almost always report a history of panic that preceded development of their avoidance. For example, only 6% of 562 patients with episodes of panic and/ or agoraphobia met criteria for agoraphobia without history of panic disorder in the HARP study. There are at least two explanations for the contrast between population and clinic-based data. First, epidemiological data may vastly overestimate the prevalence of agoraphobia due to misdiagnosis of specific phobias, generalized anxiety, or "normal" cautiousness about certain situations (e.g., walking in unsafe urban districts) as agoraphobia. The degree to which this applies to the most recent epidemiological data is not yet known. Second, individuals who panic are more likely to seek help.

In addition, not all persons who panic develop agoraphobia, and the extent of avoidance that emerges is highly variable. Agoraphobia tends to increase as history of panic lengthens; however, a significant proportion panic for many years without developing agoraphobic limitations. Nor is agoraphobic avoidance related to age of onset or frequency of panic. Some find more intense symptomatology during panic attacks in individuals who are more agoraphobic. Others fail to find such differences. Although not differing in fears of dying, going crazy, or losing control, more agoraphobic individuals may be more concerned with social consequences of panicking. Also, anticipation of panic in specific agoraphobic situations predicts agoraphobic avoidance. Whether the latter two variables are precursors or are secondary to agoraphobia remains to be determined. In an interesting recent set of findings, Williams, Kinney, Harap, and Liebmann reported a general absence of danger appraisals as patients with agoraphobia and other phobias confronted their most-feared driving and claustrophobic situations. That is, patients reported perceiving very little danger in the possibility of panicking or in the situation itself while confronting those situations. The authors conclude that appraisals of danger may not be important for fear and avoidance. On the other hand, they measured appraisals in the height of fear; danger appraisals are probably more apparent during anticipatory anxiety, given restrictions on cognitive processing during fear.

Occupational status also predicts agoraphobic avoidance, accounting for 18% of the variance: "The more one is forced to leave the house by means of employment, the less one is likely to suffer from agoraphobia". Perhaps the strongest predictor of agoraphobia is gender. Females increasingly predominate the sample as agoraphobia worsens. Sex role expectations and behaviors may contribute to these effects.

Rarely does the diagnosis of panic disorder, with or without agoraphobia, occur in isolation. Commonly co-occurring Axis I conditions include specific phobias, social phobia, dysthymia, generalized anxiety disorder, major depressive disorder, and substance abuse. Twenty-five to 60% of persons with panic disorder meet criteria for a personality disorder, mostly avoidant and dependent personality disorders. However, as noted previously, the reliability of Axis II diagnoses is questionable.

Mean age of onset ranges from 23 to 29, although a substantial number of adolescents panic. Treatment is usually sought around 34 years of age. A large percent (approximately 70%) report the presence of identifiable stressors around the time of the first panic attack. Fortunately, they respond well to specifically targeted treatments, described below.

Theoretical and Empirical Developments

An extensive literature on the neurobiology of panic is reviewed by Stein and Uhde and Johnson and Lydiard and an integrated neurobiological model is presented by Goddard and Charney. Current directions are reviewed briefly below. A particularly notable feature is that despite consistently elevated self-reported symptoms and distress among panic disorder patients, evidence regarding neurobiological dysfunction is highly contradictory. Contradictions may be in part due to methodological inconsistencies, particularly concerning psychological and environmental conditions surrounding neurobiological testing. For example, instructional sets and safety signals may significantly impact physiological indices, but have been relatively ignored. In addition, cardiovascular fitness, panic severity, and the influence of impending laboratory procedures have been inadequately controlled despite their potential major impact on measures of interest. Other weaknesses include reliance on nonanxious controls for comparison, so that specificity of effects to panic disorder versus other anxiety or mood disorders is unclear. Cross-sectional findings are often misrepresented as evidence for etiological neurobiological pathways for panic disorder. Also problematic is the wide net across which neurobiological disturbances are detected. The major neurotransmitters implicated in panic disorder are reviewed next.

The noradrenergic hypotheses arose largely from the work of Redmond and colleagues, who found that stimulation of the locus coeruleus in monkeys induced anxiety reactions that were very similar to human panic attacks. Subsequently, researchers investigated reactions to pharmacological probes of the noradrenergic system (e.g., yohimbine and clonidine infusions) and markers of noradrenergic functioning, such as elevated neuropeptide Y. In general, the results are mixed but suggest some type of dysregulation, such as alpha-2 hypersensitivity or peripheral beta-adrenoceptor sensitivity. The data suggest some type of abnormality in serotonergic function in panic disorder as well that is not yet fully understood. A postsynaptic serotonin receptor supersensitivity has been suggested, for example, although the data are equivocal. Despite the efficacy of benzodiazepines, research of the GABA/benzodiazepine complex is limited. Roy-Byrne and colleagues reported a series of studies showing that benzodiazepines have less effect on saccadic eye movement velocity and plasma catecholamine levels in panic patients versus normal controls, although no differences were found in neuroendocrine responses. This suggests that panic disorder may be associated with decreased reactivity of benzodiazepine receptors in some but not all areas of the central nervous system. Finally, neuropeptides such as cholecystokinin and adrenocorticotrophic hormone responses to corticotropin-releasing factor challenges may be dysregulated. This is consistent with the noradrenergic hypothesis and dysregulation of the hypothalamic-pituitary-adrenal (HPA) axis.

HPA Axis and Autonomic Functioning. Overactivation of the HPA axis has been widely viewed as central to panic disorder. Previous research is mixed, but Abelson and Curtis examined secretions of corticotropin and cortisol over 24 hours, while attempting to control the myriad of confounding factors from previous studies. Blood samples were drawn every 15 minutes over 24 hours of bed rest in 20 patients with panic disorder and 12 normal controls. Patients had significantly higher overnight cortisol levels, particularly more severe patients who were referred rather than recruited for the study. In addition, patients showed more episodic secretory bursts. The groups did not differ substantially on corticotropin levels, although patients with low panic frequency had higher daytime levels than either patients with high panic frequency or controls. The authors attributed these findings to chronic overdrive of the HPA axis with frequent panic attacks that reduces corticotropin secretion.

Autonomic functioning (e.g., heart rate, skin conductance) is one gauge of the HPA axis. However, evidence for autonomic hyperactivity is very mixed. Data gathered in the natural environment via ambulatory devices show that *some* panic attacks occur in the absence of autonomic activation, although severe panic attacks are more autonomically based. Lint, Taylor, Fried-Behar and Kenardy present an interesting set of results. Ten women with panic disorder were monitored over five days, during which time 23 panic attacks and 96 tachycardia events were recorded. Twelve tachycardia events occurred during panic attacks, but 84 occurred in the absence of the report of panic. Interestingly, mean heart rate during tachycardia events was considerably higher than during panic attacks (131.8 bpm versus 87.8 bpm), and yet more symptoms of shortness of breath, rapid heart beat, and chest pain were reported during panic attacks (78% versus 48%, 83% versus 51%, 61% versus 30%). These data suggest that symptom reporting is not directly linked to physiological state but may be influenced by an array of psychological and environmental context variables. For example, sensations of a racing heart may be reported more often in threatening contexts, such as when alone. Also, although some ambulatory studies show that panic attacks are preceded by autonomic arousal, others do not. Similarly, some ambulatory studies report no baseline differences between panic disorder and nonanxious controls in respiratory and cardiovascular functioning and others find differences.

Results from laboratory-based studies are mixed also. On the one hand, despite higher baseline heart rates, skin conductance, and startle reflex, panic disorder patients do not react abnormally to mental arithmetic, cold pressor tests, carbon dioxide stressors, postural challenges, isometric exercise, Valsalva maneuvers, or threat of shock relative to nonanxious controls. Higher baseline heart rate is attributed to anticipatory anxiety or poorer cardiovascular fitness. Thus, although autonomic dysfunction may occur during panic attacks, "an inherently unstable 'ANS' is not a necessary precondition for the occurrence of panic".

On the other hand, the autonomic system may reestablish a balance over long periods of stress, such that dysfunction is no longer apparent except during acute panic attacks. In accord, Friedman, Thayer, Borkovec, Tyrrell, Johnson, and Columbo compared recent panickers to individuals with blood phobias on parasympathetic (immersion of face in water) and sympathetic (threat of shock) tasks. Recent panickers evinced heightened sympathetic control and lowered vagal or parasympathetic tone, as shown by higher heart rate coupled with low heart rate variability. Lowered vagal tone is found in panic disorder patients not selected for recent onset as well. Although Asmundson and Stein attributed vagal deficiencies to lack of exercise levels, the fact that signs of autonomic dysregulation, including lowered vagal tone, are corrected via imipramine and cognitive therapy is hardly attributable to habitual exercise. Middleton and Ashby found that treatment increased plasma noradrenaline, produced significantly *less* reductions in systolic and diastolic blood pressure in response to standing for 10 minutes, and increased heart rate variability and peak frequency. Also, in direct contrast to Stein, Hauger, Dhalla, Chartier, and Asmundson, Boulenger, Jerabek, Jolicoeur, Lavalee, Leduc, and Cadieux reported plasma neuropeptide Y levels that were more than 50% higher among panic disorder patients than controls, suggesting chronic overdrive of the HPA axis. Finally, Faravelli found an exaggerated drop in cerebral blood flow that was attributed to autonomic dysregulation. Thus, Papp, Klein and Gorman conclude that "the complexity of the research data and the wide variety of symptoms demonstrated by panic patients are most consistent with the theory that panic disorder is the result of an inherently unstable autonomic nervous system coupled with cognitive distress".

Respiratory Functioning. Initially, panic was attributed to chronic hyperventilation. Indeed, voluntary hyperventilation induces panic in 30 to 50% of panic patients. However, hyperventilation does not always induce panic, panic attacks that occur in the natural environment are not always accompanied by objective indices of hyperventilation and evidence for chronic hyperventilation is mixed.

Extensive research on the effects of lactate infusions and carbon dioxide inhalations have culminated most recently in a specific respiratory hypothesis, called the "suffocation false alarm theory". Administration of sodium lactate induces panic attacks in approximately 67% of panic disorder patients versus 13% of nonanxious controls. Similarly, inhalation of 5 to 35% carbon dioxide in air induces panic attacks in a large proportion of panic disorder patients in comparison to fewer patients with obsessive compulsive disorder and relatively few nonanxious controls. Papp attributed these findings to hypersensitive brain stem carbon dioxide chemoreceptors.

More specifically, Klein proposed that "out of the blue" panics are triggered by an abnormally low threshold for suffocation that in turn is activated by rising carbon dioxide and lactate levels. In this model, chronic hyperventilation is understood as a strategy for keeping levels of carbon dioxide below threshold, thereby preventing panic, whereas acute hyperventilation during panic is viewed as a response to breathlessness. Central to Klein's theory, and in contrast to ideas expressed throughout this book, is the belief that "spontaneous" panic attacks are different from fear. This distinction is based largely on the claim that heart palpitations or activation of the HPA axis are frequently absent from unexpected panic attacks but are common to fear.

Furthermore, the suffocation false alarm theory is based on only indirect evidence. For example, Goetz, Klein, and Gorman examined symptoms during lactate inductions that discriminated those who panicked from those who did not. Logistical regressions showed that dyspnea and dizziness significantly predicted panic status over and above other variables. The authors concluded, "Because dizziness/lightheadedness is a symptom frequently reported in association with hyperventilation, it is a confirmation of the suffocation false alarm theory that other outstanding physical symptoms such as palpitations, trembling, sweating, nausea, depersonalization, numbness/tingling, flushing and chest pain proved superfluous to declaring panic and made no significant independent contribution". However, these conclusions are limited to lactate inductions that directly induce respiratory disturbance. In other words, different symptoms may emerge from different panic inductions. Verburg, Griez, Meijer, and Pols found more evidence for respiratory disorders in histories of panic disorder patients relative to other anxiety groups, in the absence of other medical differences. They suggested that history of respiratory diseases predisposes toward panic disorder by causing dyspnea and derangement in the respiratory receptor set point and lowering of the suffocation threshold. However, a clear alternative interpretation is that respiratory diseases generate fear of respiratory symptoms that in turn generates panic attacks.

Indeed, fear of respiratory disturbances is an obvious contender to the notion of suppressed suffocation thresholds. For example, Taylor and Rachman found that high scorers on a measure of suffocation-fear were more likely to panic during a "suffocation" test (breathing through a narrow straw). Also, fears of suffocation and beliefs that bodily sensations are harmful strongly predict anxiety and symptomatology in response to a carbon dioxide challenge of breathing deeply and rapidly into a bag for five minutes.

Furthermore, there is no direct evidence that panic disorder patients have abnormally high sensitivity to carbon dioxide (calculated as change in minute ventilation against end tidal carbon dioxide, divided by body surface area) relative to nonanxious controls. Finally, Schmidt, Telch, and Jaimez argued that indices of a hypersensitive suffocation alarm (i.e., dyspnea symptoms, increased respiration, and decreased baseline carbon dioxide levels) should predict lowered fear and panic in response to hyperventilation, which reduces carbon dioxide levels, and elevated fear and panic in response to carbon dioxide inhalation, which increases carbon dioxide levels. They found no support for these hypotheses. In general, results regarding physiological responding to carbon dioxide inhalation and other respiratory tests are not consistent. In some studies, panic disorder patients do not differ from nonanxious controls. Differences are reported in other studies. Patients who are responsive to induction procedures may reflect a more severe or more genetically loaded subgroup. In accord with the latter hypothesis, first-degree relatives of persons with panic disorder, who themselves had no history of panic, were more likely to panic following inhalation of carbon dioxide than were relatives of persons with mania or depression or relatives of controls. Nevertheless, the largest and most reliable differences occur in self-reported anxiety and symptomatology, a finding that is consistent with psychological models described below.

Psychosocial Functioning

Psychobiological conceptualizations of panic disorder emphasize fear of bodily sensations. In a seminal paper, Clark proposed,

> *Individuals who experience panic attacks do so because they have a relatively enduring tendency to interpret certain bodily sensations in a catastrophic fashion. The sensations that are misinterpreted are mainly those involved in normal anxiety responses (e.g., palpitations, breathlessness, dizziness, paresthesias) but also include some other sensations. The catastrophic misinterpretation involves perceiving sensations as much more dangerous than they really are and, in particular, interpreting the sensations as indicative of an immediately impending physical or mental disaster for example, perceiving a slight feeling of breathlessness as evidence of impending cessation of breathing and consequent death, perceiving palpitations as evidence of an impending heart attack, perceiving a pulsing sensation in the forehead as evidence of a brain hemorrhage, or perceiving a shaky feeling as evidence of impending loss of control and insanity.*

Other theoreticians emphasize the interaction between fears of sensations and autonomic and central nervous system instability.

Vulnerability Factors. A proposed psychological vulnerability is anxiety sensitivity, or the tendency to perceive anxiety as harmful. The anxiety sensitivity may be best viewed as a second-order, or lower level, trait as compared to the higher-order trait of neuroticism or trait anxiety. That is, whereas it is more likely to develop in individuals who are highly trait anxious, anxiety sensitivity is only one facet of trait anxiety one that has to do with perceived negative consequences of bodily sensations. Thus, anxiety sensitivity predicts panic attack history over and above more general indices of trait anxiety and negative affect. In support of the role of anxiety sensitivity as a predisposing variable, Maller and Reiss found that three-fourths of individuals who experienced panic attacks for the first time between 1984 and 1987 scored high on the Anxiety Sensitivity Index in 1984. In a naturalistic, one-year follow-up study, anxiety sensitivity predicted maintenance of panic disorder in an untreated panic disorder group and panic attacks in a nonclinical panic group. Similarly, anxiety sensitivity predicted development of panic attacks five weeks after an acute military stressor.

Most likely, anxiety sensitivity is acquired insidiously from a lifetime of direct aversive experiences (such as personal history of significant illness or injury), vicarious observations (such as exposure to significant illnesses or death among family members, or family members who display fear of body sensations through hypochondriasis), and/or informational transmissions (such as parental warnings or overprotectiveness regarding physical wellbeing). In accord, Ehlers found that parents of panic disorder patients were more likely to suffer from chronic illnesses that required treatment and physical symptoms typical of anxiety, in comparison to parents of patients with other anxiety disorders and controls. In addition, patients with panic disorder observed sick-role behavior related to panic symptoms in their parents more often than control participants. This was not true for non-panic-related sicknesses.

Associated with anxiety sensitivity is enhanced attentional selectivity or interoception for physical cues. Panic patients appear to have heightened awareness of, or ability to detect, bodily sensations of arousal although discrepant findings exist and whether they are more *accurate* in their detection is questionable. Nevertheless, Ehlers and Breuer attribute discrepancies to methodological artifact. Ability to perceive heart beat, in particular, appears to be a relatively stable individual difference variable, given that it does not differ between untreated and treated panic disorder patients or from before to after successful treatment. Thus, along with anxiety sensitivity, ability to detect interoceptive cues may predispose toward panic disorder.

Earlier theorists emphasized separation anxiety as a specific precursor for agoraphobia and panic. Bowlby suggested that abnormal parent-child bonding induces a specific form of anxious attachment in children, resulting in enduring separation anxiety, which in turn leads to agoraphobia when the individual is confronted with personally threatening situations as an adult. Recent evidence exists for neurobiological effects of disturbed attachments as well. In support of separation anxiety as a predisposing factor, Silove, Harris, Morgan, Boyce, Manicavasagar, Hadzi-Pavlovic, and Wilhem found that patients with panic and agoraphobia score higher on a scale of separation anxiety than individuals with social phobia, specific phobias, and generalized anxiety disorder. Unfortunately, this type of research is plagued by retrospective biases. Furthermore, Moreau and Follett concluded from their review that separation anxiety is nonspecific to all anxiety disorders as well as depression. Thus, separation anxiety may be best viewed as a component of a broader vulnerability.

Initial Panic Attacks. The large majority of initial panic attacks occur outside of the home, while driving, walking, at work or at school, in public in general, and on a bus, plane, or subway or in social evaluative situations. Furthermore, settings for initial panic attacks are often rated retrospectively as somewhat difficult to escape. This may be particularly so for patients who subsequently develop more agoraphobia. Barlow suggested that situations that block escape behavior, the natural action tendency associated with panic, intensify urgency to escape and associated fear and panic. In a recent review paper, my colleague and I took a broader perspective, proposing that initial panic attacks are most likely to occur in situations in which feared physical sensations are perceived as particularly threatening due to possible impairment (e.g., driving), entrapment (e.g., air travel, elevators), negative social evaluation (e.g., job, formal social events), or distance from safety (e.g., unfamiliar locales). That is, certain contexts are more likely to be associated with negative personal consequences of experiencing anxiety than others.

Many (48%) panic patients report similar but less intense or less frightening sensations prior to the first panic. Also, previous experiences of cardiac symptoms and shortness of breath predict later development of panic attacks and panic disorder. Perhaps such prior experiences reflect a state of autonomic vulnerability, which only develops into full-blown panic when instances of autonomic instability occur in threatening contexts or stressful conditions (i.e., when the sensations are more likely to be perceived as threatening). In addition to autonomic instability, an array of factors may account for physiological sensations on the occasion of the initial panic attack. These include benign physiological events (ranging from normal variations in state to illnesses), distal and proximal stress (e.g., impending divorce, rushing to an appointment, meeting a deadline), stimulants (e.g., caffeine, hallucinogenic drugs, prescription medications), environmental conditions (e.g., heat and humidity), and anticipatory anxiety about the immediate situation or an upcoming event (e.g., receiving a work evaluation).

Maintenance Factors. Acute "fear of fear" that develops after initial panic attacks refers to fear of specific bodily sensations associated with panic attacks (e.g., racing heart, dizziness, paresthesias). This fear is attributed to interoceptive conditioning and misappraisals of bodily sensations (i.e., misinterpretation of sensations as signs of imminent death, loss of control, and so on). (Note, however, that fear of sensations is moderated by "occasion setters," which vary greatly across individuals. For example, elevated heart rate may be feared while sitting and not feared while running, depending on the individual. Furthermore, if the bodily sensation occurs in association with an established safety signal or a safe context, fear responding will be diminished) Thus, fear of fear can be construed as sensitization of the predisposing trait of anxiety sensitivity due to the experience of panic attacks.

Evidence for fear of sensations is considerable. For example, patients with panic disorder have strong beliefs and fears of physical or mental harm arising from bodily sensations that are associated with panic attacks. They are more likely to interpret bodily sensations in a catastrophic fashion and to allocate more attentional resources to words that represent physical threat, such as disease and fatality and catastrophe words, such as death and insane. Also, they are more likely to fear procedures that elicit bodily sensations similar to the ones experienced during panic attacks, including benign cardiovascular, respiratory, and audiovestibular exercises, as well as more invasive procedures such as carbon dioxide inhalations. Furthermore, they fear signals that ostensibly reflect heightened arousal, even in the absence of actual heightened arousal, as shown through false physiological feedback paradigms. Not only is misappraisal associated with fearfulness, but reappraisal lessens fear. For example, persons with panic disorder and nonclinical panickers report significantly less fear and panic during laboratory-based panic provocation procedures, such as hyperventilation and carbon dioxide inhalation, when they perceive that the procedure is safe and/or controllable, when accompanied by a safe person or after cognitive-behavioral treatment that reduces fears of bodily sensations. Failure to replicate these effects by Papp, Welkowitz, Martinez, Klein, Browne, and Gorman is attributable to methodological factors.

As an aside, it is noteworthy that appraisals of danger and expectations of panic and anxiety are generally absent from ongoing tracking of thought content as patients with agoraphobia confront feared situations. This issue is discussed with a review of the role of conscious cognition in phobic responding. However, the fact that appraisals of danger and expectations of anxiety are very strong in anticipation of phobic situations and generally weak in the midst of fearful confrontation with phobic stimuli is entirely consistent with the threat imminence continuum model. That is, worry and anticipatory anxiety allow more conscious and elaborative cognitive processing, whereas cognitive capacities are limited and primitive during states of fear.

Several features distinguish fear of bodily sensations from fears of external stimuli. First, autonomic arousal generated by fear of sensations in turn intensifies the sensations that are feared, thus creating a reciprocating cycle of fear and sensations. Presumably, the cycle is sustained until physiological arousal is exhausted or perceptions of safety are achieved. In contrast, fears of external stimuli do not intensify the object of fear. Second, cues that trigger panic attacks (i.e., bodily sensations) are not always immediately obvious, thus generating the perception of unexpected or "out of the blue" panic attacks. Even when interoceptive cues are identifiable, they tend to be less predictable than external stimuli. Third, bodily sensations are more difficult to escape, on average, than external objects; that is, sensations are relatively uncontrollable. Upredictability and uncontrollability elevate general anxiety about upcoming aversive events and panic attacks. Consequently, the unpredictable and uncontrollable nature of panic is hypothesized to contribute to high levels of chronic anxious apprehension and maintain anticipatory anxiety about the recurrence of panic. In turn, anxious apprehension increases the likelihood of panic, by directly increasing the availability of sensations that have become conditioned cues for panic or by increasing attentional vigilance for these bodily cues. Thus, a maintaining cycle of panic and anxious apprehension develops. Also, anxious apprehension develops over specific contexts in which the occurrence of panic would be particularly troubling (i.e., situations associated with anxiety about impairment, entrapment, negative social evaluation, and distance from safety). These anxieties contribute to agoraphobia. Note, however, that agoraphobia is predicted by other variables as well, as described earlier. Finally, subtle avoidance behaviors are believed to maintain negative beliefs about feared bodily sensations. Examples include holding on to objects or persons for fears of fainting, sitting and remaining still for fears of heart attack, and moving slowly or searching for an escape for fears of acting foolish.

Nocturnal Panic

Recently, colleagues and I have been studying nocturnal panic (NP), or waking from sleep in a state of panic. NP does *not* refer to waking from sleep and panicking after a lapse of waking time, nighttime arousals induced by nightmares or environmental intrusions, night terrors, sleep paralysis, sleep seizures, or flashbacks to traumatic events. NPs occur without apparent reason and are similar symptomatically to daytime panic attacks. They tend to occur in non-REM sleep, particularly in the transition between late Stage 2 and early Stage 3 sleep. Although epidemiological studies have not been conducted, surveys of select clinical and nonclinical groups suggest that NP is a relatively common phenomenon. From 44 to 71% of panic disorder patients report having experienced NP at least once and 18 to 45% have regular and frequent occurrences.

NP has been viewed as panic in its purest form: a purely biological event for which cognitive and behavioral conceptualizations are inadequate. However, I propose that cognitive-behavioral factors and treatments may be as applicable to NP as they are to daytime panic.

Biological models of NP emphasize respiratory disturbances, such as centrally based hypersensitive carbon dioxide receptors and chronic hyperventilation. That is, extreme hypercapnia, as a result of carbon dioxide sensitivity in central medullary carbon dioxide receptors combined with increases in partial pressure of carbon dioxide that usually occur during sleep, is posited to cause NP. Ley suggested that NP results from chronic hyperventilation, or breathing volumes of air in excess of metabolic demand. Chronic hyperventilation reduces levels of carbon dioxide, which in turn leads to compensatory plasma biocarbonate release. Over time, the resultant insufficiency in plasma biocarbonate levels and increased blood alkalinity is posited to create vulnerability to ventilatory irregularities. The combination of natural reductions in respiration with increased levels of carbon dioxide during sleep produces an acute reduction in alkalosis that cannot be compensated for because of the chronic state of plasma biocarbonate deficiency. Hence, a state of respiratory acidosis may trigger hyperventiltory hypocapnea, acute reduction in carbon dioxide, and panic.

In contrast to these hypotheses, patients with NP do not exhibit carbon dioxide hypersensitivity or chronic hyperventilation in a laboratory setting. Of course, respiratory disturbances may be fully sleep dependent and only observable via continuous respiratory monitoring during sleep. In the only report of respiratory patterns prior to NP, Hauri et al. found no evidence for hyperventilation or dysregulated respiratory drive. However, this study was limited to only four instances of NP. We found that shallow or irregular breathing preceded four out of five instances of NP, but measurement was limited to respiration rate and volume. Thus, the role of respiration awaits further investigation.

In addition to increased REM latency, there is some evidence that patients with NP have reduced movement time. Thus, Uhde speculated that increased movement during sleep may confer a degree of compensatory protection against NP, especially given that panic disorder patients who do not have NP tend to have increased movement time relative to controls. This is consistent with the evidence that nocturnal panickers are more vulnerable to relaxation-induced panic and the notion that decreased arousal contributes to the pathogenesis of NP. My colleagues and I understand these effects within a psychobiological model, described next.

Fears of bodily sensations are hypothesized to contribute directly to NP. In support, individuals who were reassured that episodes of physiological arousal during sleep were safe and expected were less fearful of signals of such arousal than individuals who were not reassured and who did not expect episodes of arousal to occur. That is, the latter group awoke with more self-reported distress, panic, and symptoms. Further study is ongoing in which the sleep stage during which signals are presented is standardized and the specificity of effects is established by comparisons with signals that do not relate to physiological arousal but to which NP patients may simply be more reactive. Nevertheless, the previous set of results support the role of cognitive sets about arousal that are formed prior to sleep.

Table 9.1. Reactions of Panic Disorder Patients with Nocturnal Panic Attacks and Matched Healthy Controls to Audio Signals that Ostensibly Measured Autonomic Arousal During Sleep

	Group			
	Nocturnal panic (n = 18)		Control (n = 18)	
Measure	M	SD	M	SD
Anxiety rating (0-8)				
ER	1.1	1.4	1.3	1.2
UN	4.5	1.8	2.7	1.6
Sum of symptom ratings (0-52)				
ER	2.1	2.0	4.0	4.9
UN	11.7	7.7	4.3	4.7
Latency to press event button (min)				
ER	28.1	16.6	37.3	9.1
UN	27.3	17.1	34.3	11.6
Abrupt awakening				
ER	22	11		
UN	44	11		
Abrupt symptoms				
ER	22	0		
UN	67	11		
Abrupt fear				
ER	11	0		
UN	44	0		
Panic				
ER	11	0		
UN	44	0		

Note: Panic disorder patients who were led to believe that the signals were unexpected and who were not given reassuring information about arousal during sleep (UN) were more anxious and symptomatic and were more likely to waken with abrupt fear and panic than patients who were led to believe that the signals were to be expected and who were given reassuring information about arousal during sleep (ER). Fewer differences existed between control participants.

The notion that information can be processed throughout sleep is supported anecdotally and experimentally. For example, recent earthquake victims often report fearful awakenings in response to subtle vibrations, caused by tremors from heavy motor vehicles, events that would not have induced arousal and waking prior to the earthquake. Spouses of sickly patients are particularly prone to wake to sounds of discomfort or lack thereof (e.g., breathing cessation) in the patient. The ability to selectively process and distinguish among different auditory stimuli during all sleep stages has been empirically demonstrated, using evoked potential recordings.

Additionally, habituation to auditory stimuli has been shown to occur during Stage 2 sleep, suggesting that information processing continues in a sleeping state.

Thus, we hypothesize that panic disorder patients are able to process relevant internal stimuli (e.g., increased heart rate) during sleep as a function of their fears of bodily events that may happen to them while asleep.

In summary, we propose that NPs are triggered by changes in physiological state that elicit fear, especially if those physiological stimuli occur in the transition between Stage 2 and 3 sleep, when arousal to full consciousness is more possible. Physiological triggers may or may not be respiratory, given that heart rate changes (usually acceleration), body movements, increased EEG frequency, respiratory changes, and increased sweat gland activity have all been observed in the minutes and seconds preceding waking. What predicts which patients will develop NP? We hypothesize that one important factor is appraisals that render sleep, and other states that are characterized by loss of vigilance, as a dangerous context. Sleep is a state in which vigilance is at its lowest. Other states in which vigilance is significantly compromised include relaxation, fatigue, and substance-induced altered states of consciousness. In accord, patients with NP are more prone to panic during relaxation than daytime panickers, and proportionately more panic in reaction to sleep deprivation (71% versus 21%).

The development of fear of loss of vigilance is attributed to life experiences particularly significant traumas, or the experience of serious threat to the integrity of self or witnessing a serious threat to the integrity of another person. We have some preliminary data to support the notion that patients with NP have experienced more traumas than panic disorder patients without NP, despite the fact that their NPs are unrelated to traumarelated dreams. An archival study found that 85% of 79 patients who ever experienced NP reported a history of traumatic life events in contrast to only 28% of 75 patients who never experienced NP. Interestingly, only 13.3% of the first group met criteria for post traumatic stress disorder. Although these data are very preliminary, they point to the need for further investigation of traumatic life events and their relationship to daytime and NP attacks.

Finally, severity may contribute to propensity for NP. For example, college students are more likely to report NP the more fearful they are of bodily sensations and the more physiologically reactive they report being in general. in patients, NP is associated with more severe and more frequent symptoms, in general and during daytime panic attacks, and more frequent daytime, unexpected attacks. A higher percentage report a history of depression compared to patients without NP (71% versus 29%). Finally, Labbate, Pollack, Otto, Langenauer, and Rosenbaum found that patients with NP had more comorbidity with generalized anxiety disorder, social phobia, and major depression; tended to have lengthier durations of panic disorder; and were more likely to have experienced anxiety disorders during childhood.

Treatment of Panic Disorder and Agoraphobia

The following cognitive-behavioral treatment is detailed in several manuals and several similar treatment protocols exist. The standardized protocol described below can be tailored to meet individual needs in a clinical setting, although structure and focus should not be sacrificed, given that "unstructured" formats for behavior therapy are less effective than structured formats.

Treatment is conducted individually (one hour per session) or in groups of three to five patients and two therapists (90 minutes per session). Ideally, treatment is scheduled twice a week initially, followed by once per week, and extending to once every two weeks toward the end of treatment to facilitate consolidation of learning and generalization. The number of treatment sessions ranges from 11 to 16, depending on degree of agoraphobia, and "self-treatment" is conducted between sessions through homework assignments. The treatment is divisible into three components. The first two components are strategies for managing anxiety and panic (education and cognitive restructuring plus breathing retraining); the third component is exposure to internal and external cues that trigger panic and agoraphobia. An overview of the treatment is provided in Table 9.2.

Table 9.2. Outline of Cognitive-Behavioral Treatment for Panic Disorder and Agoraphobia

Session 1	Education about the nature of anxiety and panic Introduction to three-response systems (cognitions, behaviors, physiology)
Session 2	Education about physiology of anxiety and panic, and "fear of fear" model Introduction to monitoring of cognitions
Session 3	Hyperventilation demonstration Education about physiology of respiration Breathing retraining: diaphragmatic breathing
Session 4	Introduction to principles of cognitive restructuring Probability overestimation identification and countering Breathing retraining: slowed breathing
Session 5	Catastrophizing identification and countering Breathing retraining: application to distracting conditions
Session 6	Review of cognitive monitoring and challenging Hypothesis testing for cognitive challenges Breathing retraining: application to anxiety and panic Introduction to interoceptive exposure rationale and symptom induction testing
Session 7	Review of cognitive monitoring and challenging Hypothesis testing for cognitive challenges Repeated interoceptive exposure

Table Contd.

Session 8	Review of cognitive monitoring and challenging Hypothesis testing for cognitive challenges Repeated interoceptive exposure
Session 9	Review of cognitive monitoring and challenging Hypothesis testing for cognitive challenges Assignment of naturalistic interoceptive exposure Hierarchy development for in vivo exposure
Session 10	Review of cognitive monitoring and challenging Hypothesis testing for cognitive challenges Review of naturalistic interoceptive exposure and design of future exposures Assignment of in vivo exposure
Sessions 11-16	Review of cognitive monitoring and challenging Review of naturalistic interoceptive exposure and design of future exposures Review of in vivo exposure and design of future exposures

Education and Cognitive Restructuring

The first two sessions provide education about the nature of panic and anxiety. They are highly didactic and accompanied by bibliotherapy. Education serves to correct misappraisals of bodily sensations and to develop a personal scientist model. Encompassed within the educational module is the "three response systems model" to describe panic and anxiety. That is, each panic attack and episode of heightened anxiety is described in terms of what "one thinks," "one does," and "one feels." Patients are taught to recognize the way in which those three systems interact. For example, when sensations are cognitively misinterpreted as dangerous, they may intensify (as fearful arousal elicits stronger sensations), which in turn provides further confirmation for the perception of danger and an urgency to escape. In turn, urgency to escape is likely to contribute to accelerating arousal, and so on.

Respiratory and autonomic physiology are described in detail to correct misperceptions of sensations as dangerous. The goals are to normalize fear and anxiety, provide a realistic explanation for physiological sensations of panic, and recognize that fear and panic are time limited. A main premise is that sensations experienced during panic attacks derive from protective physiological mechanisms. For example, heart rate and breathing accelerations are designed to speed the flow of oxygen to the muscles, which are gearing up to "run or fight." Blood flow is redirected away from the periphery and toward the central organs, where most energy is needed, resulting in cooling of temperature in the extremities. Thus, panic attack symptoms represent "side effects" of these protective physiological changes. Finally, the "fear of fear" model of panic is presented.

Cognitive restructuring begins around Session 4, with the notion that interpretations influence emotional reactions. Principles of automatic and discrete thought processes are described. "Automatic" refers to habitual thoughts that occur without full conscious awareness. Examples are to immediately search for exits upon entering a movie theater; to assume that any elevation of heart rate is potentially dangerous; or to be constantly monitoring symptoms of arousal, without full awareness. Also, thoughts are discrete, meaning they shift with the parameters of each situation. For example, fears of embarrassment may prevail in crowded situations, whereas fears of death may dominate when the individual is isolated. Consequently, identification of anxious thoughts for a given episode of fear or anxiety requires careful and detailed questioning.

Next, errors in thinking are categorized as overestimations of probability (i.e., risk inflation) and catastrophic estimations of consequence (i.e., blowing an event out of proportion or viewing events as unmanageable and disastrous). Patients are helped to categorize their own thoughts as overestimations or catastrophizations. Once categorized, thoughts are questioned within a hypothesis-testing framework, by examining realistic probabilities (e.g., "What is the actual likelihood of a heart attack?"), gathering evidence (e.g., medical status), exploring alternative interpretations (e.g., attribution of heart rate elevations to anxiety), and considering realistic consequences and concrete ways of managing events should they occur (e.g., "How would I realistically cope if I were to faint?").

Therapists help patients make guided discoveries using Socratic means. Questioning and challenging are extended through behavioral experiments designed to test predictions and gather more data to disconfirm fearful predictions. For example, fears of falling when unsupported by a surrounding structure may be tested by standing away from walls the next time sensations of dizziness arise.

Cognitive restructuring is emphasized throughout Sessions 4, 5, and 6, during which concepts of overestimation, catastrophizing, and methods of countering negative thoughts are introduced and practiced sequentially. Thoughts and restructuring are continually monitored for the remainder of treatment, particularly in relation to exposure exercises.

Breathing Retraining

Regardless of whether patients actually hyperventilate or not, breathing retraining appears helpful. The purposes of breathing retraining are to decrease symptoms of acute hyperventilation that sometimes occur during panic, reduce vulnerability to such symptoms, and develop a self-control technique.

Breathing retraining begins around Session 3 with a demonstration hyperventilation exercise, where patients are asked to stand and breath deeply and fast for up to 90 seconds (assuming appropriate medical screening). Following assessment of the degree to which the sensations are similar to panic attacks, patients are educated about the physiology of hyperventilation to correct misinterpretations (e.g., "I cannot breathe" or "I will suffocate"). The main educational points are as follows. First, it is natural to overbreathe when anxious or panicky as the body searches for more energy in the form of oxygen. Second, if the oxygen is not used at the rate at which it's consumed, a state of hyperventilation can ensue. Third, hyperventilation refers to lowering of the proportion of carbon dioxide to oxygen in the blood, which in turn increases alkalinity of the blood, oxygen stickiness of hemoglobin, and constriction of blood vessels. These changes lead to slightly less oxygen reaching the tissues and resultant sensations of lightheadedness, dizziness, depersonalization, and paresthesia. Fourth, these effects are not dangerous.

The next step is to teach "correct" breathing. This entails maximizing breathing from the diaphragm (or abdomen) relative to the chest, because chest breathing is believed to contribute to hyperventilation. A meditation component involves concentration on counting during inhalation (e.g., "one, ") and the word "relax" during exhalation, proceeding up to 10 and back down to 1 in a continuous cycle. The first homework exercise is to repeat the diaphragmatic counting exercise for approximately 10 minutes, at least two times a day, for a week, without attempts to either slow the breathing or to apply the exercise at times of elevated anxiety. After one week of practice, slowed breathing is approximated, by gradually reaching a six-second cycle (three seconds inhalation, three seconds exhalation). After another week of slow diaphragmatic breathing practice, practice is instituted in distracting environments, such as at work or in the car. The last step (at Session 6) is to apply slow breathing as a control strategy at times of anxiety or panic.

Interoceptive Exposure

The purpose of interoceptive exposure (as in the case of exposure to external phobic stimuli) is to disrupt or weaken associations between specific bodily cues and panic reactions. Interoceptive exposure is introduced at Session 6, and continued through Session 11. Exposure is graduated and proceeds from simulated exercises to more naturalistic activities.

Sensation-induction exercises are conducted initially to identify ones that produce sensations that are similar to panic attack symptoms. These exercises include hyperventilating, spinning in a swivel chair, holding the breath, muscle tensing, and breathing through a small tube. Relevant exercises are ranked in terms of anxiety levels. Beginning with the least anxietyprovoking exercise, exposures are repeated a sufficient number of times for anxiety to decrease. With each exposure, patients are instructed to experience the sensations as fully as possible, to tolerate them for a period of time before terminating the exercise, and to tolerate them without their usual safety behaviors. For example, patients may be asked to hyperventilate until they feel sensations of lightheadedness or dizziness, continue the hyperventilation exercise for at least 30 seconds longer, and then remain standing rather than lie down. By so doing, they gain opportunities to learn that feared outcomes do not eventuate (e.g., passing out, losing control, or dying). Cognitive strategies and breathing strategies are applied *after* each induction.

In addition to within-session practices, interoceptive exposure is practiced every day between sessions. Not only does homework practice consolidate learning, but it facilitates generalizations to conditions where the therapist is not present as a safety signal. After extinguishing fears of these types of exercises, naturalistic exposure activities are identified, ranked in a hierarchy, and practiced repeatedly at least three times per week. Naturalistic interoceptive exercises include aerobic classes, fun-park rides, running up flights of stairs, steamy showers or saunas, humid weather conditions, watching suspenseful movies or sporting events, consuming caffeine or chocolate, and any other activities that induce feared physical sensations.

In Vivo Exposure

In vivo exposure is intended for agoraphobic avoidance and is introduced after the panic control interventions (i.e., from Session 9 onwards). However, the best way in which to sequence the various treatment components is yet to be empirically demonstrated. As described below, there is even evidence that in vivo exposure alone is sufficient for the treatment of agoraphobia.

As with interoceptive exposure, a hierarchy of individually relevant agoraphobic situations is generated, and exposure practice is graduated, beginning with the least anxiety provoking. Exposures are encouraged at least three times per week. Included among the more challenging items are situations associated with the very first or very severe panic attacks, or situations in which panic attacks are likely to occur in the future. The difficulty of exposure is further increased by including exercises to elicit feared sensations. For example, driving might be combined with heat from the car heater or from closing windows, and walking might be combined with caffeine ingestion. During every exposure exercise, patients identify and challenge negative cognitions and apply breathing retraining where appropriate. In addition, commonly used but maladaptive methods of coping with agoraphobic situations are addressed. The first is the use of safety signals, such as other people or objects (e.g., phones or phone numbers, money, medications). Safety signals maintain erroneous beliefs of danger (e.g., "I would have gone crazy if my husband had not been there to help me" or "I might have fainted if it hadn't been for the knowledge that the medication was in my pocket"). Thus, patients are gradually weaned from safety signals. A second negative coping strategy is unnecessary precautions (e.g., sitting in the aisle in a movie theater so faster escape is possible, tightly gripping the steering wheel to prevent losing control of the car). Mastery behavior is encouraged in place of these unnecessary precautions (e.g., sitting in the middle of the row at a movie theater and appropriate loosening of the grip on the steering wheel). A third strategy is distraction (e.g., pretending to be elsewhere, using music or games to keep one's mind occupied), which tends to alleviate anxiety in the short term but *may* not be effective in the long term. Thus, patients are encouraged to maintain an objective focus on the situation and their feelings (e.g., "OK, I am in the elevator, the doors are closing, and I can feel it moving, my hands are sweaty, and I would judge my anxiety to be about 3 on the 0-8 point scale). Note that an objective focus is very different from what is termed subjective focus, which tends to be negative and fear provoking (e.g., "OK, I am in the elevator, and it feels as if I can't breathe -the doors may get jammed shut, and I could be stuck in here forever").

To maximize the benefit of exposure, practices are planned and rehearsed with the therapist. That is, each session is devoted to reviewing exposure practices during the preceding week, learning from those experiences, and planning new exposures for the coming week. Planning involves consideration of situational factors (e.g., how many people are likely to be there, how much traffic will there be) and sensations that are likely to occur and how they will be managed. Rehearsal is given to likely negative cognitions and how they can be countered. Wherever possible, in vivo exposures are conducted in-session, with the aid of therapist coaching and feedback. These might include exposures to elevators, heights, stores, walking, and other situations that are in close proximity to the clinical setting. Of course, therapist-directed exposure is followed by self-directed exposure.

Efficacy of Cognitive-Behavioral Therapy

Cognitive-behavioral treatment of panic disorder has proven highly effective. To date, the percent of panic disorder patients who are panic free, or free of panic as well as maladaptive anxiety, after cognitive-behavioral therapy is reported in 20 independently conducted and controlled studies. On average, using outcomes from the most effective condition when variants of cognitive-behavioral treatments were compared, 76% of treatment completers are free of panic at posttreatment, as are 78% at follow-up (up to two years), after 11 treatment sessions, and a 10% attrition rate. However, outcome estimates based on panic-free status alone may be inflated. On average, 52% are free of panic and excessive anxiety at posttreatment, as are 66% at follow-up. It is noteworthy that status is maintained or continues to improve over the follow-up interval, after active treatment is terminated. These treatments also significantly improve quality of life.

Despite these very promising results, close inspection reveals two caveats. First, panic-free rates are generally reduced in samples with higher levels of agoraphobia, and as most of the studies above excluded patients high in agoraphobia, they may overestimate the benefit of cognitive-behavioral therapy for panic sufferers as a whole, many of whom have substantial agoraphobia. Second, tracking the status of each individual patient over time in one study showed that cross-sectional data may misrepresent long-term outcomes. Brown and Barlow reported that more than one third of patients who were classified as panic free 24 months after treatment experienced a panic attack in the preceding year. Also, 27% of their sample had received additional treatment for panic over the follow-up interval. This suggests considerable return of fear and the value of strategies outlined in Chapter 5 to minimize return of fear. On the other hand, more favorable results were obtained from survival analyses over two to nine years after exposure-based treatments: Only 18.5% of 81 patients who were panic free after treatment relapsed. Agoraphobia and personality disorders predicted more relapse.

The previous 20 studies targeted fears of bodily sensations and panic attacks, although some samples included patients with agoraphobia. The following data were summarized from 13 controlled studies that reported percentages of clinically significant improvement from agoraphobia and panic as well as agoraphobia. On average, after 12 sessions and a 17% attrition rate, 50% show substantial improvement, defined as normative levels of functioning or mild or less distress across a variety of measures, at posttreatment, as do 59% at follow-up. Finally, early behavioral interventions dramatically offset the development of agoraphobia.

Treatment Dismantling

Current research efforts focus on determining which cognitive and behavioral components are necessary or most essential. Michelson, Mavissakalian, and Marchione published their first of a series of investigations comparing different behavioral treatments to various cognitively oriented treatments for agoraphobia. They compared paradoxical intention, graduated exposure, and progressive deep-muscle relaxation, although all participants conducted self-directed, graduated exposure between sessions. At posttreatment and three months later, paradoxical intention demonstrated equivalent rates of improvement, but significantly more remained symptomatic compared to graduated exposure and relaxation. Michelson, Mavissakalian, and Marchione replicated this design with almost twice as many participants. Contrary to the first study, few significant differences were detected between treatments. Lack of differences was replicated in a third study. Thus, cognitively oriented treatments appear as effective as behaviorally oriented treatments, although the cognitively oriented treatments were heavily behavioral given that all participants engaged in self-directed exposure.

Without the self-directed exposure component, Emmelkamp and colleagues found that cognitive therapy (rational emotive therapy and self-instruction training) was significantly less effective than prolonged in vivo exposure for agoraphobia, on an array of behavioral and self-report measures of anxiety and avoidance. However, more recently developed cognitive approaches that target fears of bodily sensations seem more successful for severe agoraphobia, even when conducted in full isolation from exposure and behavioral procedures. The more recently developed cognitive procedures that incorporated behavioral strategies (e.g., hypothesis testing) were more effective than guided mastery procedures for inpatients with moderate to severe agoraphobia who received six weeks of treatment and equally effective for patients with varying levels of agoraphobia over the course of eight weeks. Recently, Bouchard found that cognitive therapy was only slightly less effective than exposure therapy for patients with varying levels of agoraphobia. In addition, recently developed cognitive therapies are clearly effective with samples with mild to moderate agoraphobia, producing results that are either superior to or as effective as applied relaxation.

It is unclear whether the combination of cognitive and behavioral strategies is more effective than either alone. Marchione, Michelson, Greenwald, and Dancu found a clear superiority of combination treatments (cognitive therapy plus graduated exposure, relaxation training plus graduated exposure, versus graduated exposure alone) for agoraphobia. In contrast, Emmelkamp and Mersch reported no superiority from the combination of rational emotive therapy, self-instruction training, and prolonged in vivo exposure. In a follow-up analysis, the exposure component of the combination treatment was determined to be responsible for treatment effects. Similarly, although the addition of self-statement training may result in use of more coping thoughts for agoraphobics with severe driving phobias, in vivo exposure without self-statement training was as effective overall. Several more recent studies similarly find no benefit for the treatment of agoraphobia from the addition of cognitive treatments that target fears of bodily sensations or panic attacks. Finally, breathing education, retraining, and repeated interoceptive exposure to hyperventilation did not increase benefits from in vivo exposure for agoraphobia.

Treatment Matching

Some have attempted to match treatments to response profile. Based on reactions in a naturalistic agoraphobic situation, ost, Jerremalm, and Jansson classified participants as either behavioral (i.e., high self-rated anxiety) or physiological (i.e., high heart rate) reactors, who were then randomly assigned to 12 sessions of in vivo exposure therapy or applied relaxation. Both treatments produced significant gains, but improvement was not related to an individual's match to treatment. Mackay and Liddell classified agoraphobics as cognitive responders or non-cognitive responders based on a self-report symptom questionnaire. Individuals were assigned to either cognitive therapy plus in vivo exposure or relaxation training plus in vivo exposure. Of the four groups created by crossing response type with treatment mode, three demonstrated significant treatment gains; the non-cognitive responders who received cognitive therapy failed to improve. These results are not clearly supportive of the treatment-matching hypothesis, although they do suggest a possible individual trait (i.e., non-cognitive responder) that may suppress the efficacy of cognitive therapy.

Efficient Treatments

Most treatments described above are conducted individually, with a therapist, over the course of 10 to 20 treatment sessions. Given cost, unavailability of specialized treatment centers, and restrictions on travel, attempts have been made to increase treatment availability through group treatment, self-directed treatment, minimal therapist contact treatment, and brief treatment.

Several studies reviewed above utilized group treatments. Their outcomes were comparable to outcomes from individual treatments. In a direct comparison, Neron, Lacroix and Chaput compared 12 to 14 weekly sessions of individual or group cognitive-behavioral therapy (n=20), although the group condition received two additional one-hour individual sessions. The two conditions were equally effective for panic and agoraphobia measures at posttreatment and six-month followfup, although generalized anxiety and depressive symptoms were more improved by follow-up in individually treated participants. Another study found that group treatment and individually conducted self-directed treatment were equally effective. Obviously, there is need for more investigation of the efficacy of group treatments relative to individual therapy, but extant data suggest that groups are generally effective for targeted symptoms of panic and agoraphobia.

Barlow compared group treatments for agoraphobia that either fully incorporated partners in every treatment session or excluded partners from treatment. Although these findings are limited to patients with partners who are willing to be involved in treatment, groups that incorporated partners achieved superior outcomes. This finding was even stronger two years after treatment completion. In fact, several studies support the efficacy of involvement of partners in treatment for agoraphobia.

Self-directed treatments appear to be effective with less severe and highly motivated patient samples. In a single-case, multiple-baseline design with six severe agoraphobic women, Holden, O'Brien, Barlow, Stetson, and Inffantino found that 4, 6, or 10 weeks of cognitive restructuring and graduated in vivo exposure, via a manual with brief therapist contact, was of relatively little benefit, whereas an additional 4, 6, or 8 weeks of therapist-directed, home-based treatment was moderately effective. The failure of the self-help phase was attributed to patients' failure to comply with exposure instructions. Ghosh and Marks found that a less severe agoraphobia group given book instruction and seen only three times by a therapist over 3 to 10 weeks improved as much as a therapist-instructed group and complied well with self-exposure practices. These studies targeted agoraphobic avoidance. Bibliotherapy and self-help manuals that target panic directly have been evaluated recently. Gould, Clum, and Shapiro compared four weeks of bibliotherapy, individual therapy (eight one-hour visits), and a wait-list control condition. The bibliotherapy group were contacted twice, for 10 minutes each time. By posttreatment, the bibliotherapy group did not differ from the individual therapy group, and both improved more than the wait-list group.

Brief treatments have been examined also. Evans compared a two-day group cognitive-behavioral treatment to a wait-list condition, although without random assignment. The two-day program was composed of lectures (three hours); teaching skills such as breathing, relaxation, and cognitive challenging (three hours); in vivo exposure (nine hours); and group discussion, plus a support group of two hours for significant others. Eighty-five percent of treated patients were reported to be symptom free or symptomatically improved, and these results were maintained one year later. In contrast, the wait-list group did not demonstrate significant changes after four months. Finally, the efficacy of condensed cognitive-behavioral therapy for panic disorder was tested in a group of patients who were seeking medication treatment. Four weeks of cognitive-behavioral therapy was somewhat effective, particularly with less severe patients.

Cognitive-Behavioral Therapy and Pharmacotherapy

The mainstays of pharmacotherapy for panic disorder have been tricyclic antidepressants and monoamine oxidase inhibitors (MAOIs) in the 1960s and 1970s, high-potency benzodiazepines in the 1980s, and selective serotonin reuptake inhibitors in the 1990s. The efficacy of tricyclic antidepressants (e.g., imipramine), particularly for panic relative to anticipatory anxiety and phobic avoidance, has been widely replicated. However, tricyclics are not well tolerated in comparison to benzodiazepines, probably due to side effects, including elevated heart rate and blood pressure. Similarly, MAOIs such as phenelzine are effective, but have negative side effects. At least eight placebo-controlled, double-blind trials have found alprazolam (a high-potency benzodiazepine) to be superior to placebo, with 55 to 75% of patients free of panic at end point. Whereas maximal effect is usually obtained from weeks 4 to 8 for tricyclics, the superiority of alprazolam to placebo is usually evident in the first week or two. Other effective benzodiazepines are clonazepam, lorazepam, and diazepam. Concerns about the development of tolerance and abuse with long-term use of benzodiazepines have been mitigated by the finding that dosage levels tend to decrease over time. Selective serotonin reuptake inhibitors, including fluvoxamine, paroxetine, and sertraline, are also effective for panic disorder, with more controlled studies under way. Finally, beta blockers are not supported as a single-treatment option although they may be useful as adjuncts to other pharmacological agents.

Meta-analyses show that cognitive-behavioral treatments yield larger mean effect sizes (averaging over all dependent variables) (ES=.88) than either antidepressants (ES=.55) or benzodiazepines (ES=.40). In refute of these statistics, Klein claims that studies that support the efficacy of cognitive-behavioral therapy are seriously methodologically flawed by failing to establish efficacy in samples shown to be drug responsive. Specifically, given that previous comparisons of cognitive-behavioral therapies to pharmacotherapies find pharmacotherapies to be no different from placebos (e.g., Klosko, Barlow, Tassifnari, & Cerny and given that pharmacotherapies are generally very effective relative to placebos in drug trials, Klein concludes that samples in the former studies are drug nonresponsive. McNally criticizes this position as unfair: "Although CBT researchers are obligated to include drug and pill placebo conditions in their designs and to demonstrate a significant drug effect, Klein exempts pharmacological researchers from parallel obligations to include a CBT condition in their designs and to demonstrate a significant CBT effect"; and "Interestingly, Klein seems more willing to accept negative evidence against 'established' psychosocial treatments than against 'established' drug treatments". Examination of the series of critiques provided by these two authors illustrates the widely different interpretations placed on the same data sets and speaks to the value of more collaborative research from each discipline to provide more comprehensive and mutually satisfying outcomes.

Cognitive-Behavioral Therapy and Other Psychotherapy

Finally, research comparing cognitive-behavioral therapies to alternative therapy models is extremely sparse. Brief (four sessions) cognitive-behavioral therapy was more effective than brief nondirective therapy. On the other hand, Shear found few differences between cognitive-behavioral therapy and nondirective supportive therapy over 15 weeks of treatment. However, their cognitive-behavioral therapists were rated as somewhat less than ideal in competency, and their nondirective condition included psychoeducation about the nature of anxiety and panic that overlapped considerably with the cognitive-behavioral condition.

Summary

Recently developed treatments that directly target fears of bodily sensations are highly effective for panic disorder, although there are at least two noteworthy caveats. First, there may be more fluctuation over time, after treatment is over, than first thought, and greater attention should be directed toward return of fear-prevention strategies. Second, panic attacks are generally more successfully controlled in patients with only mild agoraphobia. Treatments for agoraphobia are also generally effective, although there is considerable room for improvement. Comparisons among cognitively and behaviorally oriented treatment approaches suggest that cognitive approaches that directly target fears of bodily sensations may be as effective as exposure-based approaches, and that the combination of these two approaches is no more effective than either alone. However, comparative research with severely agoraphobic samples is clearly lacking. In addition, large benefits seem obtainable with more efficient treatment delivery. However, outcomes from briefer and self-directed treatments may be limited with more severe samples and may be based on lower completion rates. Finally, comparisons with pharmacotherapy are controversial and comparisons with alternative psychotherapies are sorely lacking. Obviously, future research directions abound, and yet, as seen in the remaining chapters, treatment outcome research with respect to panic disorder and agoraphobia is by far the most developed of all the anxiety disorders.

Bibliography

Acharyya, S. (1996). Practising cultural psychiatry: The doctor's dilemma. In T. Heller, J. Reynolds, R. Gomm, P. Muston & S. Pattison (eds) Mental Health Matters. Basingstoke, UK: Macmillan.

Acocella, J. (1999). Creating Hysteria: Women and Multiple Personality Disorder. San Francisco: Jossey Bass.

Adityanjee, R. & Khandelwal, S. (1989). Current status of multiple personality disorder in India. American Journal of Psychiatry, 146, 1607-1610.

Adler, D., Drake, R., & Teague, G. (1990). Clinicians' practices in personality assessment. Comprehensive Psychiatry, 31, 125-133.

Bandura, A (1969). Principles of Behaviour Modification. NY: Rinehart & Winston.

Banister, P. et al. (1994). Qualitative Methods in Psychology: A Research Guide. Buckingham, UK: Open University Press.

Banyard, P. (1996). Applying Psychology to Health. London: Hodder & Stoughton.

Barkley, R. (1981). Hyperactive Children: A Handbook for Diagnosis and Treatment. NY: Guilford Press.

Barlow, D. (1977). Behavioural assessment in clinical settings. In J. Cone & R. Hawkins (eds) Behavioural Assessment: New Directions in Clinical Psychology. NY: Brunner Mazel.

Cardena, E. & Spiegel, D. (1993). Dissociative reactions to the San Francisco Bay area earthquake of 1989. American Journal of Psychiatry, 150, 474-478.

Daly, M. & Wilson, M. (1994). Some differential attributes of lethal assaults on small children by stepfathers versus genetic fathers. Ethology and Sociobiology, 15, 207-217.

Davey, G. et al. (1998). A cross-cultural study of animal fears. Behaviour Research and Therapy, 36(7-8), 735-750.

Davison, G. & Neale, J. (1994). Abnormal Psychology. NY: Wiley.

Dawson, J. (1999). The alter as agent: Multiple personality and the insanity defence. Psychiatry, Psychology and Law, 6(2) 203-206.

Edgerton, R. (1971). The Individual in Cultural Adaptation. Berkeley: University of California Press.

Eich, E. (1995). Searching for mood-dependent memory. Psychological Science, 6(2), 67-75.

Erdberg, P. & Exner, J. (1984). Personality assessment: Rorschach assessment. In G. Goldstein & M. Hersen (eds) Handbook of Psychological Assessment. NY: Pergamon Press.

Falek, A. & Moser, H. (1975). Classification in schizophrenia. Archives of General Psychiatry, 32, 59-67.

Faris, R. & Dunham, H. (1939). Mental Disorders in Urban Areas. Chicago: University of Chicago Press.

Fewtrell, W. (1981). Variations in Clinical Opinion Between Psychologists Treating a Single Case of Sleep Dysfunction. Annual conference, British Psychological Society.

French, A. & Schechmeister, J. (1983). The multiple personality syndrome and criminal defence. Bulletin of the American Academy of Psychiatry and the Law, 11(1), 17-25.

Frick, W. (1995). The subpersonalities controversy. Journal of Human Psychology, 35(1), 97-101.

Fryer, D. (1995). Labour market disadvantage, deprivation and mental health. The Psychologist, 8(6), 265-272.

Ganaway, G. (1989). Historical versus narrative truth: Clarifying the role of exogenous trauma in the etiology of MPD and its variants. Dissociation, 2(4) 205-220.

Garb, H. (1997). Race bias, social class bias and gender bias in clinical judgement. Clinical Psychology: Science and Practice, 4, 99-120.

Hacking, I. (1995). Rewriting the Soul: Multiple Personality and the Sciences of Memory. NJ: Princeton.

Halgin, R.P. & Whitbourne, S.K. (1993). Abnormal Psychology: The Human Experience of Psychological Disorders. NY: Harcourt Brace.

Jablensky, A. et al. (1992). Schizophrenia: Manifestations, course and incidence in different cultures. Psychological Medicine Monograph Supplement20.

Jahoda, M. (1958). Current Concepts of Positive Mental Health. NY: Basic Books.

Karno, M., Hough, R., Burnam, M., Escobar, J., Yimbers, D., Santana, F. & Boyd, J. (1987). Lifetime prevalence of specific psychiatric disorders among Mexican Americans and non-Hispanic whites in Los Angeles. Archives of General Psychiatry, 44, 695-701.

Kelly, K. (1993). Multiple personality disorders: Treatment coordination in a partial hospital setting. Bulletin of Menninger Clinic, 57(3), 390-398.

Kraepelin, E. (1883). Lehrbuch der Psychiatrie [translated by A. Diefendorf]. Delmar, NY: Scholars' Facsimiles and Reprints.

Landrine, H. (1991). Revising the framework of abnormal psychology. In P. Bronstein & K. Quina (eds) Teaching a Psychology of People. Washington, DC: APA.

Langer, E. & Abelson, R. (1974). A patient by any other name: Clinician group difference in labelling bias. Journal of Consulting and Clinical Psychology, 42, 4-9.

Mann, A., Graham, N. & Ashby, D. (1984). Psychiatric illness in residential homes for the elderly: A survey in one London borough. Age and Ageing, 113, 257-65.

Nasser, M. (1986). Comparative study of the prevalence of abnormal eating attitudes among Arab female students of both London and Cairo universities. Psychological Medicine, 16, 621-625.

Obeyesekere, G. (1977). The theory and practice of psychological medicine in the Ayurvedic tradition. Culture, Medicine and Psychiatry, 1, 155-181.

Orne, M., Dunges, D. & Orne, E. (1984). On the differential diagnosis of multiple personality in the forensic context. International Journal of Clinical and Experimental Hypnosis, 32, 118-169.

Patterson, G., Chamberlain, P. & Reid, J. (1982). A comparative evaluation of a parent training program. Behaviour Therapy, 13, 638-650.

Paul, G. (1966). Insight vs. Desensitisation in Psychotherapy: An Experiment in Anxiety Reduction. Stanford, CA: Stanford University Press.

Reitan, R. & Davison, L. (1974). Clinical neuropsychology: Current status and applications. Washington, DC: V.H. Winston & Sons.

Rieber, R. (1999). Hypnosis, false memory and multiple personality: A trinity of affinity. History of Psychiatry, 10, 3-11.

Saks, E. (1994). Integrating multiple personalities, murder and the status of alters as persons. Public Affairs Quarterly, 8, 169-182.

Sampath, H. (1974). Prevalence of psychiatric disorders in a Southern Baffin Island Eskimo settlement. Canadian Psychiatric Association Journal, 19, 363-367.

Taylor, C. et al. (1996). A comparison of the background of first time and repeated overdose patients. Journal of Accidents and Emergency Medicine, 11(4), 238-242.

Taylor, W. & Martin, M. (1944). Multiple personality. Journal of Abnormal and Social Psychology, 39, 281-300.

Wakefield, H. & Underwager, R. (1992). Recovered memories of alleged sexual abuse: Lawsuits against parents. Behavioural Sciences and the Law, 10, 483-507.

Walker, C.; Bonner, B. & Kaufman, K.. (1988). The Physically and Sexually Abused Child. NY: Pergamon Press.

Warner, R. (1985). Recovery from Schizophrenia: Psychiatry and Political Economy. NY: Routledge.

Zeigob, L., Arnold, S. & Forehand, R. (1975). An examination of observer effects in parent-child interactions. Child Development, 46, 509-512.

Index

M

N

O

P